Deborah Cassrels has been a journalist for over 40 years. She has been based in Bali since 2009, and has written extensively for *The Australian* newspaper on refugees, politics, terrorism, crime and the Bali Nine Australian drug smugglers, among other issues. She covered the 2015 executions of the two Bali Nine ringleaders and was a finalist for the Walkley Freelance Awards in 2016 for her work on terrorism in Indonesia.

Previously a features writer at *The Weekend Australian Magazine*, she contributes to *The Times* of London, *The Guardian* and SBS. Her work has also appeared in *The Sydney Morning Herald*, *The Age* and *The Australian Financial Review*.

After beginning her career as a reporter for *The New Zealand Herald*, she moved to Australia in the mid-1980s to work for *The Australian* and *The Courier-Mail*. She has freelanced in the US, Europe and Central America.

Deborah has two children and divides her time between Indonesia and Sydney.

GODS AND DEMONS

Deborah Cassrels

ABC
BOOKS

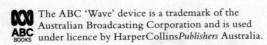 The ABC 'Wave' device is a trademark of the
Australian Broadcasting Corporation and is used
under licence by HarperCollins*Publishers* Australia.

HarperCollins*Publishers*
Australia • Brazil • Canada • France • Germany • Holland • Hungary
India • Italy • Japan • Mexico • New Zealand • Poland • Spain • Sweden
Switzerland • United Kingdom • United States of America

First published in Australia in 2020
by HarperCollins*Publishers* Australia Pty Limited
Level 13, 201 Elizabeth Street, Sydney NSW 2000
ABN 36 009 913 517
harpercollins.com.au

A catalogue record for this book is available from the National Library of Australia.

ISBN 978 0 7333 3890 8 (pbk)
ISBN 978 1 4607 0913 9 (ebook)

Cover design by Hazel Lam, HarperCollins Design Studio
Cover image by Cheryl Ramalho /Getty Images
Photograph of Deborah Cassrels by Sonny Tumbelaka
Typeset in Adobe Caslon Pro by Kirby Jones
Unless otherwise credited, all photos are taken by or are from the collection of
  Deborah Cassrels
Printed and bound in Australia by McPherson's Printing Group
The papers used by HarperCollins in the manufacture of this book are a natural,
recyclable product made from wood grown in sustainable plantation forests. The fibre
source and manufacturing processes meet recognised international environmental
standards, and carry certification.

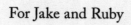

For Jake and Ruby

contents

PROLOGUE

*'Indonesia defies definition, almost. Its diversity is its identity.
Unfortunately, there are some who cannot tolerate that reality
and that's why there's a sense of wanting to impose identity
politics. There has never been in our history a suggestion to define
our identity by uniformity – more by our diversity.'*
—Marty Natalegawa, former Indonesian foreign minister, 2018

I didn't travel to Indonesia with huge expectations; rather it was in the spirit of possibility, self-preservation, adventure and an abiding interest in the unknown. I had worked in many countries, and it was in this peripatetic vein that I set out.

Then there was the other variable – hope. I was looking to clear the cobwebs and stagnation that follows a relationship breakdown.

If people in Indonesia inquired about a plan, I was 'in limbo'. I was dipping my toes in the unknown. In the process, I created a new life for myself. I saw things afresh, became absorbed and found my journalistic feet.

As short holidays morphed into months on an island that took me by storm, so the possibilities widened. Writing for *The Australian*, the paper on which I had worked in many capacities largely since the 1980s, I had a broad canvas on which to cover sometimes tumultuous and invariably fascinating narratives.

I had arrived in Bali with little knowledge of Indonesia, one suitcase and a finite list of story ideas. My language tutor in Australia, who had a long career teaching officials posted to Indonesia, had pulled out a map and quizzed me on the nation's vast and sprawling geography. Nothing was familiar. But once I was ensconced, the nation-state took on real proportions. Its magnitude, people, diversity, struggles and beauty drew me in. Straddling both sides of the equator, it comprises 17,500 islands and hundreds of islets. The world's most populous Muslim-majority nation, with 273 million people, it is the largest archipelagic country in the world. In appearance, ethnicity, culture, politics and religion – and, not least, food – the fledgling democracy was wildly eclectic and intoxicating.

My stories loosely segued from politics to terrorism to court dramas to travel. From Javanese extremist enclaves I boarded majestic Sulawesi *pinisi* schooners for remote, eastern islands. The spice-growing Malukus, West Papua, Flores, Lombok and others yielded a microcosm of the resplendent, shambolic archipelago.

As configurations of this complex nation grew more familiar, I came to see Bali as a tenuous part of a giant chameleon. The archipelagic chain, variously prone to outbreaks of ethno-religious conflict and natural disasters, was interconnected historically and culturally. Lurching from one mammoth challenge to the next, the country rumbled along.

In Lombok, Bali's eastern neighbour, I met expatriates who had been forced off their properties, their houses burnt down. Land feuds were common among locals too, and flare-ups broke out unpredictably. Lombok was branded cowboy country.

But if all of the Indonesian islands were in a beauty contest, Lombok would be a contender for first place.

On assignment to Manado, on North Sulawesi's jungly northern tip, south of the Philippines, I was stunned by a different emerald beauty, its Christian stronghold and Jewish sanctuary – and by the distance from Bali. My midday flight returned to Bali at two the following morning, after refuelling in Jakarta. I could have travelled to another country.

A few months into my Bali tenure, I saw the challenges of the developing world mainly as an adventure. I was enamoured of many things, including my large garden villa – with staff. Never a fan of high-rises, I felt grounded in my tropical surroundings.

When I moved to a new abode, I was beset by daily power outages. And the odd rat ran amok – on those occasions, I enlisted staff help. We would entice the rodent into a rubbish bag, then bash it until it was stone dead. In another ploy, a guard dog was unleashed on a hunt through my villa, much to the excitement of the owners, a local family.

More seriously, I was run down by a motorbike rider who had belted towards me on a severely degraded tourist thoroughfare.

Stories imbued with potent social and political trajectories seemed to fall into my lap. Frequently it was a case of sliding doors: one contact or story led to another. A web of connections, even from remotest Indonesia, would strangely lead to the person I sought. It was as if the thought triggered its manifestation – what sort of magic was this? With minimal effort, casts of interviewees would fall into place, frequently generating several different stories during one remote assignment.

The broad range and depth of subjects I covered over my years in Indonesia always left me hankering for more. The juggling of hard news, feature and magazine writing was a rewarding discipline. I never took days off, as such. There were natural troughs. A non-journalist friend once asked me, 'Do you remember all of the stories you've written?' I thought it was an odd question, given stories are more than memories; they're part of me, an intrinsic part of my life. In addition, my archives – scores of notebooks, diaries and tapes –

bear witness. Behind each story is the research that I like to think remains largely indelible.

This book isn't only about the joy of a new journey, with the grab-bag of quirky surprises encountered and relationships made along the way. It's about mystery, power, corruption, violence, loss and unnecessary death. Deaths of Indonesians. Deaths of foreigners far from home, killed in abhorrent ways, and the devastating aftermaths.

It's about life outside the Western comfort zone and finding ways forward in a tough, complex land.

1

THE UNRAVELLING

Touching down in Bali in May 2006, I was beguiled by the traditional welcome at the airport. Gamelan percussion regaled arriving passengers, its pentatonic scales the backdrop to ancient Hindu sculpture and cultural narrative. Everything in Bali felt soft and sensuous, the balmy air sweet, the people gentle – the opposite of the fraught life I was escaping. I didn't realise an abnormal lull had settled over the island due to the mass tourist exodus after the 2002 and 2005 bombings. To me, the tranquillity in upmarket Seminyak was welcome.

In 2004, my de facto marriage to Chris Mitchell had imploded. In the aftermath I packed the sad vestiges of our family life into scores of labelled crates and boxes. They stood like scattered tombstones through our house – itself in the throes of extensive renovations.

One afternoon I stood alone in one of our sad little rooms, which was stuffed to the gills. Stacked furniture from several lifetimes lined the walls. Framed happy snaps were piled haphazardly upon photos – a children's beach scene here, a child's birthday party there, glittering nights out with dignitaries over there. Shelves groaned under books; mementos spilled over the floor. The ruins of two decades of shared lives built on stalwart trust lay discarded, crammed into our office. Stylists had swept through most of our two-storey home with a sanitising broom, erasing all traces of us as though they could betray a dirty secret. The house now reflected a submissive *Stepford Wives* beige. Real estate agents, accustomed to distressed sales, had acted with brutal efficiency. Through the double glass doors the blue ocean, dimpled with driving rain, stretched to Sydney's headlands.

Tears blurred my vision. I reached for the phone. My then mother-in-law, unswervingly direct, exceeded herself this time. 'I suppose it would have been better if he had died,' she blurted over the line from Queensland.

The thought had occurred to me. But I didn't expect mindful collusion despite her son's tawdry and very public midlife crisis. Chris had strayed into an extramarital affair, abruptly leaving me and our two teenagers to cope with the detritus. The girlfriend was now pregnant.

I stood cradling the phone, waiting for more. But there was silence. At least, I thought, insight had triumphed over blood as she mulled over what had been inflicted on me. It should have been her last comment. Instead, apparently overcome with rage, she snapped, 'You didn't invite me to lunch.'

Admittedly that would have been beyond the pale. But, when had I *not* invited her to lunch? I pondered this impatiently and sniffed. 'What do you mean?'

I could imagine her fist raised in righteous indignation across the phone line as I smarted under the ill-timed rebuke.

Suffice to say, I never heard from my mother-in-law again.

*

Chris, a News Corp veteran, had climbed the ladder to editor-in-chief of *The Australian* from the paper's finance section. We'd met in the early 1980s after I arrived in Australia after years of living and working in Europe.

We had both started in journalism at seventeen. I'd landed my first job on *The New Zealand Herald* as a cadet reporter after graduating in journalism from the Auckland University of Technology. Our relationship cemented over a mutual passion for newspapers, deadlines and an irregular lifestyle. We went on to spend the next twenty years together. Building up from the bottom, we scrimped and saved for many years, especially after our children were born. Amid frenetic daily news cycles, increasing work functions, overseas conferences and two children, schedules were upended at a moment's notice.

But we were tight, inseparable almost. There were ups and downs, but we were generally happy, I thought. We had planned for retirement and in 2001 bought a Byron Bay property from which eventually to write books. In the meantime, our work and social lives converged. They were filled with politicians, from premiers to prime ministers, to other journalists, artists, corporate and media moguls, among others.

In 1995, Chris was promoted as editor-in-chief to Queensland Newspapers, a News Limited subsidiary, and we moved to Brisbane. We rented a colonial house in Yabba Street, Ascot – nothing grand, in fact, rather rundown, but a good family home – from a former state governor, Peter Arnison, after he relocated to Government House.

Lachlan Murdoch, the eldest son of media tycoon Rupert Murdoch, was then general manager of Queensland Newspapers. He lived in nearby Hamilton Hill and occasionally popped in for breakfast. Chris, donning an apron, would whip up bacon and eggs, passing a heart-stopping fry-up through the serving hatch from the kitchen of our Federation home. Lachlan, sitting alone at our grand ten-seater table, chatted to Chris and waited to be served. 'Can I get some more eggs?' Lachlan would yell through the hatch after mopping up his plate.

At a Murdoch family dinner the same year, held at Lachlan's house before a Hayman Island News Corp conference, we were two outsiders along with a couple of top rugby league players. The next day, Tony Blair, then an aspiring British Labour PM who had indicated media ownership rules would work to Murdoch's favour, travelled to the island to deliver a keynote address. As the story goes, Murdoch went on to back Blair in the 1997 election campaign, ending eighteen years of conservative rule.

The Murdoch clan, including children James and Elisabeth, their half-sister Prudence and her husband Alasdair MacLeod, had assembled from all points of the compass. It was coincidentally the day of the Queensland election, and Chris would have preferred to be at the office directing staff. Rupert, then married to his second wife, Anna, a statuesque, handsome woman, was taking a nap when we arrived.

We sat at a table of about a dozen. Rupert, still visibly sleepy, his hair tousled, ambled in greeting people and assumed the head of the table. During dinner he regaled us with a colourful account of his proficiency at Australia's national gambling game, two-up, demonstrating his prowess: it entailed flipping two coins at once – traditionally pennies, played on Anzac Day. The idea was simple: two heads you win; two tails you lose; one of each, toss again. The tale was interspersed with his early newspaper days in the 1950s. It showed a charming side to the man who loved to gamble.

Around this time we bought an exquisite 1900s colonial Queenslander in a cul-de-sac down the road from the governor's house sporting a pool, tennis court and orchard, purchased substantially with my inheritance. We entertained such people as the Australian poet Les Murray, the well-regarded art dealer Philip Bacon, and the founder of the *Adelaide Review* and columnist for *The Australian*, Christopher Pearson. An aesthete, Pearson was also a corpulent, dry-witted intellect, and then a newly minted, devoted Catholic. Equally devoted to the long lunch, he tagged our traditional lunches bohemian 'salons'. Pearson's friend, Tony Abbott, then parliamentary secretary to the Minister for Employment, and Kevin Rudd, director-general of the state cabinet office, popped in sometimes. Rudd reciprocated the hospitality at his Brisbane home and in Noosa, northern Queensland, on holiday with his wife Thérèse Rein. Rudd would hold court over a bottle of red, long after Thérèse had retired for the night.

It wasn't unusual for colleagues from *The Courier-Mail* and the ABC to drop in after work for late-night drinks, including Chris's protege, Paul Whittaker, or 'Boris', who went on to take over as *The Australian*'s editor-in-chief in 2016.

Our children, Jake and Ruby, raised in this milieu – and lucky enough to score personal odes scribbled by Les Murray over lunch – mostly took it within their stride, notwithstanding some hiccups. The interstate transfers took their toll in their most vulnerable adolescent years.

The strain was portentous. Shortly after Chris was promoted to editor-in-chief of *The Australian* in 2002, he suffered extreme insomnia and stress-related delusions, possibly triggered by too many sleeping pills. His disturbing condition landed him in a Sydney hospital as he tried to ease into the new position, and the children and I stayed in Brisbane. It was a well-kept secret. By all accounts, he had suffered a 'heart condition'. When I was alerted, I immediately flew to Sydney to be by his bedside. It was some months before he recovered sufficiently to take the helm of the national newspaper.

A defining moment came when I arrived at the hospital to find Chris whispering about visual and auditory hallucinations, one of which entailed Rupert Murdoch talking to him from the TV set at the foot of his bed. I had just written a feature article about schizophrenia, and he worried he was suffering typical symptoms.

But after several weeks and an army of specialist help, the most serious indications blew over and we returned to Brisbane. Chris rested. He recovered. It was a blip, it seemed, on our otherwise bright horizon.

We sold our grand house and packed up for the Sydney job. I left my feature-writing position at *The Courier-Mail* and joined *The Weekend Australian Magazine* as a staff writer. The hard, frugal years were behind us.

*

Our relationship more or less unravelled overnight. It was a cliché. Despite no overt signs of a breakdown or affair, at least from my position, Chris arrived home from work one evening announcing his departure. He already had a love nest. Like an interloper, he strode upstairs to his wardrobe, stuffed a few clothes into a black plastic garbage bag, twisted the top into a knot and marched out with it. 'You didn't even ask me to stay,' he later remarked.

Suddenly the man I'd known, loved and trusted for twenty years was a stranger. Our little family unit died. My mothering role, as it was, ceased. I felt robbed as much as our children were robbed of a secure home in their early teenage years. They floundered in this stark, denuded landscape in which they had no fixed address.

That was the most devastating aspect of the situation. In forfeiting my own full-time career to support Chris's, I felt I had been utterly betrayed. I found myself unable to accommodate my own children.

For about eighteen months I felt eviscerated, unable to function. Unable to concentrate, I quit my job at *The Weekend Australian Magazine*. It was as though a death had occurred, without a body. Our children wondered how to navigate this new paradigm. I couldn't be regarded as reliable – I was unable to see beyond the end of a nearby wharf which, to me, offered a painless escape into the watery green depths. How could I offer soothing words about their father flying the coop in flagrante delicto, so to speak?

I wasted hundreds of dollars on psychiatrists and psychologists, one of whom told me to list all my lovers. 'Why?' I asked the sleazy man lounging in his expensive suit. A woman who prescribed Seroquel (for schizophrenia) at the Sydney clinic – after binning pages of my story she'd requested – was lucky not to be deregistered after I suffered violent side effects from the drug. And the last one said my only chance of salvation was in a wealthy man. I *paid* for all that 'advice'. Little wonder I regarded therapists as shysters.

Chris had scarpered six months before my fiftieth birthday. It was a milestone I should have celebrated with him. But dispirited I would not be. I splurged on a diaphanous salmon Akira Isogawa dress and threw a lavish party at the family home before it was sold. I had lost so much weight, the dress almost hung off me; I was under forty kilos. But people rallied: colleagues and friends from *The Australian*, and others who flew from Brisbane, alongside Ruby and Jake and his schoolmates, all treated me like a queen, plying me with champagne till dawn. I nailed that.

The chickens eventually came home to roost. 'These gen Xers are selfish,' Chris told me a few years later when his relationship collapsed. 'It couldn't work,' he said. 'Each night I came home from work she was ensconced in herself, writing her book. She wouldn't even lift her head to say hello when I walked through the door. She never cooked. It's a totally different generation, Debbie, they don't share *our* values, they're not like *us*.'

*

I needed to escape my personal war zone in Sydney. The impetus for a new identity, a new life, geographically separated, developed in a bright moment after I holidayed in Bali for the first time in May 2006.

I was seeking light. The hard edges began to dissolve in the calm of my Seminyak beachfront hotel canopied by emerald gardens and soaring palm trees. Sometimes I woke at 5 a.m., sat on the balcony and listened in the dark to the first eerie birdsong before daybreak shattered the cool. I hired a driver, visited tourist hotspots and took in Bali's natural beauty. It felt dreamy, distant from my troubles.

It lured me back in September 2006, and again in 2008, for extended breaks, both times feeding my career aspirations.

One of Bali's original expats, my new Kiwi friend Ross Franklin, remarked that I was obviously in thrall to the unassailable 'pull' of Bali. Ross was a renowned architect, twice married to Indonesian women, and a wealth of information; he seemed the ideal source to quiz on the vagaries of Bali life.

But I tried not to appear impressionable. I replied that perhaps I was susceptible. The warmth of the people, the cultural change, the tropical environment and the fact I didn't need to commute each day were alluring. The strictures of Western society fell away. Formalities became less pronounced – new friendships could form in a *warung* (restaurant) or even at the supermarket.

Most propitious was my meeting with the then-managing editor and owner of *The Bali Times*, Irishman William Furney. It led to an enduring friendship, and we covered some of the same stories, particularly in court, for our different markets.

Bali offered me a cathartic, liberating respite. I awoke from a crippling funk. I seemed to have shed old skin, to be re-energised, walking on air. An intense joy gripped me in a rush of freedom and gratitude. I was falling for Bali's fabled charm.

The island's charisma – *taksu* – or divine Hindu spiritual energy, manifest in artistic and cultural riches, is epitomised in the phrase, 'morning of the world', coined in 1954 by Jawaharlal Nehru, then prime minister of India. Bali was a scenic, sensual environment in which to rejuvenate.

I did not need to look far for stories and I had already found my journalistic feet in 2006.

On my last two vacations I ventured into Kerobokan Prison to interview members of the infamous Bali Nine drug gang, producing my first lead stories from Indonesia. They were the catalyst for my new path.

As the scope for work expanded, I became preoccupied with the idea of living on the island. At the same time, my personal life filled with new people and invitations to parties and dinners. All I had to do was stand still: everything came to me. And if it fell in a heap, I could return to Sydney.

While some friends perhaps thought a permanent move would be extreme – one of them jibed, 'Are you opting out?' – I didn't regard it as a seismic shift. I had trial runs; I wasn't going cold. Most importantly, it was only a six-hour flight from my children. But during my years in Indonesia, my absences from them – despite the fact they were at university and living independently – were gut-wrenching.

I procrastinated over a permanent move until after the death in 2008 of my older sister, Diana, from brain cancer at the ridiculously young age of fifty-four.

While holidaying in southern France with her husband she had collapsed one night after stepping out amid World Cup revelry. There was no forewarning.

In our twenties we had both lived abroad, connecting spontaneously in far-flung places and odd circumstances. Our bond was very close; I'd sometimes had extraordinary premonitions about her. When she fell ill I received an ominous text from France imploring me to 'call urgently; I have to speak to you'. I was driving home from work and I pulled over. I stared at my phone, shivering.

'We wanted to talk to you first,' she said, referring to our two other siblings. 'We knew you would know what to do.'

Later I recoiled from her confronting texts, one which read: 'I want to be ready when death comes at me.'

Yet when I saw her, she was strangely detached from her impending non-existence. She read voraciously. She revealed that the best sex she had with her husband was in her last months. Why wouldn't it be? Framed in urgency. Drenched in need. A last hoorah.

Despite a valiant battle from London to New Zealand, six months later she was gone. She remained lucid to the end. When a close friend asked to visit in her final hours, she shot back, exasperated, 'Not while I'm dying.'

When, then? I wondered stupidly.

Her death came exactly a decade after our mother's.

What was I waiting for? It was a final kick: time was of the essence. I instigated a move as *The Australian*'s first Bali-based stringer.

2

BALI: A FORCE

During my second visit to Bali in 2006, I found out that Kerobokan Prison was virtually on my hotel's doorstep. Kerobokan had become an Australian household name thanks to the dubious claim to fame shared by the Bali Nine gang of heroin smugglers and the convicted drug trafficker Schapelle Corby. I hadn't travelled to Bali with the intention of visiting the jail, but as a journalist I naturally gravitated there once I learnt it was so close by.

More or less on a whim, I went as a visitor, unsure of what would unfold but realising I would regret it if I didn't challenge myself to pursue a story. I knew Australian media outlets would be interested in more information on the Nine. After their Denpasar trials and subsequent appeals earlier that year, other media had retreated; it was an opportune window for an exclusive story.

I didn't expect to see Corby, the photogenic Gold Coast beauty therapist who has never admitted guilt. She'd been a perennial media sensation since her 2004 arrest at Bali's Ngurah Rai airport carrying 4.2 kilograms of cannabis in her boogie board bag, and was already renowned for her reclusiveness and dislike of journalists. The closest I came to her that day was via bags of groceries and toiletries delivered by her sister Mercedes — these passed through security in a reverential hush, with everyone peering at the contents.

Tourists didn't yet include the jail on their bucket lists. A couple of years later, many turned up to view and 'make friends' with the notorious Nine who had conspired to courier 8.3 kilograms of heroin from Bali to Australia in 2005. The Australian Consulate-General put a halt to the circus farce: only those vetted by the Nine would be allowed on visiting lists. In 2006, though, I could meet them firsthand.

Between the prison's entrance and the inner courtyard were security posts. There was also a serene rockpool and a small Hindu temple upon which a Balinese person draped in a ceremonial sarong prayed and placed offerings with musky incense. I learnt no Hindu building is exempt from religious rituals and a shrine – even a jail, despite its pluralist population.

Entry to the inner courtyard, where inmates sat with visitors on hard white tiles littered with cigarette butts and discarded food, was a long, painstaking process. The Australian prisoners' families, who flew over on shoestring budgets, were not prioritised. They queued like everyone else in the sweltering heat, sometimes for hours, initially waiting for a designated number – yelled out in Bahasa Indonesia – from a guard behind a barred window. You had to listen intently to not miss your number.

If morning visitors had a prolonged wait, their access time would be truncated. Afternoon visits were unbearably steamy, and visitors sweated profusely amid clouds of cigarette smoke. That day, I felt I would faint.

At several security thresholds, I joined the queue for the checking of illicit goods by armed guards. As a visiting tourist, I had to surrender my passport, phone and voice recorder behind a counter, which I did uneasily. At the final post a bulky female guard gave my fully clothed body a fairly thorough search, in a heavy-handed, awkward procedure. I wasn't intimidated but I entertained a niggling thought that someone could plant drugs on me.

I'd only ever visited one other prisoner, at the sterile Los Angeles county jail where visitors spoke to inmates via phone through thick glass. In comparison, Kerobokan appeared relaxed – when, in fact, it had a history of vicious gang riots, violent and unexpected deaths, extortion and sweeps. Day-to-day, though, guards were easygoing, bantering with prisoners who later told me they feared the gangsters – whose drug rackets thrived inside – more than the guards. I was intrigued by their jovial rapport.

Wandering into the circular, open-air enclosure for the first time, I felt momentarily overwhelmed. Packed with inmates and visitors, some sitting on straw mats with hand-held fans, eating *nasi* (rice) wrapped in brown paper or burgers and chips, the yard resembled a Sunday picnic.

I was standing in a sea of Indonesians amid a loud chattering chorus, scanning for Westerners, when I zeroed in on a man with scruffy, longish blond hair wearing shorts and a T-shirt. He looked like a surfer minus the tan. Parked against a wall, he was entwined with an Indonesian woman, rather obscenely for a public place. Both wore tiny earpieces, appearing to listen to music.

I bent and tapped the man on his arm. 'Are you one of the Bali Nine?'

'Yes.' He disentangled himself and jumped up, politely introducing himself as Martin Stephens. The then thirty-year-old, keenly engaged, briefed me on his respiratory problems and his fear of contracting bird flu for which his mother Michelle Stephens had provided the antidote, just in case.

He'd met his visiting love interest of nearly a year, Christine Puspayanti, when she was visiting another inmate; Stephens had made eye contact and amorously poked his tongue out at her. He said to me blithely, 'She brings my food; you've got to have someone.'

It had been a gruelling week. Stephens and fellow courier and cellmate Michael Czugaj had their life sentences upheld on appeal in Indonesia's Supreme Court while, shockingly, death penalties were imposed on four couriers. The death sentences for the gang's organisers, Andrew Chan and Myuran Sukumaran, remained.

Stephens had been trying to commute his sentence to a set term to earn remissions like his friend Renae Lawrence, the sole woman of the gang and the only one serving twenty years. He told me, 'I am quite lucky. It would have been nice to get twenty, the same as Renae, but I just thank God that I haven't got the death penalty.'

A flash of horror swept his face, swiftly replaced by relief. In that instant, we connected.

He went on: 'It's a stink. Everyone's in shock. They don't know if it's true or definite, nothing's on paper. We don't get told nothing. I can't see them doing it though [carrying out the executions], not for that many Australians. The government won't let them do that.'

Stephens introduced me to 28-year-old Renae Lawrence, who had done two previous drug trips to Bali. The pair were close: they had worked in a NSW catering company with Chan and another Bali Nine member, Matthew Norman. In jail they supported each other; if either sank to suicidal depths, the other would come to the rescue.

'I feel like this is a bad nightmare and sometimes I forget I'm here, then I wake up and look through the bars,' Stephens told me in a moment of regret.

Shortly before visiting finished at 3 p.m., Lawrence, smiling shyly, sidled up to me. Sporting shorts and a T-shirt, she had an upper tooth missing – she wouldn't disclose why, only that she had visited the dentist. But it was her strikingly masculine haircut and a tribal tattoo snaking down her left forearm that made the biggest impression on me. She confided seriously that her parents would be upset about the tattoo she'd had inscribed in jail. This former panelbeater seemed like a paradox: hard and soft simultaneously.

I was surprised to hear her speak haltingly, as if English were not her native tongue. But she conversed easily with fellow inmates in Indonesian. Her friend Stephens had not mastered the language.

Lawrence had attempted suicide twice in the relatively brief time she'd been imprisoned, but she professed to be coping. 'I read, talk. You just cope, otherwise you'd climb walls or go crazy, like some do in here,' she said casually.

Then, giggling self-consciously, the pair said they'd pledged emotional support for one another. When either one was distressed, guards summoned the other for support. 'It's therapeutic. I've been strong for Renae,' Stephens told me. 'You look after each other.' In turn, Stephens relied on his partner in crime: 'I really needed her to get through this.'

I asked him, hypothetically, what he might be doing were he free. The former barman who had worked in Wollongong, New South Wales, replied wistfully, 'I wish I was back working at the bowling club.' Brief silence.

A bell cued the end of visiting. Lawrence slipped into the dark interior, while Stephens showed me the exit. Inscrutable guards ensured the yard emptied quickly; like a stage set, the convivial Sunday picnic reverted to a littered, unsavoury prison yard. I hurried out and collected my belongings behind the front desk.

The door swung open to stark sunlight. A sense of exhilaration swamped me: I had cracked my first story out of Kerobokan. It was an exclusive in *The Sydney Morning Herald*. I freelanced and subedited for the paper around this period, after leaving my magazine job. But it was a thrill to see this story in print. The freshness of their ordeal, their close shave with the death penalty, along with the banality of prison life, gave a human face to cases that lodged in the Australian psyche. Everyone had a view but the public spectacle of the visiting grief-stricken families struck a raw nerve.

Before I left the jail, Stephens asked me to bring him shampoo 'and maybe some groceries … it means so much in here' because the jail food was rancid slop. The following day I made the sought-after delivery. In turn, Stephens slipped me his calling card. His name was printed in bold capital letters above his address: c/- Kerobokan prison (in lower-case letters) with banking details, all upper case. It was the prelude to more than a decade of following and reporting the gang's bleak journey. I routinely brought food, cigarettes and phone credit money to those I visited. Sometimes, they would call me to top up their phone credit or just to talk.

In my early days in Bali, Stephens called me often, furnishing me with the dynamics of daily life inside, dramas concerning his fellow inmates, his fear of gangsters and the personalities of the constant parade of new wardens, most of whom he liked.

Some details seemed implausible – not least, the toilet policy. Inmates used a crude hole in the ground within their cells, partitioned by a privacy curtain. When it was full, inmates would pay outside authorities to empty the unalloyed effluent. If inmates could not afford the fee, the sewage simply overflowed into cells. It was different for those with money – they had proper toilets.

Sometimes Stephens would appear overweight, bloated with telltale glassy eyes, obviously medicated; at others, trim and clear-eyed as he had been when we first met, even boasting he'd lost 25 kilos. I grew to understand that he was a pariah among the Bali Nine. He admitted to feeling lonely, but he leaked inside stories, and his backbiting bluster and carping made the others consider him craven and not to be trusted. 'I don't like to mix with the others, I don't like them,' he told me. 'I get on with Matthew Norman and [cellmate] Michael Czugaj' – teenagers at the time of their arrest – 'but there is bad blood with the others. We cross paths when I hang out playing a bit of tennis and basketball with the Indonesians.' In 2011, Christine Puspayanti became Stephens's devoted wife, taking on much of a caring role after a lavish 'in-house' wedding, with the couple wearing traditional Javanese garb.

Over the years I got to know all of the Nine, some pretty well. These relationships went outside the job. I tried to comprehend what made them tick, how each coped and what went on inside. Mostly, I felt sympathetic to their plight. Had the Australian Federal Police not tipped off their Indonesian counterparts, enabling the arrests, the Bali Nine would have been jailed in Australia. I imagined the seething emotions they harboured against the AFP, which knowingly exposed them to the death penalty.

With time, the group hardened. Tan Duc Thanh Nguyen, Si Yi Chen and Matthew Norman lived under the shadow of death until 2008, when their sentences were reduced to life. Scott Rush excruciatingly waited until 2011 for his sentence's reduction to a bittersweet life term. I watched the rawness of their ordeals slide into frustration, despair, hope and the daily grind. The spectre of death and life sentences haunted them.

But Lawrence never crumpled. She worked her way up through the system, later rebuffing the media's advances for fear of thwarting her release when it came in 2018.

3

ESTABLISHING A FOOTHOLD

Soon after my separation, my kids had moved out. I was alone and unanchored, living in the family home for over a year before it sold. Sydney seemed to turn on me with contempt. Each place became a memorial to times past, echoing stages in the children's development: days at the beach, walks in the park, a rowdy house full of schoolfriends. Now they were sullied memories.

Out of necessity, to retain my sanity, I left it all behind. I walked through the entrance of Sydney Airport with my suitcase in my hand and my heart in my mouth. When the plane began its ascent, I watched with a sense of dread Sydney's vanishing blue ocean and hours of monotonous scrubby red desert. Then, on the horizon like a flashing light, came the tropical azure of Bali.

In May 2009 I had packed up my Sydney apartment. Armed with journalist visa documents, I returned to my previous Bali hotel. Staff greeted me in a sort of homecoming and assigned me my favourite room by the pool. I was a notch up from being a backpacker. Until 2009, I tapped out stories on my hotel bed or from a beachside café facing groundswells of foaming surf. Everything was a novelty: I enjoyed living in a hotel for a couple of months and eating at local *warungs*, and it was almost dreamlike to conduct interviews and write from an oceanside café. If I wanted a dip, the staff minded my laptop.

Outside my hotel, souvenir stalls were stuffed with everything from clothing to giant wooden phalluses catering to ethnic preference. I befriended a stallholder, Wayan. A slight, cheerful middle-aged man who came from a village in Singaraja, north Bali, he had good English picked up from the passing tourist trade. We chatted almost every day, me practising my Indonesian. He was the father of two daughters, and his wife toiled in a tiny, stifling laundry across the road.

Eventually, I made Wayan an offer: to supplement his income, I would pay him a monthly wage in return for motor-scooter rides to my interviews. This would allow me to cut through heavy traffic and be assured of a punctual lift back before a deadline. Wayan acceded. But he couldn't wait for the monthly salary, so I paid him daily.

He always arrived early at the hotel reception, greeting me with a wide smile. I would hop on the back of his motor scooter, sometimes with one of his daughters perched in front, Bali-style. We ripped down the main road in the mornings – still crisp before the sun belted down – with the blue sky overhead, emerald-green vegetation either side, the wind in my hair.

Whenever I introduced him to the local government officials I interviewed, he was so overawed that he was lost for words. In mid-2009, I visited the *bupati* (mayor) of south Bali for a story on the progress of the commemorative Bali peace park planned for the site of the 2002 Bali bombings. Wayan, wide-eyed, looked child-like in the presence of the high-profile official but was secretly chuffed, later telling his friends about his unlikely meeting.

Our arrangement worked for some months, until the school run and Balinese ceremonies overlapped, and sometimes after dropping me, he forgot to return or, I suspected, something else came up.

Wayan remained in my life like a family friend. In 2019 he proudly told me his eldest daughter had graduated in accountancy from university. He wanted an education for his kids, he said, so their lives would be better than his. I had contributed a laptop in 2010 that I no longer needed, pleased it had some value left in it.

Wayan continued to help me with chores like house-hunting. When I outgrew the hotel novelty several weeks after my return in May, we zipped about on his bike, searching for a quiet, serviced villa. I found one at Seminyak's iconic Golden Village compound but I could only secure a three-month lease. Mine was the most rundown in the traditional complex, but the renovated bedroom doubled as an office. I loved the compound's history and its vast tropical gardens.

Much of early Bali had revolved around Golden Village, the first villa community in Seminyak. Steeped in hippydom, it was built in 1973 as a rudimentary *losmen* (hostel) before expats started renovating. Villas looped in a circle around swaying coconut palms and lush gardens, an anomaly on today's built-up island. Back in the day it was an electricity-free oasis wedged between boundless rice paddies where expats held legendary wild parties on magic mushrooms while living like lords on a pittance.

One day, standing in my open kitchen, I thumbed through my empty contact book, suddenly panicked. I was accustomed to having decades of people at my fingertips, but in Bali I had no fixer, or assistant, like other correspondents who relied on them to organise interviews, translate and keep abreast of news events, and I was seldom briefed by editors at *The Australian*'s Sydney headquarters at that time. It was free-style on a very modest salary. At least – after more than thirty years of working largely in city newsrooms – I was my own boss, far afield on assignment, dropping in on uncanny situations that involved inspiring and sometimes unhinged characters.

On my doorstep was an archipelago spanning 1760 kilometres from north to south. Its strange island shapes arc onto the Pacific

Ring of Fire with around 120 volcanoes, reflecting the conundrums and complexities of each. One of the most seismically active zones in the world triggering regular, devastating natural disasters, hundreds of thousands of people have died in earthquakes, floods, tsunamis and landslides.

From late 2009, when I first ventured to other islands, I flew on death-defying small aircraft. They were the cheapest but, flying low, they offered extraordinary incandescent views. Flying in to the eastern island of Flores in 2011, I was struck by the aqua fluorescence bounding scores of surrounding coral atolls. Further east the following year I visited remote chains on a *pinisi* yacht leading to the prehistoric-looking atolls of West Papua. Each with unique histories, people and narratives. There was nowhere I wouldn't go. From the jungles of north Sulawesi in 2013 to hundreds of trips to the heaving city of Jakarta and back to incongruous Dickensian pockets in remote Bali. At face value, I found few similar features between islands. Bahasa Indonesia is, for instance, the official language but more than seven hundred languages and dialects are spoken.

My remit as a correspondent for *The Australian* in 2009 was all-encompassing. With no frills. Some years on, however, when an irked editor-in-chief Chris Mitchell threatened to 'shut down the Bali bureau', I smiled wryly. The newsroom was my villa and the open road.

Gradually my contact book filled up, and I built a wide network throughout Indonesia. Jakarta correspondents came and went. Western journalists parachuted in to Bali for sensational yarns on crime and drugs. Australian tourists, in particular, jumped lemming-like into punishing drug sentences. I stayed for the long haul.

Throughout all my years in Bali, I purposely accumulated little, always renting furnished villas with linen and kitchenware.

My uncluttered life was liberating, and I figured that if I wanted to leave the island or quickly move to another villa it would be uncomplicated. I felt easier living in this temporary zone, not courting unnecessary headaches and free to focus on work. My possessions comprised work tools and light clothes suitable for the tropics. At the drop of a hat, I would race out the front door carrying a small backpack, with camera and laptop, to report from locations Bali-wide or in remote Indonesia for a couple of weeks. Living semi-communally also made sense; I was a single woman in affordable, relative luxury, with a pool, restaurant, other expats and security guards on my doorstep.

Each day a woman (it is women's work unless she is menstruating, or considered spiritually unfit) placed offerings of rice, fruit, petals, tiny biscuits and a stick of smouldering incense in a *canang*, a small woven basket made from coconut leaves – a magnet for hungry dogs and birds – to placate unseen lower spirits that lurked outside my door, through the lush grounds, on the streets, on high street shelves to please the Hindu gods and on the ground to appease demon spirits. Each item in the basket represented a religious offering to different gods. Thus, harmony was achieved by balancing the negative with the positive. A Balinese acquaintance told me that once the offerings were placed and a prayer recited, the ritual was complete. It was inconsequential if the offerings got trodden on or ravaged by animals.

Domestic chores became a thing of the past. I never cooked or cleaned, as I had staff like other expats. Strains of the last days of the Raj resonated. I had no reservations about the novelty of this pampered lifestyle; that was the way people made a living and many of the old expats treated staff as family.

*

Though I missed my kids, I didn't miss my old life, which I saw as a sterile shell of stark highrises and monotonous daily routines with glum commuters trudging to work.

But from the start of my new job, the Indonesian foreign affairs department wasn't so happy: it wanted all foreign correspondents under its thumb, and it pressured me for years to relocate to Jakarta, a teeming metropolis of more than ten million people. To me, its skyscrapers and eye-stinging pollution held little appeal. Bali, by comparison, was enchanting, with its easy lifestyle, appealing culture, beaches and startling tropical vegetation. I held out; the pressure blew over.

Reflecting on expanding my contact network, I turned to the basics of a reporter's tools: police liaisons. But navigating a labyrinthine, arcane bureaucracy was a struggle hampered by my scant Bahasa Indonesia. I became more proficient over the next few years, thanks to an array of home tutoring.

In my first months I gained useless police contacts passing through a well-oiled revolving door. Sometimes they re-emerged on far-flung islands. Often, precincts were dysfunctional; officers would spend hours tapping out reports with one finger on clunky typewriters, or playing Nintendo. I passed days in dank corridors of smoke-filled police stations, waiting for people who had gone home after lunch or hid out behind their desks.

In 2010, the Australian consul general to Bali, Lex Bartlem, lost his usual self-composure while helping me retrieve my stolen laptop. It had been plundered with bags of spoils from my street. I was at the north Kuta police station when officers dragged in two battered transvestites, sobbing and wailing. Blood streamed down their pulverised faces; mobs of locals had beaten them before police arrived, as was the brutal custom. The suspects sat by police, their mascara-blackened cheeks adding to their macabre appearance, before being led into a private room. The police station was packed with locals and foreigners who had been robbed and we all sat in shocked silence absorbing the strange and ugly spectacle.

Officers then brought in the bags of stolen goods – but when I spotted my laptop and tried to extract it, chunky fingers closed over mine. 'You have to leave it here. It's evidence for the court trial.' I was well aware cases took many months to come to trial and I couldn't wait. I was working on several stories and my files had not been backed up.

Lex took a cavalier approach, initially. But his laborious calls to police, speaking through a translator, were in vain. His pleas on official consulate letterhead, reiterating the importance of my laptop to my job, went unanswered. After about ten days, he seemed exhausted of further ideas. When he suggested I enlist weightier officialdom at Australia's Jakarta Embassy, I disclosed I was a Kiwi. It was the last straw. (Months later, after I had bought a new laptop, my old one was retrieved from a police cupboard – it was encased in mould and resembled a volcanic relic.)

So, naturally, when I found an efficient cop, I was overjoyed. I first contacted Denpasar's police commissioner, Djoko Hari Utomo, in 2013. Without persuasion, he relayed tip-offs and sent me reams of crime reports in real time, simplifying my life exponentially. I never figured out why he was so helpful; he asked for no return favour, which, in my experience, was uncommon – officers sometimes asked me to dinner, for instance (meaning I would pay).

I came to rely on Djoko too much, for in 2015 he became globally known and ostracised and I lost him as a source for reasons later explained.

Tourism officials were no less fundamental to my work. Again, it took a year before I was in the happy position of instantly accessing a quote.

In the early days, I was constantly challenged by the ruling forces of *jam karet* (rubber time). It was one of the first

Indonesian cultural terms I learnt – the hard way. It meant the island moved to the rhythm of its own clock with a lack of punctuality. This was not just acceptable but constant. It was not conducive to being a functioning journalist. Whenever basic work staples – internet, telephone, TV, even light bulbs – died, repairs always happened *besok* (tomorrow), a loose word that frequently translated to months, or never. Critical documents sent from Jakarta to my villa never arrived. A sudden death in a Balinese family or a week-long Hindu ceremony prolonged tasks until they dissolved. Phone calls on deadline rang out, or I was told, 'Call back next week.' Scheduled government interviews led to abandoned offices.

I initially found it difficult not to take this personally but I was operating outside Western ideas of time.

In Balinese life, *jam karet* is, by association, intimately entwined with the spiritual world. Everyone is immersed in beliefs and ceremonies incorporating *sekala* – the seen or tangible – and *niskala* – the unseen or mystical – or the intersecting of the material and spiritual worlds that frequently upend daily routines.

Fred B. Eiseman Jr, in his book *Bali: Sekala and Niskala*, writes: 'a major portion of their (Balinese) thinking and activities revolve around the existence of these forces and how they can best control and adjust to them.'

How could my plans not be derailed?

Let me take you into this realm. As part of a piece on Bali's ramshackle infrastructure and overdevelopment I arranged to meet the head of the Denpasar tourism office early one morning in late 2009. When I arrived, at its entrance were profusions of scattered petals and towering bowls of Hindu fruit offerings. Throngs clad in ceremonial garb filled the grounds, praying and chanting in a spiritual manifestation. Curling fingers of musky incense suffused the air.

I became increasingly sceptical of clinching an interview. The chief, shrouded in white, was making supplications before a sumptuously adorned temple. I touched his shoulder and asked, 'Did you forget our appointment?' Reluctantly, he led me to his office. There we were: me, him and a couple of sidekicks wearing ceremonial sarongs and the ritual *udeng* (Balinese head-dress), knotted at the centre of the forehead and dedicated to the gods.

The chief regarded me quizzically from behind his desk and asked, 'What do you want?' During our phone exchange, I had overestimated his command of English, and now I realised that my still kindergarten-level Bahasa Indonesia made an interview unworkable. But why, if he couldn't speak English, was he Bali's government tourism chief?

Mainly, my failed interview was an early first-year lesson in the cultural vacillations of island life, and the need for an assistant – *the* most valuable asset in a reporter's arsenal in Indonesia. For the next few years I employed an array of Indonesian fixers, mainly for translation in court cases, but many were inexperienced and I worried the interpretations were incorrect. Sometimes I was able to 'borrow' *The Australian*'s Jakarta correspondent's assistant, Telly (Lia) Nathanial, who was a godsend.

*

When my short lease finished at Golden Village in late 2009, I chose another villa compound close by in the central Legian district. It had the same communal set-up and convenience, though it lacked the charisma of Golden Village. I could still walk to the beach, restaurants and shops.

But the south was rapidly changing. Seminyak's charm and green belt gave way to a flourishing concrete jungle, with constant bulldozing and building. Despite my dismal sortie to the tourism office, in January 2010 I wrote the first of several pieces on Bali as a ticking environmental time bomb, using comment from my new – and abiding – contact, the affable Ida Bagus Ngurah Wijaya, chief of the private Bali Tourism Board. Someone dubbed my piece a 'thesis'. True, it was forensic, but it remains relevant. Integral to the story was Yuyun Ismawati, a leading Indonesian environmentalist who later drove my investigation into the ravages of artisanal goldmining on other islands.

On my immediate doorstep, Seminyak had become a minefield. Infrastructure wasn't keeping up with development, and new sewage and drainage installation along the tourist strip of Jalan Legian, a showcase street of fashionable shops and restaurants, had already taken a year. Open trenches replaced footpaths, endangering pedestrians and drivers, and business plunged.

That's when I became a victim of the degraded landscape. On my way to dinner in October 2009, I was mowed down by a baby-faced motorbike rider. I had joined pedestrians forced to share the road with gridlocked traffic, picking our way through huge swaths of rubble and mud. Blinded by glaring headlights, I was hit front-on. I fell back, my head hitting the bitumen. I was surprised to be breathing. I asked the stunned Balinese rider to wait for police, but he picked up his bike and skedaddled, of course. An expat friend from Golden Village took me in, in case I should lapse into unconsciousness. I stayed up all night, icing an ever-expanding egg lump on the back of my head, petrified it would turn fatal. Reality hit home: Bali wasn't as soft and fuzzy as it had seemed.

Westerners frequently misjudge Bali as a bubble separated from Indonesia. I wrote some of their stories – the ones ending in tragedy. Some were self-inflicted, others terrible accidents related to the shortcomings of a developing country; one young tourist was fatally electrocuted by touching a street pole linked to crude power lines. I concluded that it's best to maintain a cautious awareness in a developing country.

One of the most insightful chroniclers of the island was Jason Childs, an expatriate Australian cameraman who I met in mid-2009. He frequently worked with me, covering the jail, anniversaries of the Bali bombings and environmental stories, to name a few. An avid surfer, his deep affinity to the archipelago was at the core of his work. His astute eye could uncover layers of hard truths with grace and humility. He once aptly described the conundrum of Bali, telling me, 'There's a sense of freedom ... and the Balinese are so accepting, but when it goes bad it's diabolical.'

I have witnessed that schizophrenic ride many times, personally and professionally.

Noting with dismay the fading allure of the island, with its appeal to surfers, small-town vibe and unique culture, Childs lamented its reckless destruction. 'As a photographer, it's one of the most amazing places to live in the world. But I didn't come to live in a city and all the other problems that come with it. The pace slowed after the [2002 and 2005] terrorist bombings but it has accelerated since 2005 at a pace nobody could have planned for. It's a scary thing ... for the amount of development that's going on there's no infrastructure being put in.'

When Childs and his family, after living on the island for two decades, returned to Australia in February 2016, I missed him. I had wonderful Indonesian snappers, but invariably the picture editor said, 'Can you ask Jason?'

4

BALI HEALING

A few months after I settled in Bali in 2009, William Furney, my friend from *The Bali Times*, suggested I visit Pak (Mr) Dewa in Bedugul, the picturesque fruit and veg bowl at the island's centre. Pak Dewa was a reflexologist and a *dukun*, or shaman, whom Furney, a fitness junkie in his thirties, consulted for his painful joints. Furney had a generous habit of suggesting ideas he deemed suitable for the Australian market.

So it was that I sought out Pak Dewa at Furney's advice — not for his restorative therapies, but for the secrets he held about the Indonesian dictator Suharto, who died in 2008. Suharto, a devotee of Javanese mysticism, had been known to consult *dukuns*, meditate at sites of mystical power and collect *pusaka* (sacred heirlooms) throughout his life. He was thought to draw power from spiritualists' advice. One of his Balinese *dukuns* was purportedly close to Pak Dewa. My mission was to extract an exposé on the pair's confidences. This was my introduction to a country steeped in ancient mysticism, superstition and paranormal intrigue. The assignment was a long shot, and one that proved tricky.

Pak Dewa's house was isolated, at the end of a nameless potholed track facing a lake. But he was obviously worth the trouble because Indonesians travelled from all corners of the archipelago, queuing before dawn to consult him.

Furney had organised my guide for the three-hour trip north of Seminyak. Who better than Pak Dewa's nephew, Gusti? Small snag: Gusti, who'd enthusiastically agreed, overlooked the impending birth of his child. He phoned on the scheduled day to say his wife had just given birth. Next came Pak Putra; we were to travel on a motor scooter – until his wife forbade him from travelling with another woman on the back. The next contact refused point-blank to go near the *dukun*; he shuddered, saying he was afraid of black magic. Finally a practical bloke, who was moonlighting from his hotel job, stepped into the breach. He was a large man, perhaps a bouncer, and managed to find Pak Dewa's place.

It was about 9 a.m. I queued with locals in the dirt courtyard where extended family wandered among scratching chickens, ducks, pigs and crowing roosters. No one seemed curious about the 'tall' *bule* (foreigner) among them – I was amused to find myself, at only 162.5 centimetres, towering above them. They were keenly guarding their places, and it was a long wait. My bored driver stood in the yard chain-smoking kreteks, Indonesia's sweet clove cigarettes, simultaneously spitting.

In fact, we were in one of the most stunning rustic parts of Bali, in the unspoilt central highlands. This was the first time I had ventured outside the tourist zone, and the cooler higher-altitude climate was an exhilarating change. In the valley where I stood, mountain ranges soared above Pak Dewa's house, adjoining the glassy Lake Beratan which lies beside the seventeenth-century Hindu-Buddhist water temple Pura Ulun Danu Bratan. So iconic is the temple it then graced Indonesia's IDR50,000 banknotes.

The locals seemed apathetic towards the view. They patiently awaited therapy, at a fraction of a GP's fee, to exorcise demons, equip themselves with black or white magic, or with *susuk* (talismans inserted beneath the skin for good luck) and alleviate pain with reflexology. Pak Dewa was a one-stop shop.

Finally it was my turn – by this time, my anticipation and the sun were high. Pak Dewa ushered me into his house. A wiry, short man of seventy-four, he had two front teeth missing and most of his black hair intact. He sported a sarong, singlet and a black leather bomber jacket. Adroitly avoiding questions about Suharto, he claimed he was 'media-shy'. I asked for a reflexology treatment, hoping he might loosen up.

He led me into a tiny, stifling room and pulled crimson curtains across the windows to conceal us from outsiders pressing their faces to the grubby panes. *Lie on the floor*, he gestured, before targeting anatomical pressure points. Alarming flashes of agony swept through me as he poked and stabbed my feet and legs with a wooden reflexology stick, the pointy end resembling a freshly sharpened pencil. As a yelp escaped my lips, he upped the pressure and smiled beneficently, until I raised my hand in protest.

Next I submitted to *tirtha* (holy water) for spiritual wellness, my driver helping to translate. In one hand, Pak Dewa held a pale pink bougainvillea flower between thumb and forefinger; in the other, a half glass of water. He closed his eyes and recited a prayer while sprinkling the holy water over my head several times. He then dropped the flower into the water and told me to drink it to invoke the divine powers of the Hindu gods.

'Is it tap water?' I asked, wondering if it was sterile.

He replied with a sort of guffaw, my guide translating. 'Don't worry about the water quality; faith in the holy water is omnipotent.' (For the record, I didn't get sick.)

Till the end, Pak Dewa remained tight-lipped about Suharto's secrets: it was a fait accompli.

William Furney had, of course, already tried to unlock the mystery of these conversations with Suharto. Confounded, he had sent me along for a second go. He was probably disappointed with the result, yet gave little away.

But the experience piqued my interest in shamanism – especially after several expats breathlessly told me of their own encounters.

*

Bali was, for years, the Coles supermarket of spiritual healers, *dukuns*, *balians* and soothsayers believed to possess occult powers.

For Indonesians, healers are essential in a prosaic and practical way, as Adrian Vickers points out in his 2012 book *Bali: A Paradise Created*, 'Magic and exorcism are important topics on an island like Bali, where tropical diseases and a high infant mortality rate have been part of the basic experiences of people on all levels of society.'

After the 2006 publication of Elizabeth Gilbert's bestselling romantic memoir *Eat, Pray, Love* and the 2010 film adaptation – partly set in Ubud's spiritual mecca and starring Balinese healer Ketut Liyer – the Walmart version emerged. Tourist demand for transformative traditional healing surged, and Westerners swore by its emotional and physical powers manifested in trances and the spirit world.

But in the absence of regulations, questionable practices have mushroomed. It's impossible to know how many healers operate in Bali. One estimate tips eight thousand, far exceeding the number of medical doctors – though Indonesian statistics of any kind are dubious.

Spiritual tourism is a godsend to healers who make a living from an ancient craft that traditionally caters to the poorest stratas of society. For locals unable to afford medical treatment, the healer deals with stigmatised conditions including cancer, leprosy and HIV/AIDS. A small donation is expected, to keep the healer fed; the meal of choice for most Indonesians is a rice and vegetable staple that costs about a dollar. I wonder if Westerners referencing *Eat, Pray, Love* expected too much for their buck.

At the height of spiritual mania following the release of the film, my Balinese friend Puspa took me to Tjokorda Gede Rai – a well-regarded *balian* – for a 'check-up'. We visited him on the outskirts of Ubud. The patrician-looking, bearded healer was clad in the *mangku*'s (high priest's) attire of pure white sarong and shirt. At seventy-eight, he was still handsome, tall and upright, with the high cheekbones and fine features typical of the Balinese. He had been a *dukun* for almost half his life, he declared proudly. Holding aloft heavy wooden scrolls 'of wisdom', he would consult one of two hundred for me, he said, gazing from rheumy yet gimlet eyes.

It was quiet; a couple of locals loitered. I lay down in an open-air wooden *bale* (hut) on a flaxen mat, and Tjokorda executed the sharp stick routine. 'You have blocked energy on the left side,' he told me, prodding to unblock my bad energy. Miraculously, back pain – from too many hours at the computer – subsided. He smiled. 'Already the good energy is flowing.'

What of my spiritual concerns? The subtext seemed to be: was I another lovelorn, divorced Western woman seeking new love?

'You are still young,' he said convincingly. 'Today your new life begins. You will have good luck in love and work.' Yes, I definitely felt more energised, happier and younger, in that devil-may-care way – for about fifteen minutes.

I wonder how many shamans rode the wave after Elizabeth Gilbert schlepped from New York on her journey of self-discovery, enlightenment and love. The most prominent one was Ketut Liyer, elevated to his career apotheosis, ensuring his windfall. He even began to charge devotees in US dollars for consultations.

Foreigners have long been susceptible to the forces of Bali's exalted magic and karma. Faced with fantastic stories and entranced Indonesians, I was intrigued. During my first months in Bali in 2009, out of curiosity I consulted *dukuns* and clairvoyants recommended by expats. But I found them to be mostly scam artists – and not very good ones.

Work was invariably the prism through which I gained insights into ingrained Hindu beliefs and rituals. When a fixer challenged a work-for-pay matter with me, spitting venom in a barrage of texts, it culminated in this: 'I will cast a spell on you. I am Hindu. We believe in karma. You'll see, you will get what you deserve.' This went on for days, and it got quite nasty. I was intrigued it came from someone using facts as their stock-in-trade. The more I ignored it, the more inflammatory the rhetoric.

Thankfully, I wasn't touched by the wrath of these curses – not that I am aware. But many expats told me they attributed misfortunes such as illnesses, accidents and thefts to curses from imagined enemies. Taking themselves off to the *dukun* for an exorcism was as common as a supermarket trip. Wellbeing restored, they were relieved, certainly of many rupiah.

How easy it is for charlatans to proliferate in this climate. In 2009 I read a warning from a disenchanted foreign woman in a Bali expat paper: 'There are many charlatans out there who are happy to make empty promises that you will be healed … if you faithfully follow their instructions, and pay a large amount of money. There are other *balians* who are very charismatic and have convinced parents that their daughter[s] will be in good hands, while they blatantly abuse their power to do inappropriate things.'

You don't have to be a young girl, as I found out in 2011 when I was touched up by a creepy old *balian* in Denpasar. There were no protective laws.

Bali authorities were quick to crack down on Western 'alternative therapists' exploiting cancer patients. But the humble *balian* was unassailable.

*

After my session with Tjokorda, an influx of foreigners arrived seeking his sage advice and healing hands. They crammed into the small *bale*. It was church-like silent, bar the odd reverential whisper.

He summoned an impatient middle-aged Swedish woman. 'You have cured my stomach cancer,' she said deferentially. 'It's completely gone. Thank you so much. I came to see you last year, and a few months later my cancer was gone. Do you remember me?' He didn't, but he betrayed no surprise. It seemed to me that Ketut Liyer was an insipid second to this dynamo.

Among those waiting were some in advanced stages of cancer. Desperately seeking spiritual panaceas, they told me they had renounced science-based Western medicine, believing it more toxic than therapeutic. Childlike, they sat in a circle on bamboo mats watching, in hushed thrall, the elderly Tjokorda diagnose and work on one prostrate 'patient' after another. He was standing in a type of pulpit. After each 'patient' was 'cured' and dismissed, they were so grateful they half-genuflected. It was a fairly stock procedure: a good poke around the head, toes, feet and internal organs with a reflexology stick revealed vulnerable pressure spots or health issues. Acute pain – identified when the 'patient' yelped – was said to be connected to a particular illness.

A Frenchwoman lay on the floor and waited while Tjokorda, deviating from the stick routine, gathered medicinal herbs from his garden to treat her blood ailment. He placed a bunch on her stomach, stuffed a lot more into her mouth and ordered her to chew, and placed the rest in a plastic bag for her to take home.

Then there was the wan elderly American man whose multiple Western operations and treatments had left him enervated and anxious. His wife, at first harried and upset, smiled gratefully as they left with a tiny plastic bag that contained the herbal medicine – they carried it as though it were gold bullion.

In every nook were tiny baskets with offerings to the gods. And money. Money stuffed into jars, offering bowls, under spiritual books, overflowing. Although I'd been told the healer didn't take money, it is de rigueur to contribute. Most payments were at least IDR100,000 ($10), though many 'patients' gave up to IDR500,000. Where did the money go? Tjokorda apparently had no earthly use for it.

Among his admirers were three Western students hoping to glean healing skills. One was a Frenchwoman in her forties who'd arrived in Bali a few months previously with little hope as a mastectomy and chemotherapy had failed to eradicate her breast cancer. But she vowed the cancer had shrunk since she'd seen the healer. 'It's a miracle,' said Puspa, who deeply believed in harmony and balance, clairvoyants, traditional healing and *balians*.

A group of French people had flown in from Paris especially to see the *balian*. Many wanted check-ups; others were in varying degrees of ill health. There was a keen sense of theatre, and I suspected Tjokorda found it thoroughly gratifying as he periodically sank into a chair to smoke a fag, surveying his minions while they waited for him to resume duties. When several more groups arrived and squeezed into the small space, it was overwhelming, the heat stifling. Tjokorda glanced at his prospective workload and disappeared into his garden.

On his return, he had a plan. He selected one person in each group. The atmosphere changed; people became testy, and a scuffle nearly broke out. Tjokorda, seeing it was about to get ugly, swiftly picked his patients. The rest slunk off, promising to return in the morning. I asked a young German student if she thought his popularity had grown since the *Eat, Pray, Love* hoopla. 'Definitely,' she said enthusiastically. 'Groups come every day. It's big business. The hotels arrange drivers and ask people if they would like to see a healer.'

I learnt that Puspa – who donned many hats as a sometime journalist, translator and guide for French TV channels – arranged healer trips for large French groups. I met some during my own trips with Puspa. They would visit for a week, specifically for spiritual consultations. They were modern-day pilgrims seeking meaning in their suburban lives. Spiritual tourism filled a gap, Puspa said. It's a microcosm of the island in which magic is not only tied to the tourist dollar but also to innate Indonesian mystical beliefs.

5

SLOW BURN

During my early Bali years, the only other island-based Australian journalist was Justin Hale. Then in his late thirties, he had been covering cut-and-thrust stories since 2002, including the Bali bombers' trials, the Aceh tsunami, the Bali Nine trials and so on. Fluent in Bahasa Indonesia, Justin was a stringer for Australian commercial radio and TV outlets.

It was during my reporting of the Bali Nine appeal cases and other trials that we formed a friendship based on my ignorance of the Indonesian judicial system. Court seemed intimidating to me, the characters dour and oddly theatrical, their words laced with a degree of faux indignation. I imagined the menace reverberating through the Bali Nine. Equally vulnerable were their families, struggling to comprehend the catastrophic consequences pronounced on their children by prosecutors and judges in a language they didn't understand in stifling, media-packed courtrooms. The trials could be just as opaque to journalists.

In the early days, if Justin didn't show, I sometimes called him for help or relied on English-speaking lawyers. No matter how small the case, proceedings were excruciatingly protracted. By the time I emerged, editors were scrambling for copy. Once, Justin blithely suggested I pad out a story with the judge's concluding summary: the offender had damaged Bali's exemplary tourist reputation. 'They always say that,' he chirped. And so they did, and so journalists kept churning it out.

It wasn't unusual for hearings to be delayed until after lunch or postponed for a week or more if one of the judiciary didn't show. On good days, I'd nervously calculate how much time I had to write the story if the hearing finished by 3 p.m., while allowing for a three-hour time difference that would make it 6 p.m. in Sydney – pretty much on deadline. I would have about half an hour, so I usually wrote an outline in advance, fleshing it out later.

In time, I realised much of the judges' marathon preambles were as arcane to me as they were to the most astute ears. Local reporters rushed for seats but paid little heed until later, unless it was a significant trial. The key was to have a good Indonesian fixer, which wasn't easy in a small pool already snapped up before my arrival in Bali. Jakarta correspondents typically did three-year stints, and then their Bali fixers – like their contact books – seamlessly flowed to the next team. Unhelpfully, I was limited to employing fixers on a freelance basis – whenever I knew an important story was about to unfold. The fixer's job of checking court schedules and alerting 'bosses' to stories was my responsibility. As my contacts grew through the years, and I eventually employed a steady fixer at my discretion, my situation became less problematic.

*

Bespectacled and fair-skinned, at 188 centimetres tall, Justin towered above the Indonesians, an advantage in a milieu of pushy local media. He had been in Indonesia so long he knew the foibles and strengths of a long line of Australian correspondents, and he enjoyed filling me in on Fairfax veterans such as Lindsay Murdoch and Mark Forbes. In my time, Matt Brown (ABC), Tom Allard (Fairfax) and Adam Gartrell (AAP) turned up to court from Jakarta with their fixers. Alone, I must have cut a slightly strange figure.

*

By 2010, when Bali Nine courier Scott Rush, the poster boy of the gang, prepared to lodge his final appeal against his death sentence, I'd gained confidence in deciphering the foibles of the Indonesian court system. I had interviewed Rush and his lawyers many times, and, occasionally, his anguished parents, though they were wary of the media. All the Bali Nine parents were paranoid their personal comments might adversely affect their child's cases. This seemed wise, as there was often no logic to verdicts; sometimes journalists would check with one another that we didn't mishear the prosecutor or the judge. Though parents tried to present a positive front, they were in an invidious position. Amid the turmoil, there was such strain and grief, it was painful to see.

In May that year, I had joined Martin Stephens's mother Michelle on a spartan wooden bench at the prison's grim waiting area. Overcome by the oppressive heat, sweat beaded on her flushed face. It was difficult even to breathe.

Stephens was about to lodge his final appeal to commute his life sentence. I was disconcerted by Michelle's businesslike attitude to her son's sentence – as though it were a bad dream that would pass. When I asked her how she felt his appeal would go, she replied crisply, 'We've always been confident.'

Wasn't she just a bit nervous? I pressed.

'No.' She appeared surprised by my question. 'We have everyone praying for him. I don't know why this had to happen,' she told me huffily, 'but it has, and it's obviously happened for a reason, so we just have to get on with it.'

She was staying with Stephens's fiancée Christine Puspayanti and her twelve-year-old daughter from another relationship.

Michelle continued, 'When this is over, we'll arrange the wedding and get them married.' They did marry, but behind bars the following year after Martin's life sentence was upheld in January 2011.

The mother of Rush's schoolfriend Michael Czugaj, Vicki – a warm, outgoing woman from the Sunshine Coast, who I came to know well – told me on one trip to the prison, 'This is my life.' She was really mourning a lost child. At eighteen, Michael was one of the youngest of the group when he was arrested with 1.75 kilograms of heroin strapped to his body. To Vicki, a single mother of eight who cleaned kindergarten toilets for a living, the situation was surreal. When she was in Bali we would go out for dinner and drinks to lighten the mood for a few hours. I admired her courage and sense of humour; how many parents could carry that off amid the sorrow and fear?

In her modest hotel room with a kitchenette, she cooked for her son on her annual fortnightly visits, and poured out her heart to me. 'He has changed so much since his arrest. He was just a boy, now he's a man. The years haven't been kind. He's gone from a very good looking teenager to someone who's drawn in the face. He's lost a lot of weight and his skin and teeth aren't good. To see your child in this situation is not pleasant. It doesn't matter what they do, they're still your baby, your flesh and blood. The last day is the worst, walking away … it's so lonely. I cry and cry.'

As one of the few Western reporters to monitor the gang long-term, I often saw their state of mind reflected in their physical transformations. I had seen Rush's appearance fluctuate wildly. In 2008, he was thin, his skin so wan it looked virtually translucent.

On 18 August 2010 he was almost unrecognisable when he arrived at the densely packed Denpasar District Court for his last-chance reprieve. He wore a large wooden cross around his neck, and when he removed his sunglasses his black-ringed eyes were glazed. His face was pallid, spotty and bloated, and the guards, his lawyer and the Australian consul general had to help him to a holding cell.

Australian TV crews had flown in, and in the media crush Rush was virtually mobbed as though he was a rock star. But when addressing the panel of judges, he acknowledged the interest, declaring, 'I accept I am a criminal, not a celebrity.'

Ripples of concern spread throughout the courtroom as he sat rubbing his face and eyes excessively.

At one point he broke down in tears while reading his statement, apologising for his drug crime and fixing his gaze on his indomitable parents, Lee and Christine Rush, sitting calmly in the courtroom's front row of the public gallery. Only later during the protracted hearing did the emotional strain take a visible toll on Lee, who was overcome with grief.

The high stakes of his case had conferred an unwelcome spotlight on the tearaway Brisbanite whose history of teenage drug use, theft and fraud eventually led to his squalid Bali jail cell. But his sentence was a bizarre anomaly. Of the six couriers arrested at Denpasar airport in April 2005, Rush – who had 1.3 kilograms of heroin strapped to his body – was the only one who remained on death row. Even the prosecutors regarded him as a simple courier.

After a 2006 appeal against his life term, he was strangely handed the death sentence. Now he was fighting for his life, facing the prospect of the firing squad.

At the time, Rush was quite open with me. We had an easy rapport, and I liked him. I had tried to help him repair a romantic relationship with a Melbourne woman, Laura Pemberton. I'd met her in 2008 after I noticed her visiting the then twenty-two-year-old – they sat with their arms entwined, deep in conversation.

I gave her a lift from the jail back to her hotel; she was returning to Australia that night.

Back in Sydney, I interviewed her by phone and asked what drew her to Rush. Four years his senior, she had on a whim visited him on holiday, singling him out as one of the more receptive to visitors. They had fallen for each other and pledged eternal love. She said, 'I wanted to visit one of the Australians ... I had read that Scott welcomed visitors, he wanted people to visit him; a lot of the others don't particularly. And I've always thought the death penalty is rubbish. Obviously, he had quite an impact on me. He was very charismatic, very positive, very kind. I wanted to keep in contact. We both wear an eternity knot round our necks. Whatever happens, our feelings for each other will be eternal. I love him. He calls me his angel.'

Then, Laura revealed some surprising personal details. 'It's not a conventional relationship of course but I do love him and I care about him a great deal. It's more of an emotional connection rather than a physical one, obviously. Luckily, I don't have a particularly large libido so it doesn't come into it much.'

The Sydney newsdesk was mesmerised by her comments but omitted running the last sentence.

When I broke this story on 15 November 2008, the tabloids went into paroxysms. I had returned to Sydney after a couple of months in Bali and I was receiving hyped calls while I walked around a supermarket. *The Daily Telegraph* was the first to hound me for Laura's details, and though I respected her wish not to reveal her surname, they found her. Overwhelmed by the media's relentless pursuit and subsequent stories, she went into hiding a few months later and changed her details. At various times I was still able to reach her.

I believe it was Rush's death sentence that came between them. There was no future in the relationship, Laura told me.

'They're on death row – *they're all going to die*,' she screamed down the phone in March 2010. The flush of new love had descended into dark reality.

Rush was psychologically tortured under the shadow of the death sentence. He suffered nightmares about the firing squad. Drugs were a coping mechanism, he told me. 'I was affected massively. That's why I'm messed up all the time. I couldn't sleep at night. I was really screwed up. I dreamt about Myuran and Andrew [the other Bali Nine members sentenced to death]. I took tablets to try to calm me down. I felt kind of hopeless.'

It was widely reported that it was Rush's father, Lee, who first tipped off the Australian Federal Police to the smuggling operation. The AFP rejected this and claimed it was already aware of and investigating a syndicate recruiting couriers to import narcotics to Australia. Lee said that he had asked the AFP to prevent his son from leaving Australia so that his son could not get involved in any drug-related crime. The AFP denied promising him that his son would be prevented from leaving Australia or be warned he was under surveillance.

Instead, on the day Rush left Australia, the AFP alerted the Indonesian authorities, crucially telling them to 'take what action they deem appropriate'.

Rush was dogged by the AFP's role, asking me, 'Do you think that they … can say they don't deserve any responsibility at all?'

Former AFP chief Mick Keelty, who retired in 2009, copped flak over his part in the arrests.

Then, as Rush's legal team mustered a string of expert witnesses for his final appeal, we heard Keelty and deputy commissioner Michael Phelan would testify for him.

In Denpasar's District Court in September 2010, Keelty, clad in a traditional, brightly printed Indonesian shirt, quietly told judges that Rush played a very minor role in the smuggling plot.

Likewise, Phelan stressed Rush's part as a lowly courier. But they denied they knew before his arrest that Rush had been involved in the operation.

Among the other Bali Nine members there were recriminations over Lee Rush's tip-off, and Rush was long racked with guilt. Martin Stephens told me, 'Everyone did bear a grudge, but either way we would have been caught. But if we had been caught in Australia we'd be out of jail by now.'

I had assumed incorrectly the group was tightknit after sharing five years in Kerobokan, but Stephens disavowed me of that idea. At best, they resembled a dysfunctional family. 'We're not friends, we weren't in the beginning and we're not now. I don't trust anyone in here. I only talk to my girlfriend [now his wife, Christine Puspayanti]. When we get out I'm sure we'll never see each other again.' The men shared a separate area called the Tower, and the atmosphere was claustrophobic and often antagonistic. Michael Czugaj, who battled depression, had become quite chatty with me, and over the phone he described the difficulties, 'We're all in here together, there's a lot of hostility and conflict. You have to ignore it and try to be polite. We don't have a choice.'

*

That year the mood was particularly sombre. Several Bali Nine members lodged final appeals, paving the way for Myuran Sukumaran and Andrew Chan's judicial appeals to spare their lives, which I covered less than a month after Rush's appeal in September.

Everyone watched on tenterhooks. Among the media throngs that day, you could barely move. On court days, busloads of Indonesian prisoners were also waiting for hearings; the noisy, overcrowded holding cells were like saunas. I couldn't imagine the discomfort and distress of waiting for hours behind those bars. That day, proceedings didn't get underway till after midday, and the build-up was tense.

Journalists were usually kept at bay in high-profile cases, as families and lawyers spoke to the inmates behind the thick bars and snappers jostled for the best shots. I sometimes brought the Australians bottles of cold water and asked if they wanted food.

Just before guards led Sukumaran and Chan to the courtroom, they changed their sweat-soaked T-shirts for pressed business shirts. The padlock opened, and a thunderous media circus followed, with TV crews lugging equipment on their shoulders. It was easy to fall or be shoved and injured in the stampede – which later happened to me during Schapelle Corby's release in May 2017.

After the court cases, we withdrew to corners of the courthouse with our fixers to write the story and file. It was often evening by the time I returned to the surreal tourist scenes of Seminyak I couldn't reconcile with the parallel life-and-death dilemmas I reported. Colleagues said the same thing.

*

Chan's application for life was refused the same day the court commuted Rush's death sentence in May 2011. Sukumaran's appeal was rejected on 6 July 2011. The last option to spare their lives was a presidential pardon from Susilo Bambang Yudhoyono, and he wasn't known to be merciful to drug dealers.

*

I needed to move again in early 2010. The villa I left in the Legian district is lodged in my memory as one that violently shook during an earthquake at 6 a.m. in September 2009. I awoke to swaying lamps and shelves and the disorientating feeling my bed was moving beneath me. The 5.8 magnitude quake had struck nearby, just south of Denpasar but a conflicting more powerful figure of 6.4 was also officially announced. It sparked fears of a tsunami and sent terrified residents rushing outside in various states of panic and undress, too frightened to return. Miraculously there were no serious injuries; most were caused by collapsing roofs and falling debris or Indonesians jumping out of windows. Of the countless quakes and tremors I have experienced in Bali, that was the worst.

An Australian friend alerted me to apartments in Batu Belig, about sixteen minutes north of Seminyak, and I soon moved into a garden unit. The area was less touristy and frantic, and near a wild stretch of beach where I liked to walk. The complex was tenanted by expats, a couple whom I knew. Each two-storeyed apartment was leased separately, upstairs and downstairs.

Perhaps the first bad omen came when the owner's dog bit me at a time when rabies was rampant on the island. I raced to hospital for rabies shots, but was left forever fearful of Bali dogs. The beach itself rendered a dark, slightly sinister tone over its broad foreshore and I preferred to walk there only in the mornings. One day I watched a man standing on the sand over a large skinned animal – perhaps a dog or a pig – laughing creepily at my dismay.

Above my unit was a Jekyll and Hyde character who grew gradually more unpredictable. With my workload and travel, I took scant notice. But one midnight, an enormous crash woke me: he had thrown his entire glassware and crockery collection over his balcony onto my small porch.

I had helped this man write a CV to secure a better job, and he had expressed interest in my work. One day I received a call from the Sydney newsdesk – he had sent them a letter accusing me of unethical conduct and signed his name. I was aghast at the fiction he had woven, and shaken that I should be caught in his web of instability.

Newspapers have always been targeted by kooks calling and writing in with grudges, but I found it particularly frustrating to defend myself from overseas. The same year, a man arrested with a small amount of drugs accused me of phone hacking and lies in my coverage about his case. In deep fear, from his holding cell at Denpasar's police headquarters, he told me of his dire illnesses and hopes for deportation. Some months after his release, he wrote to the paper and accused me of defamation and bribing police for information, and he threatened to sue the paper. How easy it was to pierce the reputation of a journalist. Again, I was astonished at the total fiction.

Meanwhile, I was incensed about the broken glass and crockery on my porch. There were so many shards that I couldn't even crunch my way outside in shoes in the morning. The Bali villa owner read my upstairs neighbour the riot act and made him clean it up, but didn't evict him. After that, I didn't feel safe in my villa.

On assignment later on the island of Sumba in East Nusa Tenggara province, I met a spearfishing Crocodile Dundee-type from Darwin, who promised to come to my aid should I ever need it. I filed away his offer, and years later I called him about a threatening blackmail situation I feared would escalate. True to his word, he said, 'Well, just let me know if I should send some boys.' I half-smiled – Indonesia was cowboy country, and this was one solution to a problem. But in the end it seemed too risky, so it was never pursued in any way, and I was relieved the problem organically resolved.

*

On the bright side, I rented a car and explored the island, sometimes reviewing posh resorts, spas and restaurants. These establishments had to meet the highest standards to be eligible for *The Australian*'s 'Travel & Indulgence' section, so I chose discerningly – and with some glee – though I did sneak in a couple of underdogs.

One was a decrepit hole-in-the-wall restaurant called KZU, which served delectable Japanese-Indonesian fusion food. It had a few wobbly tables and attracted strapping surfers who piled their plates for a few dollars. A few years later KZU, renamed KZU Wabi Sabi, opened in a new location in bright air-conditioned comfort, preserving the menu of its proven early success.

When Jake visited Bali for the first time in February 2011, I took him – and the bunch of schoolmates he was staying with – to authentic Indonesian restaurants. They were in their early twenties, and their primary purpose was to party in Kuta, so I enjoyed showing them more aesthetic spots. Many knew me from their schooldays, and I became one of the boys on expeditions to areas such as Uluwatu in the south.

Usually my forays to Kuta were for work: Bali bombing anniversaries, schoolies parties when tainted alcohol made the rounds, and occasionally to have dinner with Justin Hale. He lived near the former Sari Club and Paddy's Pub, the sites of the 2002 bombings, and for unspecified reasons he seldom ventured outside the strip. 'Can you slum it in Kuta?' he would ask. Then I would have warm beer and *cap cay* (stir-fried mixed vegetables) at a Formica table while he eyed the passing female parade. I have Justin to thank for my first tour of Kuta's nightlife, an introduction to a melange of Jalan Legian's tacky nightclubs that lured misguided Australian kids, pickpockets, drug touts, pimps and hookers, police stings and violent hangers-on. The tabloids and commercial TV were well served.

I interviewed many who came to blows in Kuta, over theft, methanol-laced cocktails or brutal assaults. Some were lucky to escape alive.

Four Westerners didn't in June 2009; they were among 25 people who died from drinking methanol-laced alcohol at a Kuta bar.

Richard Irving, a London expat, found his life on the line in Kuta in 2014, victim of a crime wave that had escalated since I started living on the island.

Richard had made a rare visit to nightspots at the behest of friends visiting from Britain. He was mugged by about eight Indonesians as he ventured home at 4 a.m. trying to hail a taxi. The group surrounded him on the pretext of offering transport while pickpocketing him.

I reported his story and others like it.

Richard went on: 'I noticed a hand on my wallet and grabbed his arm. They tripped me up, pushed me to the ground and started kicking and punching me.'

He was left with a broken toe, bruises and several lumps on his head – and without his phone. He retained his wallet, but the fight for it nearly cost him dearly.

At 193 centimetres tall, he reckoned he was saved by his size but as he got to his feet 'one guy had picked up a breeze block ready to drop it on my head'.

That's when he summoned the strength to flee.

The incident had happened thirty metres from a police tent parked by the Bali bombing monument in Jalan Legian. Two police officers were asleep in the tent when Richard tried to report it.

Expats and tourists took to social media each year to document increasing crimes and hotspots but some were unwilling to face reality, besmirch Bali or pay police to type out routinely ineffectual reports.

'For those people saying useless platitudes like "crime happens everywhere" … get real,' Richard said.

'This is a growing problem. Crime happens a lot here and a lot more than it used to. The police do not give one shit about it, they care more about extorting bribes from tourists without helmets.'

Weak law enforcement has remained a perennial problem, not just in Bali, but Indonesia-wide.

So I was happy when Jake, tired of running the gauntlet through the tourist hype and potential perils, realised there were better areas. He changed neighbourhoods and spent the last days of his two-week holiday at my villa.

6

THE OTHER BALI

In late 2009 and January 2010, I cast my eye to Bali's largely unspoilt eastern neighbour across the Lombok Strait. A sleepy island, Lombok had woken excitedly to land-rush fever, trading on its stunning good looks and relative bargains. The money had poured in from big and small foreign investors, but unforeseen hiccups would interrupt the best-laid plans. At the centre was an ambitious mega-development planned for Kuta, in the south of Lombok, that would jump-start new infrastructure. Serendipitously, Kuta is also the name of Bali's tourist drawcard – a name that means fortress and supposedly was the spitting image of Bali twenty years before.

For three decades, Lombok, the first in a chain of Indonesia's eastern islands, was branded the next Bali.

Administratively it is part of West Nusa Tengarra province, which includes the larger Sumbawa island to its east. During local feuds in the seventeenth century, Balinese Hindus took control of western Lombok and have been ensconced as a minority since, along with Buddhists and Christians.

Lombok's sublime rugged landscape, waterfalls, surf breaks and the giant 3726-metre Mount Rinjani volcano are good reason for tourism optimism. But apart from a small expat community around Senggigi in the north-west – the first tourist enclave from back in the 1980s, which never fully took off – and a few intrepid backpackers, mainland Lombok had little Western exposure. The island was conservative, predominantly populated by ethnic Sasaks, most of whom are Muslims and animists. The Sasaks originated in a small kingdom, predating most other Indonesian ethnic groups.

I wondered how tourism would co-exist with the poor farmers and fishermen. In the mix was internecine conflict against the minority Ahmadiyah Muslim sect, long persecuted and attacked for beliefs deemed to deviate from the fundamental principles of Islam; anti-Christian sentiment and terrorist travel warnings. Lombok was raw, Westerners found.

A past colleague on *The Courier-Mail*, UK-Australian journalist Richard Laidlaw, had once lived in Senggigi while running the now-defunct *Lombok Times*. He told me that he'd faced myriad obstacles over staff apathy and inaction, so eventually he'd relocated to Bali.

It was hard to envisage Lombok, dubbed Pulau Seribu Masjid or 'land of a thousand mosques', rivalling Hindu-dominant Bali as a tourist mecca. Bali's tourism boom had begun about fifty years earlier, while Lombok was relatively inexperienced. However, tourism was its main source of revenue, largely from a popular island trio off its mainland: Gili Trawangan, Gili Meno and Gili Air, run mostly by Western interests.

*

I flew in to the tiny, now-defunct airport near Lombok's capital of Mataram, half an hour east of Bali, to check out the investment frenzy in February 2010. The airport general manager, Erdi Nuka, was integral to my mission, and I enlisted languid staff to chase him down. Over several hours and cups of tea, I convinced Erdi my story would help to promote his island. He found a guide to drive me the forty-six kilometres to Kuta.

Next morning, Harris – a short, cheerful man from the Lombok Tourism Office – collected me from my Mataram hotel in a black SUV. I spread his map across my lap, charting the unfamiliar place names to Kuta. Within half an hour, jade rice fields, coconut groves and alluvial plains rolled by in hypnotic waves on a near-empty road. At a major turn-off, we detoured under canopied rainforest leading to Sekotong, a spectacular outcrop on the south-west peninsula.

I was hoping to track down an American man called Gerry, because of his rumoured ties to the island's grand poohbahs: *bupatis* (mayors) and development officials. I was equipped only with a description of his beach resort. Fortunately it acted as a beacon. Imposing villas with neon-blue roofs glittered under the baking sun. None was occupied, though the project had begun in 2001. Harris and I picked our way like thieves in the night through decaying, cobwebbed houses; it was the only way to the beachfront.

Under a *joglo* (open Javanese bamboo structure) was a bare-chested, middle-aged man gazing out to sea. I assumed he was Gerry; no other Western soul was about. When I called out, he turned to acknowledge me. A sinewy figure of some intrigue, Gerry was said to have served in the US Marine Corps. Without preamble, he launched into a spiel describing fanciful development plans for Sekotong, including a marina. Officials had sought his advice, he said. His vacant resort was for sale with an ambitious price tag – and on a subsequent Lombok visit in 2018, I noted the villas were still on the market.

I was sceptical of Gerry's fantastic tales. So when he interrupted himself to announce that his Swiss bankers were flying in for lunch, I was unconvinced. We were, after all, off the beaten track. Were they to land in a helicopter on the beach?

But, on cue, two male figures approached, trudging along the powder-white sand seemingly from nowhere. Sweating profusely in business attire, they seemed pleased to have two strangers in the mix. Gerry shoved beers into their hands as they wiped sweat from their faces, their clothes clinging to them like wet rags. Staff miraculously appeared bearing a five-star feast: fresh lobster, prawns, fish, salads and more cold beer from a discreet kitchen behind a table facing the sea. They set the mounds of food before the visitors.

'Time for you two to go,' Gerry cut in amid the chatter, staring at me and Harris.

An awkward silence.

Embarrassed, the bankers protested, 'We can't possibly eat all this, do stay.'

Gerry grudgingly acceded, then added, 'But *he* can eat rice in the kitchen with the staff,' pointing to Harris. Another strained pause as my guide scurried off – the poor man was clearly relieved.

That day I left pondering if the development plans were simply tall tales. (My Lombok contacts told me in 2018 they hadn't seen the elusive Gerry. I noted the resort's phone was on the blink, but the garish blue roofing remained.)

*

Back on the road, Harris and I rolled down the windows, inhaling the earthy smell of the open countryside, and continued south. On the horizon loomed Kuta's towering headlands that presided over sweeping surf beaches, coral reefs and deep bays opening to emerald valleys. Precisely the stuff on which Western dreams are built.

It was here that the Dubai-based Emaar Projects resort, slated since 2007, was planned. It drew nearly forty foreigners and one domestic investor, virtually overnight. On the back of it, small investors snapped up land and waited for critical infrastructure.

Fostering land-rush fever, authorities did everything to milk the Bali image, while vowing to avoid its overdevelopment.

Government ambitions also hung on the stalled, shambolic international airport, which locals used as a picnic ground and racetrack. When I wandered through on another Lombok visit in early 2011, I was mystified to find an eerie, deserted shell, the conditions testament to millions of wasted dollars: pools of putrid water, tangled electricity cables from open roofing, rusty equipment, concrete stairs leading nowhere while baggage conveyor belts still wrapped in plastic sat alongside shiny arrival and departure gate signs.

But it drew masses of locals. On the unfinished runway families bearing an air of wild frivolity arrived on motor scooters with picnic baskets. Men and boys used it as a race track. More than a few killed themselves, their deaths regularly reported in the local papers.

The barely functional airport opened years over schedule to much derision in late 2011.

But the promised bounty of Emaar was the catalyst for foreign investment.

So, it was catastrophic when Emaar bailed out in December 2009, beset by financial woes linked to the 2008 global financial crisis, leaving an infrastructure void and foreigners on vacant land. Though the tourism boom stopped dead many retained their land, waiting for other investors to step in.

*

Harris dropped me at the only habitable Kuta hotel and returned to Mataram. The next day I stood alone on a remote stretch of untamed Indonesian forest along the spectacular coastline, where collapsed roads might have deterred even the most intrepid travellers. Much of Kuta looked like the last or first place on earth. Sasak traditional huts, coconut and tobacco plantations, and rice paddies punctuated an almost mythical landscape. A sign incongruously advertised 'land for sale'. A real estate agency had marked out an area amid dense tropical vegetation where investors could still claim a piece of paradise – one of the last remaining blocks.

It wasn't difficult to find the monopoly agency amid a smattering of homestays and *warungs*. The tiny Exotiq franchise was run by an Australian, Neil Tate, and his New Zealand wife, Belinda Murray. It was the busiest place in town.

I came to know the entrepreneurial couple quite well. Tate had arrived in Lombok from Port Macquarie, New South Wales, for a surf in 1983, seen opportunities in the south and stayed. The landscape had scarcely changed since then.

The couple showed me the pristine scenery south of Kuta. Who would have known that every scrap of land was taken? The pot-holed road was too perilous even for our four-wheel drive.

To Neil and Belinda, Lombok was finally reaching its apogee. In anticipation, they were building palatial, clifftop marble villas, some to sell. A lift hadn't yet been installed, and I stumbled up massive steps on a sheer incline, overcome with heat and vertigo. The view at the top, facing the Indian ocean, was transcendental.

Tate said prospective buyers – many retired Australians using their nest eggs – had been so smitten by the landscape they'd invested on the spot. Those who had bought before Emaar bailed, and were hanging on, had seen the potential returns and sat tight; others had pulled out. Still others kept buying despite Emaar's withdrawal. It was the new frontier – and it was wild. Many had bought land from locals, invariably becoming ensnared in scams, bribery, inept bureaucracy and dishonesty. Tate's point of difference was if you bought through him, you wouldn't get burnt. There were foreign con artists, too, though I am not suggesting that of Tate.

The following year, I took my photographer, Made Nagi, to Lombok. As we drove about appraising Kuta's still-blank canvas, we met Jason, a Queensland surfer, sitting outside his new oceanfront budget hotel.

He was so afraid of the 'local mafia', he wouldn't divulge his surname but he allowed Made to take his photo. 'It can get me killed, that's my biggest fear,' he said. He and his wife had nearly lost their life savings through one of the land scams. It was pure tenacity and a lawyer that saved them from penury. When they'd bought the prime property through a local nominee, there was a slight hitch: 'The guy we bought the land off didn't actually own it.' I heard countless similar stories: foreign buyers burnt after unwittingly becoming immersed in ownership conflicts in the belief they had snared a bargain. Many had used their retirement nest egg and could not afford to walk away.

One who generated fees as a result of the land scams was the Tates' lawyer, Ni Luh Suarni, the director of the Lombok International Law Office. At her discreet Mataram rooms one afternoon, I found her juggling calls from aggrieved foreigners desperate for advice. A short middle-aged woman in a smart jacket, Ni Luh emerged from her office smiling. She was surely the only local not having a post-lunch siesta. Business was brisk; her firm assisted 70 per cent of foreign investors ensnared in problematic property transactions, and my interview was interrupted by streams of distressed calls. Many foreign investors had bought land without doing due diligence, she explained. 'They just meet direct with the local owner of the land and don't check the legal status or the location. A lot of land already has certificates, but the village "owner" sells it twice.'

In fact, land was frequently sold several times over – even if it didn't exist. A complex land registration system, further complicated by decentralisation from Jakarta in 2001 to autonomous regional governments, sometimes left foreigners duped or forgotten amid a sea of red tape and rampant corruption. The problems stemmed from the authoritarian Suharto era in the '90s, when the now-defunct Lombok Tourism Development Corporation had bought large tracts of land. Local farmers and fishermen were frequently unaware 'their' land had been snapped up by large Jakarta companies, the government elite and the military.

'But,' Ni Luh conceded, 'there are also many villagers who are not honest.'

The islands of Flores and Sumba became victims of the same fate. It was said the further east you went in Indonesia, the more wild, and that was true of my foreign investment investigations on those islands in late 2013.

*

My last interview in the capital of Mataram proved the most testing. I had tried several times to call Muhammad Zainul Majdi, the then Governor of West Nusa Tenggara province, for an appointment. But each time the phone rang out, or people inexplicably hung up after answering.

Frustrated, I impulsively turned up. A man viewed me with suspicion from a wall hatch and told me to wait outside on a chair in the sun. I had worn a sundress, then realised too late it was inappropriate in the Muslim corridors of power. Over several hours various men approached me, each asking what I wanted. My repeated requests – in Bahasa Indonesia – for an interview elicited different responses: the governor was in Jakarta, he was at home, at lunch, busy in his office, and so on.

While I was going quietly mad, nursing my head in my hands, I noticed CCTV cameras. And, every so often, eyes peered at me through the wall hatch. I rapped on the door again. When it swung open, I apologised for my sleeveless dress, offering to cover my arms. The man brightened and smiled. 'The governor was watching you on the cameras,' he said, possibly referring to my dress. He didn't elaborate. I smiled uneasily.

A few minutes later, I was suitably shrouded in someone's sarong. The man escorted me through a maze of cavernous, unoccupied rooms with gaudy decorations, as though set up for a festive event. Zainul Majdi, a small man in his late thirties, sat expectantly on an ornate chair, itself on a dais, in a room more colonial-era than office. I apologised again for my dress, but he seemed unaware of the problem. He raised his eyebrows quizzically. If he knew I'd been waiting for hours, he pretended not to.

Called *Tuan Guru Bajang* (young religious master), Majdi was a conservative Muslim scholar who in 2019 joined Joko Widodo's potential running mates for the presidential race – purportedly to dispel accusations the president wasn't Islamic enough. At first glance, Majdi appeared to be a man of contradictions, surprisingly Westernised with fluent English. In fact, he had graduated from the Al-Azhar University in Egypt, a renowned Sunni Islam institution. Polite and hospitable, he offered me tea. I ploughed in, asking about disputes that pitted hardline Muslims against the persecuted Ahmadiyah sect, land disputes, the uncertain future of Muslim Sasaks in a new shiny investment climate, and the toll taken by travel warnings.

Muslims in Lombok were moderate, he argued. 'There has not been a single terrorist incident, and no terrorists have originated from Lombok.'

Still, Sumbawa, part of the same province, is long known for its extremist Islamic history, and Ansyaad Mbai, a former Head of the Indonesian National Anti-Terrorism Agency (BNPT) named Bima, the largest city in Sumbawa, as a radical hotspot. When a bomb exploded in Bima in a *pesantren* (Islamic boarding school), killing one man in 2011, police said an attack had been intended for them. Before that, police found extremists hiding out in Bima.

In 2013 the crack national police counter-terrorism squad, Detatchment 88, killed five suspected Muslim terrorists on Sumbawa. Since then numerous incidents have been recorded.

Majdi talked at length about tourism. Emaar's withdrawal didn't worry him; he was promoting halal tourism, targeting Malaysian and Middle Eastern tourists as the government invited fresh tenders for the 1200 hectares of state land. Majdi aimed to quell simmering tensions, and promote stability and religious tolerance. Not long after my interview, the *Jakarta Globe* quoted him as saying the solution to tensions over the Ahmadiyah was to 'get them out of the province'. They didn't fit his tourism image, the paper reported.

On Kuta's indigenous Sasaks, Majdi showed more compassion. 'We don't want to relocate the people. We do not advocate that people sell their land. We are trying to make them contribute to tourism and hospitality.' Inevitably many didn't, and despite Kuta's wild beauty and a hodgepodge of *warungs* and guest houses, there remains an eerie, empty feel to the place.

The government's Mandalika Kuta Resort was far from complete at the time of writing in 2018. Its new foreshore boardwalk bordered a concrete jungle of unfinished buildings.

The airport, just twenty minutes north of Kuta, opened in October 2011 after years of delays and land acquisition disputes. It had undergone a miraculous transformation from the deathtrap I'd seen during construction. But the shiny facade didn't allay my fears that dodgy workmanship had perhaps been concealed each time I flew over.

When I organised a week-long holiday reunion with Ruby in September 2010, for her 21st birthday, it was not a concern. We flew into Lombok's old aiport, then boarded a speedboat to the tiny magical idyll of Gili Trawangan across the strait. I had ducked over for a quick travel piece after the complex Lombok story, and I'd mentioned the birthday to my new sources. They pulled together a superb celebration for Ruby, laying on a glorious villa, a lobster dinner and birthday cake.

Most of my Lombok contacts remained friends throughout my years in Indonesia. A couple died, a few moved on, but the Senggigi area remained an uncrowded second home away from Bali's bustle.

7

ROYAL AFFAIR

When Ruby returned to Australia, I felt bereft. It was a painful reminder that my children lived too far away from me. Though I rationalised the six-hour flight to Sydney was only a short hop, I was skipping large parts of my kids' lives. The separation haunted me. My standard coping mechanism was to immerse myself in work; my social life was quite full too, which left little time to brood.

Back on 'home' turf in Bali, I enjoyed a sedate change of pace exploring the lives of Ubud's royals in modern society – after the devolution of their real power – for a piece in *The Weekend Australian Magazine*. I figured it would be the closest I would ever get to the inner sanctum of a royal household – and I was intrigued.

One morning in 2010, I arrived at Jero Asri Kerthyasa's Denpasar home to join her extended family for one of Bali's most sacred festivals. Asri was the royal family matriarch and princess of Ubud. I arranged one-on-one interviews with each of her three children and her husband.

Asri was adjusting the finishing touches to her ceremonial finery as she called upstairs to her eighteen-year-old daughter, Maya, to hurry. We were driving north to Ubud. Maya – who, like her two brothers, had been schooled in Australia – identified as both Western and Balinese. This wasn't something I imagined to be problematic in Bali; to the outsider, the Balinese appear so accepting.

Maya chatted from the back seat, with Asri chiming in as she drove. Maya was bright, down-to-earth and charming. A typical teenager? Yes, in the way kids are excited and uncertain about their future. No, in the way she battled issues around her royal lineage and her mixed-race parentage. I learnt later that her two brothers, as males, did not experience the same pressure.

In another life, Asri had been Australian Jane Gillespie. Born in Sydney, the now sixty-four-year-old had married the dashing prince of Ubud, Tjokorda Raka Kerthyasa, forty-one years ago. At a lavish royal wedding in 1978, Jane, a preschool teacher, was transformed into Jero (the title of a commoner who marries into a high caste) Asri Kerthyasa, fully-fledged princess. She wore a *sonket*, an ornate gold-threaded sarong, with a heavy, flower-laden headdress.

No, she hadn't picked her new name, which meant 'perfect'; her brother-in-law had given it to her at the wedding ceremony because it sounded like a combination of Australia (As) and Republik Indonesia (Ri).

I'd first met Asri in Biku, the eclectic restaurant and tea lounge she'd opened a year previously in upmarket Seminyak. It was the tropics mixed with Billie Holiday's mellifluous voice and the wafting aroma of freshly baked cakes. And it was always packed, the overhead fans churning sticky air through the open Javanese *joglo*, an intricately carved wooden building.

Now we were on the road to Ubud to celebrate the start of Galungan, the ten-day Hindu festival marking the descent to earth of the gods and ancestors before their return to heaven on Kuningan. I wore the obligatory sarong for entry to the temple, and I'd arranged for a new photographer, a young Muslim woman called Eka, to meet me there. She'd travelled from Jakarta to fill in for my Balinese snapper, whose duties were in his village that day.

Asri was deftly navigating the broken roads she knew intimately. As we wound our way through small villages, the pervasive festive spirit fused in long colourful processions. The women, dressed in their best lace *kebayas* (blouses) and sarongs, carried towering fruit offerings on their heads. Streets were lined with tall, swaying *penjor*: curved bamboo poles decorated with flowers and laden with sumptuous fruit offerings. Pigs and chickens, sacrificed for the traditional feasts, were soon to grace plates as *babi guling* (suckling pig) and *ayam goreng* (fried chicken).

*

Many knew Asri's pedigree, and some even addressed her as 'your royal highness', which she found slightly amusing.

In my interview with her at Biku, she'd mused over the top of her fine china cup, 'There are misconceptions Balinese royalty is like English or Dutch royalty, but it doesn't have a lot of meaning outside Bali.' Yet a royal princess of any standing is rare, rarer still for this princess to be Australian. In her role as royal family matriarch, her duties included many such occasions as Galungan. The twice-yearly affair represents the triumph of good (called *dharma* in Sanskrit) over evil (*adharma*), and is one of the most sacred in the Balinese calendar. She told me, 'We're a big family – with about three hundred members – and there's always something on: a wedding, a tooth-filing [to keep evil spirits at bay], a cremation. The family is expected to attend.' Over the years, Bali publications charted the family's landmark occasions. They were cultural feasts, some of which the royals hospitably opened to enthusiastic public fans.

I asked Asri if she was a true believer, especially as she'd had no choice but to convert to Hinduism in order to marry her prince. 'Yes, I do believe in it,' she replied firmly. 'I was a Protestant. I converted to Hinduism but I have learnt it by osmosis; it just sort of happens around you.' She was, on the one hand, no-nonsense and practical; on the other, she had the propensity to leave me in doubt about that.

She had met her charismatic prince at the hotel where she and her mother had been staying while on holiday in Bali the year before. 'It took about a week,' Asri recalled. 'We were smitten.' She gave up her Sydney job, flicked her former boyfriend and returned to Bali to marry her prince. 'It was a whirlwind romance.' And, yes, she knew Tjok Raka was a prince.

The next part of her story was extraordinary to me. Palace life, you would think, must be a sort of cathedral of gilded grace. But over tea at Biku, I learnt palace life had in fact come as a rude shock to her. The west wing, where the couple had lived for the first six months, was dilapidated at the time (it was spruced up in the 1980s), with no electricity, running water or phone and little privacy. 'There were millions of visitors – you'd wake up in the morning and there'd be a whole village outside.'

Then there was the Balinese custom of living with extended family, which Asri found unpalatable. Many of them viewed her as an imposter. Expected to kowtow to the family's demands, rules and customs, Asri was required to share childrearing, meals and other routines. After the birth of her first son, she was expected to share him around. 'I have a degree in early childhood. I wasn't going to hand him over to the grandmother or someone with a dirty bottle. I used to lock myself in my room to get away. I was patient but I was also rude. It wasn't an enjoyable time. I'm not good at being told what to do.'

Then she had to deal with the distressing reality that her husband could enjoy several wives if he so chose, a feature of the patriarchal society she'd married into. When this was discussed early in their relationship, Asri stood her ground. 'If you want another wife, divorce me first,' she told him. It didn't end there. Many of the locals considered it inconceivable that a Western woman was an appropriate consort for a Balinese prince. The inference was: 'This is fine, but when are you going to get a real wife?' Faced with open hostility – some of which remained – friction between the couple escalated. 'I often wondered, "What am I doing here?" In Bali, the women have no rights; if they divorce, they have to leave everything behind, including the children.' The idea of deserting the marriage because of the huge cultural differences did cross her mind – luckily, 'love was the cement, the foundation that held the relationship together. Without that, it would not have survived.'

By that point, I was hanging on her every word, wondering why she hadn't thrown it all in.

There were so many challenges a novice royal faced that more famous debutante princesses took in their stride. 'The biggest challenge was knowing what to do when, and when to do what. I tried hard not to make mistakes. There's a different mindset about everything, but you can't change the way you walk and talk.' On the bright side, most people were polite and deferential, though Asri played down her acquired blue blood, contending it wasn't quite the real deal. 'It's anthropologically interesting, but a fairytale it's not,' she said with a laugh.

Years down the track, she adapted her needs to find her way through the ordeal by creating a separate life to her royal one, and by being assertive.

*

After arriving at the Ubud grounds of the family temple within their hotel, and one of their homes, at the Warwick Ibah Villas, we climbed steep steps to the stone temple, which Balinese tradition dictates must preside over everything beneath. Pointing to the home in the north and Mount Agung in the east, Bali's holiest mountain is regarded as the navel (*pusar*), or centre, of the universe. At the top is the Campuhan Ridge, a glorious green expanse of rice paddies. The land, handed down from Tjok Raka's father, is known for its sacred spring waters, a purifying elixir that drew the ailing. Sacred areas are traditionally accessed by the Balinese, even on privately owned land. During the 2009 shooting of *Eat Pray Love*, this is where producers, directors and actors – including Julia Roberts and Javier Bardem – had stayed, away from prying eyes.

My snapper Eka wore a hijab, and this had, I saw, initially surprised the royal family on this sacred Hindu day. But she was a feisty young woman and any discomfort washed over her. She put the family at ease and produced great photos.

Following prayers, a 'brunch' was served by the temple at about 11 a.m. It was a traditional, delicious feast of spicy duck, rice, assorted vegetable dishes and tropical fruit prepared by Asri's mother-in-law Gung Niang, now in her nineties. Each year she did it alone, proud of her role.

Guardians of tradition, the family, clad in elegant sarongs and lace *kebayas* for the women, then visited relatives at Ubud's palace in the town centre. A complex of gold-leafed wings furnished with opulent Dutch colonial and brocade furniture opens to a centre courtyard where we ate sweet Balinese delicacies at each family pit stop. It was a world away from Biku's 'tropical comfort food'.

On such an auspicious day, the royal family's influence was on display. Although the monarchy had held no official status since Indonesian independence in 1945, as I strolled with the family to the palace along the festive Ubud streets, it was clear they weren't only immediately recognised but also revered. Indeed, Balinese royal power appeared more potent here than its modern British equivalent.

Acting as psychologist and mediator to the locals, Tjok Raka, the head of Ubud society, freely gave his time and resources to the people who queued daily at the palace seeking his advice. He also generously gave me his time for interviews. The youngest son of his father's tenth wife, he wore numerous hats: he was a published poet, a member of Bali's legislative assembly and the president of Cricket Indonesia.

When his brother, the head of the family, Tjokorda Gede Agung Suyasa, had died in 2008, Tjok Raka had taken over his counselling and spiritual roles. The responsibility of living up to his brother's informal title, 'The Wise One', could be tiresome, reflected Asri, but her husband, whose grandfather had been the last Balinese king, was adamant the palace wouldn't be anything without the community. 'Now we [the royal family] have only one obligation: to preserve our culture,' he said. That involved upholding the principles of Tri Hita Karana (three causes of well-being), the Balinese life philosophy including harmony among people, harmony with nature and harmony with God. Derived from Balinese spiritualism and beliefs, the nurturing of harmony is manifested in the daily offerings and rituals to appease the deities.

Ubud's cachet among the seven other Balinese regencies has significance for politics, culture and tourism. The royals can trace their lineage back to ancient East Javanese kings from the Hindu Majapahit empire between the thirteenth and sixteenth centuries, before Dutch colonisation reduced their kingdoms to regencies last century, with independence in 1945 delivering the final blow. Though diluted, the royal line is far from emasculated. Advisory and philanthropic roles maintain the Balinese staples – culture and religion – and keep the peace in domestic disputes, and between conflicting village and foreign interests. Ever the pragmatist, Tjok Raka mediates between locals and foreigners in proliferating, contentious tourist developments.

Faced with diminished ancestral lands, royal family members have mostly turned their hands to businesses such as hotels, spas and restaurants in order to attract the tourist dollar. Long gone are the hugely wealthy landowners and landowning royals who were forced to cede property to villagers during reforms in 1965.

*

The cultural blend of Asri's children saw them seesaw back and forth, emotionally and physically, between Australia and Indonesia. When the family lived in Sydney from 1980 for about thirteen years, the strain was most telling on Tjok Raka, whose heart was back in Bali. He also had to adapt 'to being a nobody'. But he used his time in the West to explore the arts world, starting a Balinese section at the Australian Museum in Sydney and studying Fine Arts at East Sydney Technical College between various jobs.

On meeting the royal progeny – sons Tjokorda Gede Mahatma Putra Kerthyasa (TjokDe, for short), then thirty-one; Tjokorda Bagus Dwi Santana Kerthyasa (Max), twenty-nine; and daughter Tjokorda Sri Maya Kerthyasa (Maya), eighteen – the first thing I noticed was their Australian accents, the byproduct of their Sydney schooling. Their family name, Tjokorda, which identifies them as royalty, meant nothing at the boys' school, Chatswood High, or at Abbotsleigh, where Maya boarded. Most of their peers had no clue they were royalty. In Bali, however, the royal family is seen as more than merely mortal. 'It's nothing like the Windsor family,' Maya told me, 'but I am lucky to have my heritage.'

All had suffered discrimination, both in Australia and in Bali, over their mixed culture and light-brown skin. All had felt alienated and had agonised over their identities. Herein lay Maya's dilemma. 'It's very hard trying to please both cultures, do what's right and have fun at the same time,' she said, then the typical teen. 'The Balinese culture is a lot more modest compared to Australian culture.' What was encouraged as rite-of-passage routine for a teenage girl in Australia was typically taboo in Bali, where relationships between the sexes – even the most innocent – were relegated to post-marriage. Flirtatious mobile phone messages were about as far as it was permitted to go. Maya's extended family tried to matchmake her with, in her words, 'people far too closely related', such as first cousins, to try to ensure the royal line endured. As she was then the most eligible girl in Bali, the pressure on her was enormous. Not that she had a bar of it: 'It's kind of weird,' she told me in the car.

Ten years on, Maya is married to an Australian 'commoner', Marcus Tesoriero, and they're living in Perth with their infant son. Now a freelance lifestyle journalist, Maya never envisaged getting hitched to a Balinese man. People in Bali still address her as 'Tjok', but officially she forfeited her princess title under the island's patrilineal system by marrying out of royalty – unlike her brothers, who retain theirs regardless.

TjokDe came full circle. He married a Javanese woman, Jero Wiwied, and had a son. Since divorced and remarried, he lives with his Russian wife Mariana and their three children. Embracing his Balinese roots, he shed his Anglicised 'school' name, Adam, unlike his brother. 'It's hard. The two cultures are like chalk and cheese,' he said. 'Now I feel at home in Bali. It's a type of belonging that's very different … there's a spirituality and connection to the family land.' Yet for many years each trip from Australia to home was a challenge, with his father expecting him to slot back into the cadences and rhythm of Balinese life, master the language (he was already proficient in Bahasa Indonesia) and maintain a profound grasp of local politics. A homeopath and tea master, supplying his mother's restaurant from his Sydney tea business, TjokDe saw himself as socially and environmentally aware, drawing parallels with Prince Charles. 'If we were to have a conversation, I think we'd probably see eye to eye,' he said.

His brother Max married his actress wife from Jakarta, Happy Salma, some seven years ago. He was most comfortable with an Indonesian partner who spoke his father's tongue. 'When you can't communicate here, it's hard to fit in.' In Bali he had copped snide remarks and insults about his colour, and it was still a common affront. 'There's a bit of a bully mentality here – even when people know who I am.' In multicultural Australia he found a level of tolerance that helped to reconcile his divided loyalties.

*

After the Galungan celebration, I returned to Biku one Sunday evening to find that a delightfully mad *keroncong* band had begun its unusual weekly serenade. Ukuleles, cello, banjo, mandolin, guitar and double bass accompanied a cavorting siren in a hot pink *kebaya* and sash, belting out local tunes and a quirky rendition of 'Fly Me to the Moon'. I typed up my impressions of the music as I watched the woman abandon herself to the beat. Her hair tumbled from its prim bun and her voice reached a high-pitched, feverish screech, forcing some customers to take refuge at courtyard tables.

This was what encapsulated Indonesia – an unexpected vibe within an ancient culture that could stop you in your tracks. The young Balinese singer had done justice to this version of the *fado* music brought to Indonesia by Portuguese sailors, its sound captured by a local saying: 'You're so famished, your stomach jangles like a *keroncong*.'

At the time, Asri had the only *keroncong* band in Bali. Determined to uphold the traditions of her adopted home, she told me, 'People are glad to have something that isn't modern and soulless – so many places look like Melbourne.' It was true: Bali's southern centre was a homogenous echo of every other place. Here, Asri had found a way to blend cultures on her terms – rather like her children had. Her son TjokDe was the grand tea master, while Asri was high tea queen: she had planned Biku for years after sampling tearooms worldwide. 'There was nowhere in Bali that did good tea.'

I asked Asri and Tjok Raka, would the royal family endure? They considered the question, then replied presciently that they were sceptical their children could continue the legacy with the same commitment.

In the near decade since I chronicled Asri's story, two of her children tied the knot, her eldest son remarried and six grandchildren have been added to the brood. Not bad going.

8

PARTYLAND

In late 2010, the Balinese owner of my Batu Belig apartment had obviously had enough of expatriates and told everyone to clear out of the complex: no renewed contracts, no negotiation. That's how it was in Bali. Once again I was glad I had few possessions. My upstairs neighbour – obviously a Nick Lowe fan ('I Love the Sound of Breaking Glass') – was first to pack his bags.

While visiting a friend in Seminyak shortly after getting the boot, I stumbled on a serviced villa compound that became my home for the next nine years. The rental was a bit steep but the traditional villas, expansive tropical gardens, soaring palm trees and large central pool were captivating. Back in the day it had been another expat sanctuary; then it was rebuilt in the 1990s after being devoured by fire.

My villa was again half open to the elements, with a garden off the living room. 'Don't animals come in?' Jake asked on a second trip in 2011. The wildlife, for the most part, was harmless. Geckos slithered across my walls and ceiling, occasionally shrieking; crickets chirped, and frogs periodically hopped across my marble floor. But Jake meant rats, and he was right. I had to keep everything in the fridge, even bananas and mangoes. If not, by morning they'd be gutted, the husks and brown skins a trail of destruction.

Over the years, the villas became sadly neglected. They were a bit *Fawlty Towers*. Fittings broke after repairs, and cleaning staff doubled as cooks, plumbers, electricians and painters. I stayed because the place was spacious, green and quiet, and it was a convenient distance to the airport and the jail.

*

As I was still considered a new 'girl' in Bali, I wasn't short of invitations to dine at lavish private villas or attend outlandish parties. In a country where the death penalty is considered a deterrent against drugs, I was bemused to learn cocaine was extremely popular. On closed toilet seats of the upmarket Seminyak beachclub Ku De Ta bar, telltale white specks could be spotted in darkened cubicles. There was a revolving door of managers, beguiled by temptations on the job. The owner was a formidable businessman who, with his brother, had carved up most of the Bali club scene. He kept a tight ship.

Indonesian police knew of the thriving cocaine trade among expatriates but were thwarted by the tightknit nature of the community. Most of their drug-fuelled parties took place behind villa walls. Police relied heavily on local informants, particularly villa staff, but loyalties lay with the highest bidder.

When there was a foreign bust, Muhammad Rifan was one of the Bali legal eagles who swooped in. He had represented Myuran Sukumaran and Andrew Chan at their 2006 trials.

Rifan told me that typically foreigners who were caught with drugs paid police and some lawyers to obtain reduced sentences. 'Money has power in Bali. Everything can match with the right money. They [offenders] can get smaller penalty. But a smaller penalty is hard if the reason is not accepted by the law.'

He continued: 'Every day is a party in Bali,' where cocaine was the drug of choice among expats. No one else could afford it at its price of about Rp3 million to Rp4 million (about A$400) a gram. 'There are many freelance people selling from pubs.'

Locals were a major source of information for police but foreigners organised parties at private villas, away from local staff. 'The [expat] community is very difficult to touch by police. They can use freely in their villas; parties go on for two or three days.'

He said Bali had always been a party island for expats. 'Already, from 1970 many Australians are doing parties. Then it was the first generation. They have many assets ... surfing shops. Some locals are married with Australians.'

It was left to my imagination to which Australians he was referring.

Cocaine use wasn't confined to Bali's party set. A former Fairfax correspondent divulged that a competing colleague had a whip-around for a decent-sized bag to supply his leaving bash in Jakarta. The heaving metropolis had a notorious underbelly, and its clubs, frequented by nefarious types – people smugglers, underworld figures and so on – were drug dens. But apart from fraternising with sources, I wondered where journos found the time to party hard.

Bali's loose lifestyle gave me access to people who furnished me with lurid details by way of gossip or their own experiences. Some of those I met at parties or dinners ended up in my court stories, usually for drugs possession.

At first glow, the hype and transient expat friendships were flattering. But many had vested interests in the Bali brand and little in common with my own life, sitting in drab police stations and courtrooms. And I wasn't much good at air-kissing. There was resentment, too, about my pieces on Bali's environmental destruction and climbing crime rates that affected tourism and the value of expats' homes and businesses. Over casual drinks, people would warn their friends, 'She's a journo, watch what you say.' The island was too small, and I came to relish assignments in the vast archipelago away from Bali. My occasional travel and food reviews were bonuses I savoured.

In a sea of foreign lifestyle journalists, I was neither fish nor fowl. I was an outsider, at first misunderstood, then not to be trusted. After a few years, the party invites dried up.

*

Amid high-profile drug offenders, a line of minnows slithered through the gates of Kerobokan jail.

Angus McCaskill, a New Zealand-born expat, whose real name was Willie Rare, was lucky to escape a long jail sentence for possessing less than four grams of cocaine in January 2011. He was sentenced to seven years, but on appeal his sentence was dramatically cut to just 12 months.

New Zealand's *Dominion Post* reported McCaskill had paid about US$19,000 to Balinese authorities for a lenient sentence.

McCaskill had been caught red-handed with cocaine after a boozy night out in Seminyak with a bunch of expats. He told me that he was busted after the publication of Kathryn Bonella's 2009 book *Hotel Kerobokan* and missed making it into her popular tome. He was admitted to Hotel K, as the prison was dubbed, after being domiciled for over a month in a Kuta police cell with thirteen other men, sleeping rough on a wooden board. Nothing dented his optimism. 'I'm a very positive person. I pray every day, I didn't before but it helps. I am a Christian,' he told me from his court holding cell.

Ever resourceful, he had organised a party, texting people to bring food to the police station. The Indonesian fried rations were 'enough to take the hunger pains away', he said, but he relied on friends for fresh produce. Many were lying low, however, because they were afraid of the police.

One day during his trial, as he sweated profusely in the sweltering heat and gripped the bars of his cell, he waxed lyrical about life in the slammer. If anyone believed the jail was a crime-ridden den of iniquity harbouring gangsters and drugs, he disabused them of the notion. 'Kerobokan jail is fantastic,' he told me. 'If you can imagine a ski resort, that's what it's like. There are lots of rooms and a big common room with a TV. I have a room by myself with an ensuite bathroom; I have just renovated it. The conditions are fabulous. I can't complain. I have a room, not a cell. There are no rats. Bali jails are not what people imagine them to be. But I'd rather be in my villa,' he admitted. 'I'm hoping to get the minimum sentence. If you want a result you have to pay.'

You had to admire his opportunism. One evening I was invited to a swank oceanfront rooftop bar where a donation box flagrantly requested, 'Help Angus'. At the entrance, a couple of women sat behind a desk waiting for anyone obtuse enough to delve into their wallets. A guestbook lay beside the box. It was unclear if payment was a condition of entry, and probably some guests were duped.

*

There was always a widespread frenzied appetite for fresh drug cases in Bali, and in a system vulnerable to manipulation, no shortage of vested interests – largely the judiciary and the police.

I was in the Denpasar District Court when Dutchman Djaï Heijn, the 25-year-old heir to the Albert Heijn supermarket fortune, was handed a twelve-month sentence in Kerobokan jail for trying to traffic 225 grams of marijuana into Indonesia. Unusually, the sentence was two months more than the prosecution demanded. But Heijn wouldn't quibble, despite his outraged lawyer raising the possibility of an appeal. It was all show. Heijn had already served six months since his arrest, and he was almost free.

He had escaped a fifteen-year maximum term, and he'd avoided the death penalty because the marijuana – sent by a thoughtful friend in Spain – amounted to less than a kilogram. Police had allegedly also found a fair whack of crystal methamphetamine, also known as ice – 492 grams, to be exact – and psychedelic drugs at his home. For whatever reason, the meth wasn't mentioned in court. The Dutchman, who has always denied any involvement in the marijuana shipment, shuffled through the system virtually unscathed.

I watched Heijn in the dock seconds before the verdict was handed down. He appeared very composed, not in the least bit nervous. A slight smile played on his lips. He may well have known the verdict in advance. If true, it would have cost plenty.

Heijn was the grandson of Gerrit Jan Heijn and the great-grandson of Albert Heijn, founder of leading supermarket chain Ahold. Gerrit Jan had been kidnapped and killed shortly after a botched ransom attempt in 1987. Heijn's father, Ronald Jan Heijn, a former Dutch hockey champion, was known as a New Age spiritual entrepreneur; he had visited his father's killer in prison and forgiven him.

I was covering another court story but kept an eye on the Heijn trial. That day, a Dutch Jakarta-based journalist and I were the only reporters watching. Heijn had lived in Ubud since 2013, providing 'spiritual training' and posting stand-up 'cosmic comedy' shows of himself naked on YouTube. He also posted videos of himself lost in his own cosmic-induced wonderland, which drew torrents of derisory online comments; those videos were removed eventually but I was amazed they remained during the court case.

After Heijn's arrest, police paraded him with his drugs in front of the media, as per usual. He wore the standard clobber: a balaclava and orange jumpsuit. But, unusually, two police officers pointed rifles less than a metre from his face, as though he were a prize catch. He was, of course. However, his nationality doubtless shielded him from undue publicity. Spared the media circus that accompanies hapless Australians, he slid under the radar.

As I approached him after his trial, he was tight-lipped, firmly declining an interview, determined to avoid publicity. I never saw his family in attendance.

This was more than just a drug case, but his intriguing family backstory slipped into obscurity. It was one tale that epitomised the insular outlook of Australian media in Indonesia.

One of my pieces almost didn't run because it focused on a death-row inmate from Nigeria – not Australia. But I was able to cover alternative perspectives, on a freelance basis, for *The Times* of London and *The Guardian*. Occasionally I juggled several deadlines in a day – an adrenalin-fuelled challenge, to say the least.

9

CHILDREN OF TERROR

In May 2011, I was drawn into the murky underworld of terrorism in the first of a series over several years that spanned much of the island of Java. I found myself thrust into edgy situations, working on my terms on the road for weeks at a time.

Instrumental to my initial piece was Central Javanese filmmaker Daniel Rudi Haryanto, whose interviews with notorious Jemaah Islamiah terrorists Imam Samudra (born Abdul Aziz), Ali Ghufron (Huda bin Abdul Haq, aka Mukhlas) and his younger brother Ali Amrozi bin Haji Nurhasyim are archival gold.

Languishing behind bars on Nusa Kambangan's penal island, off central Java, with just a prayer mat, they participated in Haryanto's award-winning documentary *Prison and Paradise* before their 2008 executions for their roles in the heinous 2002 Bali bombings that killed 202 people.

I met Haryanto at a Central Jakarta café in early May, near my hotel. The spirited, genial 33-year-old had been part of the 1998 student activist movement to help oust strongman Suharto. It landed him briefly in jail and in the newspapers before authorities realised he was underage and released him. He went on to channel his rebelliousness through artistic means, stirring up political and social discourse using film.

When Haryanto handed me a copy of *Prison and Paradise*, I raced back to my hotel and, glued to a computer, watched the compelling footage.

Haryanto was among few to gain unfettered access to the Bali bombers, interviewing them between 2003 and 2007. He possessed an uncanny ability to say little and harvest much. His film captured the depraved mindset and anti-American ramblings of the homegrown Bali bombers while focusing on the life-changing legacy they left their families and their victims.

As I sat in the business lounge of my hotel, the insane exhortations of mastermind Samudra echoed from the grave.

Haryanto's camera prowled over him, sneaking up close, probing his dark eyes, bulging pools full of menace. 'If the Bali bombing did not happen it means there would be an increasingly growing evil which would undermine Islamic *aqidah* [Arabic word for "belief"]. *Kafir* [unbelievers] mentality will continue to grow if there is no resistance from the Muslims,' he asserted, sitting cross-legged in his bare cell. 'The best defence is offence ... wherever you face the infidels.' Coming back to earth, I glanced around at staff calmly working in hushed oblivion to the madman on my screen.

Samudra had regarded the bombings as a military operation against civilians in which Muslims were collateral damage. He repeatedly quoted from the Koran, stabbing a finger at passages as if to prove an argument. Yet for all his religious posturing, his aim was simply narcissistic. 'If I weren't arrested by the police I would make bigger actions ... Anywhere, my will is to find *syahid* [martyrdom] in Ambon, Poso, Halmahera [previous Indonesian conflict zones]. I want to keep fighting against the Catholic or any kafir people out there.'

'When will you be satisfied?' asked Haryanto quietly, invisible behind his camera.

'When they stop attacking Muslims.'

A couple of hours later, I slipped the DVD out of the computer and gulped down a cup of tea, the unhinged monologues ringing in my ears.

*

Just as Haryanto had probed the family narrative, so I focused on the enigmatic, furtive world of Indonesian jihadi women behind terrorist husbands, their children and their traditional roles in a patriarchal society.

I arranged to meet Titin, the 39-year-old Indonesian wife of Mubarok, alias Utomo Pamungkas, a terrorist jailed for his part in the 2002 bombings.

But meeting the wife of a jihadi wasn't easy; permission was required from her husband, serving a life sentence in the Metro Jaya Detention Centre in Central Jakarta.

Engaging with foreigners was against jihadist principles, rendering terrorists' wives and children largely impenetrable.

Which is where my contact, security analyst Noor Huda Ismail, came in. A former hardliner turned journalist and Indonesian counterterrorist expert, Ismail became an abiding source.

Titin agreed to be interviewed in Yogyakarta, Central Java, on the condition Ismail, a long-time family friend and supporter, interpreted. From the age of 12, Ismail and Mubarok had been classmates and 'close buddies' at the Al-Mukmin Ngruki *pesantren* in Solo, Central Java – the Ivy League for recruits to the al-Qaeda-linked Jemaah Islamiah (JI) terror group. Their first radicalising influence, the school's co-founder, jailed firebrand cleric Abu Bakar Bashir, also mentored bombers Mukhlas, Amrozi and their brother, Ali Imron.

A former *Washington Post* stringer, in the 1980s Ismail had aspired to fight as a mujahedin (holy warrior) in Afghanistan against

Soviet forces but chosen a different path that ultimately inspired his 2010 book *Temanku, Teroris?* (*My Friend, the Terrorist?*). In 2002 he had covered the Bali bombings, and when he found that Mubarok, his old classmate, was one of the group behind the atrocities, he was incredulous. His book was the basis for *Prison and Paradise*, in which he appeared and collaborated.

In their interviews, the jihadists all told Haryanto that they would go to paradise. He told me, 'They all said they wanted to go to Heaven where there would be seventy-two beautiful virgins ready at all times to serve them and give them sexual pleasure. They claimed to be fighters in the way of Allah, and they believed their reward would be paradise.' But Haryanto edited that bit out, fearing it might spark contentious debate about the meaning of jihad. 'I wanted to focus on the impact terrorism has on women and children.' In that he succeeded. There is no doubt the Bali bombers, in their nihilistic pursuit of violent jihad, ensured the disintegration of their families long before their deaths or imprisonments.

Haryanto was my starting point for a two-week assignment encompassing interviews across Jakarta and central Java, ultimately leading to Titin.

On my way to meet her, I returned to the story's origins – Bashir's Solo *pesantren*. My driver, who was very nervous, parked out of sight and stayed in the car, warning me to be careful. I photographed the eerily quiet buildings and strolled through deserted narrow streets to get a sense of the place. Several students emerged in Islamic garb and stared at me in open hostility. Unnerved, I decided it was time to leave. It wasn't surprising that Solo – where President Widodo was born and served as mayor – beneath its pre-colonial royal heritage and traditional batik-making, was a hotbed of Islamic fundamentalism.

The following morning I travelled a hundred kilometres south by bus past jade patchworks of rice paddies and thick vegetation to Semarang, on the north coast of Central Java. A huge port city of the Dutch colonial era with a melting pot of cultures and an extensive Chinatown, this was where Ismail lived with his wife and toddler son. He and Haryanto picked me up at the bus station. We wound our way through the city's landmarks and numerous mosques before dropping into Ismail's home.

A vibrant man of boundless energy, Ismail was keen to show me one of his deradicalisation initiatives, a literary café that isolated ex-terrorists like Mahmudi Haryono, alias Yusuf, from terror networks. The epitome of politeness, Yusuf, a clean-cut, wiry 35-year-old, appeared the most unlikely terrorist. With Ismail's aid, he had secured a job after his jail term for helping the JW Marriott Hotel bombers in 2003. Everything now looked quite rosy; he had a baby daughter and a wife. But this didn't stop the former Jemaah Islamiah militant pining for his jihadist ties. 'It's like a drug,' Ismail said.

Yusuf teetered on a knife edge. 'If it wasn't for Huda I would have been activated,' he told me while serving drinks. One phone call and he'd be hooked again. 'I became more radicalised in jail. It strengthened my cause. Jihad is still my obligation. I hate the government. The temptation of terrorism is always there.' It was the motto of thousands.

I shot some photos of Yusuf praying at the mosque, and we headed off to a restaurant from where I filed a piece to *The Australian*.

Understanding the wives and their nebulous commitment was a deeper conundrum. Ismail explained our best course with Titin. 'Wait for me in Yogyakarta,' he said, which was the closest city to her village.

From Semarang, I travelled to Central Java's cultural capital by train. For a couple of dollars I watched a rolling panorama of emerald rice terraces and mountains. The ranging, captivating beauty of Java a fertile heartland containing over half of Indonesia's population – sped by from my near empty carriage with paneless windows, the soft breeze fanning my face, before chugging into the royal city.

On the prearranged day in Yogyakarta's centre, Ismail swung by in his Range Rover and, hopping into the front passenger seat, I turned to face Titin. My first impression of the diminutive woman in the back seat was that of a giggly girl, flanked by her two young daughters. Her eyes crinkled behind optical glasses; a narrow strip across her eyes was the only exposed part of her face. She was clad in a *niqab*, the garb of the zealous Islamic Salafists, which covered her entire body.

She and her daughters had come from a remote village forty kilometres outside Yogyakarta where the family lived with Mubarok's father Harsono, who was deeply disappointed in his son.

Ismail pondered an appropriate café for our interview. Where do you take a terrorist's wife clad in a *niqab*? Surprisingly he chose a brightly lit Western joint, Dunkin' Donuts. Noticing an adjoining bookstore, he dashed in and bought gifts for Titin's daughters, Asma, eleven, and Qonita, nine.

In Dunkin' Donuts, no one raised an eyebrow at the fully veiled woman and her daughters. It was a surreal situation: here was the radical Muslim family of an infamous terrorist enjoying an American fast-food outlet, the type that attracted 'infidels' and which terrorists aspired to blow up. But Titin appeared indifferent to her environment. Settling down to afternoon tea, I was fascinated to see how she navigated a muffin with jam and a cup of tea beneath a flap covering the lower part of her face. It had not always been successful: her black *niqab*, which she'd started wearing after Mubarok's arrest in 2003, was stained with old food.

Titin hadn't told her daughters of their father's jihadic background, or why he was in prison serving a life sentence in solitary confinement at the Polda Metro Jaya Detention Centre in central Jakarta.

When the girls paid him six-monthly visits under her supervision, she pretended he was living at a university.

'They know only that their father is studying religion at a school for adults. I think they are too young to understand the truth. We can't just say that their father is jailed, now, can we?' Neither would she divulge the truth in the future, 'unless they ask'. 'I'm afraid if they know it will damage them psychologically,' she said to me. 'Sometimes it makes me cry when the younger one asks, "Why doesn't my father want to come home?"'

I tried to fathom the children's reactions if they knew their father's past. Perhaps it would be akin to discovering your father was a war criminal.

'If one day they know what happened to their father, certainly it will demolish their image of a father,' Ismail said to me. For now, Mubarok was saved by a conspiracy protecting him from condemnation by his own children.

And so, in the mysterious world of jihadists' wives, it was unknown to what extent children were indoctrinated. 'It's like a secretive sect,' Ismail almost whispered. Husbands dictated all aspects of family life, even from prison, leaving children vulnerable to radicalisation.

When I returned to Jakarta, I asked Seto Mulyadi, the chief of the advisory board of Indonesia's Commission of Child Protection, about their prospects.

'They're being brainwashed,' he replied unequivocally from his rambling home office. 'They are influenced by their fathers' jihad doctrine and beliefs from a very early age. Gradually they will become a threat to society.' Seto knew these children well; he was involved in an orphanage program separating them from radical families.

But at our Dunkin' Donuts meeting, Titin maintained her daughters were typical kids. At that moment they were leaning back in cubicles, immersed in their new books like typical kids. But the sisters' extreme Islamic dress portrayed a different picture. It followed they would, like their mother, eventually wear the *niqab* – equated with radical Islam in Indonesia – though Titin said she wouldn't enforce it. 'I don't know what will happen in the future but I don't want them to follow a radical path.'

Despite the rhetoric, Ismail shared the view that children were potential high risks. Putting it into context, Mubarok, who continued to make family decisions, told Ismail for his book, 'I was part of an underground movement organisation, the Jemaah Islamiah. Jihad is the path of my struggle, to die *shaheed* [as a martyr] is my goal.'

Titin stood by her man, claiming he had an indirect role in the crime. But Mubarok's bank account had been used to transfer money to fund the Kuta bombings. He'd helped send explosives to Bali and driven a van used in one of the blasts to the island. An Afghan war veteran trained in the southern Philippines, he and most of the other Bali bombers taught religion at the family-run Islamic *pesantren*, al-Islam, in Tenggulun village, Lamongan, East Java.

When I asked Titin if she was committed to jihadi principles, she prevaricated. She had been approached to teach at a radical Islamic boarding school and enrol her children. JI had persistently tried to recruit the family, and Titin claimed it was a constant battle avoiding its clutches. Hardcore charities aligned to Islamic networks typically offered financial aid to struggling families whose main source of income had been severed.

Enter Ismail, the avuncular surrogate father to the children, who tried to break the cycle by providing financial independence through a small enterprise for wives of terrorists. It was one of his deradicalisation programs which operated through his Jakarta-based International Institute for Peace Building.

In the end, he was afraid the funding would fall into enemy hands. But Titin's children, who attended an Islamic public school deemed moderate by extreme Muslims, were enough of a risk for Ismail to donate money for a secular education. He was afraid they would otherwise be recruited.

Titin was young and bright and had graduated from Surabaya University, East Java, with an English degree, but despite her fluent English she avoided engaging directly with me. She had never spoken with a foreigner before.

Now, a pariah, she was selling children's clothes in the village where the family lived. She was isolated and scorned, and she couldn't get a job. Her girls were bullied and couldn't go to school.

During the six-monthly prison visits, she hadn't seen the other wives of the Bali bombers apart from Ali Imron's wife, she told me.

Wives typically purported to know nothing of their husbands' activities. Hardcore Islamic doctrine allowed men to leave families indefinitely without explanation. When Mubarok left for three months to prepare for the Bali bombings, he'd simply told Titin, 'I have to go away for a while.'

In a generational handover, the eldest son of Imam Samudra perpetuated his father's legacy. He fought for Islamic State in Syria for almost two years before being killed there.

Aged nineteen, Umar Jundul Haq, nicknamed Uncu, died in October 2015.

Umar was by no means the first son of an infamous Indonesian terrorist to be killed in the Middle East. But as the son of a Bali bomber, he had cachet reserved for few other Indonesian extremists.

'These kids are preaching a heritage type of jihad. Like father, like son,' said Taufik Andrie, director of Ismail's Institute of International Peace Building. I'd met him there in 2011 and maintained contact.

'If you raise them in jihad conditioning, they will preach it. If you're a good mother and father your son should be a jihadi.

'That's why they sent them to radical *pesantrens* and to Syria and Iraq,' he said.

After five years of brutal fighting, IS's attempts to create a Middle East caliphate were defeated in March 2019 but the commitment to violence at home re-emerged.

That year an estimated 500 Indonesian men, women and children were stranded in Syria. It was feared IS returnees would use their combat skills at home, propelled toward the goal of establishing an Islamic state

*

It was at a government high school in East Java that Titin sampled her first taste of radical Islam. Proving indoctrination is rampant, even in secular schools, her teacher, connected to JI, arranged her marriage to Mubarok. Two and a half years later, he was arrested. The question on my lips was: did she still love him? She paused before answering. 'There is only one in my life; I am still in love with him.'

Apart from the scores of innocent victims Mubarak left in the wake of the blast, his own daughters will never know him. 'Does he regret that?' I asked her.

There was an unreal quality to her answers as she spoke through Ismail and her *niqab*. 'He never expresses anything, but I can see he is sad. One time he wrote me a letter saying he almost cries to see his children growing up without him.' Of the bombing, he told her, simply, 'I made a mistake and this is the big lesson for me in my life.'

Titin told me she'd only discovered Mubarok was involved after police released his name on TV three months after the bombing. 'When he said he had to go away, I did not ask why. I started to make a connection when I saw Amrozi [Mukhlas's younger brother] arrested on TV. My husband and Amrozi were very close friends.' What Amrozi lacked in brains, Samudra made up for. Ismail told me, 'He had the best rhetoric, he was clever and technologically savvy, but Mukhlas was the leader. He was charismatic with a deep religious understanding.'

*

For my piece I also contacted Mukhlas's widow, Paridah Abas, through her brother, Nasir Abas, a former key JI militant turned police collaborator. I had met him in 2011 incidentally at an official lunch in Jakarta, later interviewing him. He often gave me inside information, always insisting we meet in plush Jakarta hotels over expensive lunches; sometimes he brought a friend. I'd come to know him quite well, and he gave me Paridah's details with her permission. She agreed to an email interview. The 41-year-old lived in Malaysia with the couple's six children, then aged between eight and twenty. Her youngest was chillingly named Osama.

Paridah followed the pattern of denying her husband was a terrorist, despite the fact he'd confessed to being operations chief of JI; he had ordered and planned the 2002 Bali bombings, and had ties to Osama bin Laden. Mukhlas had admitted to recruiting his brothers Amrozi and Ali Imron to help assemble and transport the bombs used in the attacks. How could she have been in the dark?

Paridah, who had worn the *niqab* since she was nineteen, described her husband as a mujahedin, a warrior perception shared by the couple's six children. 'My husband was not a terrorist. My children see their father as a mujahid, someone who fought for Islam in Afghanistan,' she wrote in her email to me. Then, incredibly, she said, 'As for the Bali bombing, we still believe that he is innocent, that he was not the planner-bomber, whatever the government accused him to be. My children see him as ... a very good father, a genius in Islamic studies.'

When Mukhlas was executed in 2008, Paridah stayed at her mother-in-law's house in Lamongan, East Java. '[I was] surrounded by his big family and my eldest son was with me. I read [the] Koran.' A kindergarten teacher, she denied that her children, who attended a public school and studied Islamic knowledge, were motivated by violent jihad, or that JI has approached them, but 'as Muslims, they do believe they should live in an Islamic state. We are grateful we're living in Malaysia.' The country's dual legal system allows Muslims to live under a diluted version of sharia law.

Paridah didn't mention that she had taught at the Luqmanul Hakiem school in the 1990s, a radical JI-run madrassa in Johor where her late husband had been master. Typically, JI wives were involved in accounting, fundraising and propaganda for the cause. As a single mother, she accessed government financial support and community help. In stark contrast to Titin's life, Paridah's seemed good; she said people were kind and helpful. When I asked her if the family was subjected to discrimination, she brushed off the question. 'Alhamdulillah [praise to God], [we] have never been treated like that. We get full moral support from those who are aware [of their background]. I believe my husband's good image and his way with the community help us a lot.'

I asked how she reconciled her Malaysian brother's defection. Nasir Abas had evangelised on the evils of violent jihad since his jail release in 2004. His crime was an immigration violation, but his background was inextricably linked to Indonesia's radical history. Now preaching prison deradicalisation programs for Indonesia's National Counterterrorism Agency (BNPT), he is denounced by his former cohorts as an infidel and traitor. 'Nasir is my brother. For me, he is just doing what he thinks right. His activity has nothing to do with our relationship,' Paridah emailed non-committedly.

In 2001 Abas had been anointed a top regional commander by jailed JI radical cleric Abu Bakar Bashir. In his previous life he'd fought first in Soviet-occupied Afghanistan and later in the southern Philippines where he'd trained the Bali bombers.

*

In Jakarta, my routine encompassed back-to-back interviews, some leading to spontaneous ones with top brass, experts, terrorists, and so on. This was the quirkiness I loved about Indonesia – the place was studded with possibilities. Anything could happen, and did.

On this occasion, my fixer Ronna and I drove to a squalid housing compound on the outskirts of East Jakarta for which we had been given the secret address. We wandered onto quiet dirt tracks where children peeped out from behind shacks as we picked our way towards the tightly packed hovels.

A wiry man called Rahmat was slicing up chickens in a shed to sell locally for a meagre income. Piles of headless, skinned chickens littered the ground in the blood-spattered shed off his house. Buckets of water were on the tiled floor amid a gory battlefield from which wafted a raw, nauseating smell. Rahmat kept hacking and slashing the chickens studiously, speaking in a monotone, barely glancing up.

He and his family lived in the secret compound for ex-terrorists released from jail. Authorities had asked me not to disclose its existence, fearing Jakarta residents would protest against jihadis living on their doorstep. Foreign journalists weren't welcome here – Ronna and I entered cautiously, wearing headscarves and bearing gifts of hijabs for the women.

Rahmat had been radicalised by a desire to live in an Islamic state, and by his teacher Abu Bakar Bashir. The former JI member had been trained in Afghanistan by his friend Mukhlas in 1987. In the aftermath of the Bali bombing in 2003, he was rounded up with eight others and arrested. He'd spent ten days in jail.

In between his persistent chopping, he told us, 'I still believe in violent jihad if there are threats to Muslims. If something happened in [the Christian-Muslim conflict zone] Poso again, it would be a trigger.'

His wife Suryati accepted our gift and invited us into the dingy home for tea. It formed part of the shanty town behind which incongruous high-rises soared. The whole impression was one of a bizarre movie set.

Like the other wives I'd spoken to, Suryati claimed she knew nothing of her husband's radicalism. 'Whatever he does is the right thing,' she said. 'I was shocked when he was arrested.'

Several of her young children hung off the chairs. The eldest, their thirteen-year-old daughter, was participating in the intergenerational spread and inculcation of radical Islam. 'The older child knows of her father's background,' said Suryati. 'She was five when he was arrested and now understands and is supportive. She shares his radical views because she goes to an Islamic boarding school. She is proud of her father's dedication to radical Islam.'

The family of four children was included in Seto Mulyadi's University of Indonesia program under the auspices of a Muslim orphanage supporting high-risk children of ex-terrorists. The children mixed anonymously with their peers, but the issue was sensitive and secretive, and I was forbidden from entering the orphanage.

Many kids fell outside the safety net. At Indonesia's Ministry of Social Affairs, I learnt of a sweeping initiative involving about three hundred children of terrorists 'to cut off the network'. It involved removing children from extremist enclaves, to undergo therapy. When they were considered normalised the children were slotted back into families, probably perpetuating the cycle.

In my efforts to understand more about the influence terrorists have on their children, I had also tried to reach Ali Imron's wife, Nissa, but discovered she and her two children had retreated to a radical Islamic compound in East Java.

These mothers, far from the innocents they purported to be, invariably perpetuated the myth that police or the government were to blame for the fathers' imprisonment or death. Andrie told me, 'The families consider themselves victims. Every terrorist is a hero to the children. Jihad is considered holy, a good deed.'

Terrorism in Indonesia is a backlash against Suharto's repressive regime which propagated a secular state and religious pluralism. Suharto disallowed Islamic political freedom of expression. Limited religious practice and an expensive secular education system were the catalyst. 'That's when the Islamic boarding schools sprang up,' said Andrie.

10

THE GOLD DIGGERS

Back in frantic Bali, I navigated clogged traffic and tourist masses. Kerobokan prison bordered a frenetic intersection. By day the cavalcade of motor scooters and SUVs inched forward, clouded by petrol fumes; at night, the road was virtually a desert. The black shell of the prison stood shrouded in mystery.

I often pondered how the overdeveloped island would seem to the Bali Nine so many years on. As prisoners they viewed the real world only from police vans driving to and from their trials or jail transfers. 'I don't know how I would find a house [to live in] if I was released,' Michael Czugaj mused during a phone conversation.

By early 2011, the so-called paradise wasn't what it had been. The perception of a gentle tropical island inhabited largely by Hindu Balinese was eroding. I covered the escalating problems of a rising crime rate, health scares from tainted alcohol, HIV/ AIDS and rabies outbreaks, rubbish pollution, choked traffic and overdevelopment, which were repelling tourists.

Overdevelopment was proving the most difficult nut to crack because of entrenched corruption and ineffective law enforcement. At tourism meetings, where I was often the only journalist attending, the depth of concern surprised me. At one meeting I stopped the then tourism minister, Mari Pangestu, as she exited the stage. Surprised to encounter a foreign journalist, she conceded that yes, Bali was an environmental mess, but rubbish pollution was top of her list. Clearly, this was an emergency meeting before an Asia-Pacific Economic Cooperation summit that would showcase the island. The affable but no-nonsense minister had, moments before, curtly told officials to clean up Bali's image. Then she softened, speaking glowingly of promoting a 'clean, green, beautiful Bali, making it sustainable, not just for APEC, but for the future'.

The provincial government seemed impervious to the environmental stories that I, or anyone else, churned out. However, a no-plastics policy introduced in July 2019 finally acknowledged Bali's sea of plastic waste. In January an environmental and cultural tourist tax lay in the wings in anticipation of up to seven million foreign visitors largely footing the bill; jaded expats muttered it was another scam to line officials' pockets.

In my busyness, there was no sign something ominous was about to turn my own life topsy-turvy. Before it did, in mid-2011 I returned to neighbouring Lombok to cover a different crisis.

*

On the south-west peninsula of Sekotong, slightly south of Gerry's blue-roofed aberration, locals were in the grip of gold fever. Using highly toxic mercury and cyanide to extract gold in artisanal small-scale mining, they were destroying their paradise-in-waiting. The Tolkienesque idyll was transforming into hotbeds of discontent and environmental disaster. Not until I saw local homes with gold-crushing and burning equipment in their front yards did I appreciate the full import of the frenzy.

While the mercury and cyanide contaminated the water, soil and food, self-interested authorities ignored the problem. Violent clashes with police, the military and mining companies – with corrupt officials fuelling resistance and provoking killings – were common.

They were fighting for 1400 tonnes of gold in the Sekotong Hills, where thousands of illegal miners had dug up 12,000 hectares of protected forest and private land. As I drove around the winding, picturesque coastline with my guide Dewi Krisnayanti, telltale miners' tarpaulins dotted Sekotong's undulating slopes like an explosion of giant blue mushrooms.

Dewi was a Lombok-born scientist whose goldmining research was impeccable. She juggled work with family life and schoolchildren in the capital of Mataram. Indefatigable, she drove her own car to hotspots while we chatted. 'Most of the local miners came from Kuta, in central Lombok regency. They learnt how to mine from the [illegal] miners who came from Java, Kalimantan and Sulawesi. They have no background about mining; they think the more mercury they use, the more gold they can recover.'

The gold rush had driven once-sleepy villages in Sekotong since 2008. Locals earnt up to $200 a day – a windfall compared with the few dollars they picked up as fishermen or farmers. In their desperation to do better, they cast caution to the wind. They didn't care, or even know much, about the mercury poisoning that caused neurological disorders, trembling, heart and renal failure, and birth defects.

Government attempts to stop illegal miners were ignored while hundreds died in collapsing mines and landslides. More sinister, miners were misdiagnosed with symptoms of dengue fever, malaria or stomach cancer. Reports have not been released. Regional autonomy, a legal quagmire, also hampers the regulation of small miners who slip through myriad gaps into unprotected territory.

One day, Dewi and I talked to villagers burning ore outside their homes. I asked a young man called Faisal how the vapours affected him. 'We get dizzy,' he said, 'but we're okay.'

'In five years' time you could be very sick,' I said.

The man grinned. 'We don't care. It's no big deal; we drink coconut juice, that fixes it.'

We watched Faisal inhaling mercury fumes over naked flames. Obsessed with the task at hand, he maintained a steely focus so we had to huddle close to hear him.

Regulations and education on the dangers didn't exist here. The mercury was vaporised or dumped with other mining waste – including cyanide – onto land and into rivers that flushed it into the sea. This was the story I had heard, but until then it had seemed inconceivable.

We went on. Needing a cool drink, we stopped along the coast at the only luxury hotel. As we took in the plush lobby, the silvery water and the snorkelling tourists, the Malay-Chinese owner approached, insisting we stay for lunch. When I asked him the provenance of his fresh produce, he leant in and whispered conspiratorially, 'We are not buying local produce, as a protection for clients [mainly Europeans]. We get food and water from Mataram or Bali.' I'd given him my business card, so he would have assumed my reason for being in the area.

There wasn't much concern in Lombok about contamination, though an Australian expat living on the island ran an English tourist publication called the Lombok Guide that lobbied for action.

Another expat who felt irked was David Pillinger, an Australian developer whom I tracked down in Bali. Drawn into Sekotong's mining morass by a bunch of friends who owned land there and shared a love of surfing and diving, he'd suggested a sustainable cooperative mining plan in collaboration with the local government. But corruption had derailed it. 'It's like the Wild West gold rush,' he said of the charged atmosphere. 'It's like walking into a saloon.' He was incensed. 'You can't stop them mining, it's like their god-given right. Indonesia could have safe, Australian environmentally approved processes, but it's too hard. You put your money in, and they steal it.'

Pillinger had become involved with the regent of southwest Lombok, Zainy Arony, who advocated a zoning plan for Sekotong with designated community mining. Consultations between the provincial government and the national Ministry of Energy and Mineral Resources were in flux. Then, mid-negotiations, the government overturned Lombok's tourism zoning in 2010 to allow 1500 hectares of traditional small-scale mining.

Sekotong, close to Lembar Harbour, is the jumping-off point from Bali to spectacular water activities attracting foreign investors and visitors to Lombok's natural beauty. Authorities had pinned their hopes on the pristine mainland as their ticket to a booming tourist economy. They'd seen a turning point after the international airport opened in 2011, and the beleaguered development in Lombok's Kuta finally resumed. Bali's overdevelopment, along with a recent flurry of negative publicity, meant many were seeking an alternative. But gold fever, with its toxic byproducts, risked killing the nascent industry before it was born.

This was evident when I met West Nusa Tengarra's Foreign Investment Board chief, Lalu Bayu Windya. Thumbing through a list of 87 foreign investments in Sekotong, he despaired that most land was 'inactive', with tourism development flat. Much of the land had been bought in 2008 in the heat of the gold rush.

Was the gold mining a dampener? I asked. 'There are no reports of environmental monitoring carried out stating that the goldmining activities have shown a significant adverse and large impact,' Bayu replied.

Everywhere I found blanket denials of mercury contamination.

*

In Sekotong's villages, I was awestruck by the new wealth: traditional thatched huts were replaced by rows of identical smart white concrete houses. New motor scooters sparkled in the sunlight, and everyone had the latest hand phones and whitegoods. In front yards it was de rigueur to sport multiple gold-crushing machines and a burner to purify amalgam. People worked industriously, while water, mercury and tailings sloshed about, spilling on to soil where children played and animals wandered. Sacks overflowing with ore were piled outside houses and processing plants, to be crushed by the ball mills (rotating grinders). The rock had been removed by hand from narrow shafts and delivered by women carrying the sacks on their heads. Down the road at a community processing plant, a couple of locals viewed Dewi and me suspiciously as I photographed giant cyanide pumps in the otherwise derelict yard.

My contact, environmental engineer Yuyun Ismawati, warned me to limit my mercury exposure, before pulling out a map dotted with nearly a million Indonesian goldmining hotspots. Yuyun had devoted years to trying to eradicate mercury in artisanal small-scale goldmining in Indonesia. She was completing a PhD on the subject at Oxford University, where she had fallen in love with and married a Brit. But she returned frequently to Indonesia in order to continue her research and visit family. She viewed Sekotong as a looming tragedy similar to that of Minamata in Japan, which claimed nearly two thousand lives after a mercury poisoning outbreak sixty-three years ago.

Indonesia went on to sign the Minamata Convention on Mercury in 2013, seeking to curb mercury pollution, but small-scale miners slid through the cracks. 'It's cowboy country,' Yuyun said. 'There's cheating at every stage, with no records of gold trade or of gold produced at hotspots. Many shaft openings are so narrow only a child could get in. Some have died in landslides.'

In 2018, Yuyun sent me raw images from Sekatong. The mercury toxicity had taken years to manifest but there they were, scores of pictures of so-called 'Frankenstein' children who had been exposed to mercury.

Either their pregnant mothers had eaten mercury-contaminated fish, or the children had simply inhaled vapour at home. I stared at the deformed kids with club feet, mental retardation, missing limbs, cleft palates, leukaemia and much more. Still, she said, bottles of mercury lined local kitchen shelves.

*

Back on in the road in 2011, Dewi and I encountered countless signs urging *Beli Emas* (Buy Gold), in tiny kiosks beside equipment. The local traders lovingly caressed small nuggets, showing me a variety of carats from rich gold to the paler eighteen carats. The traders lamented that the most precious – twenty-four carats – was finished; they had dug it all up.

We looked for other signs of life. Stretching round the coast were a few sad, deserted guesthouses. At one in Pelangan village, we walked around the empty lobby, rang a bell and waited. To my surprise, a young man emerged and introduced himself as the operations manager. Bukran said the guesthouse embraced mining as a tourist attraction, though I couldn't see any tourists. Many, he remarked, were eager to pan for gold. I asked what he knew about the mining, and his words poured out. He described the gold fever that had killed many of his friends in the pits and the dangers that kept him away.

'In 2009, two hundred people died in a big hole. It was easy to get gold then,' he mused. It paid about A$50 for one gram. Since then, the value of eighteen-carat gold had fallen to half that but it was considerably more than the official minimum wage of about a hundred dollars per month.

Just after I left Lombok, miners swarmed to hotspots in Kuta and the more easterly island of Sumbawa. They had ravaged Sekotong's surface gold. Yuyun told me it would take up to 150 years for the area to decontaminate without financial support. Who would pay for it?

Paul Lupton, an Australian expat with property and security interests, had long enjoyed the rugged beauty of Kuta with his family, but feared contamination. They didn't eat the local food. They grew their own.

Kuta is zoned tourism, or Kawasan Ekonomi Khusus, meaning Special Economy Zone, and gold mining is not permitted. In 2017, Widodo imposed a mercury ban in small-scale mining – but locals simply switched to using cyanide.

I was eager to pursue this grim tale further in 2011, but Dewi was needed in Mataram for one of her children's school events. I flew back to Bali after a few more interviews to file another strange story.

11

A RUDE AWAKENING

In the midst of my Lombok piece, my career took a U-turn. Life veered off my dog-eared map into no-man's land. Over 2011, I'd covered stories across Bali, Lombok and Java, and even on a grand yacht passage to the eastern islands. My diary overflowed with overlapping deadlines and travel dates.

Funny how life can flip in an instant.

Which is what happened the morning I awoke with a lover to discover, from a slight touch of my own hand, a lump the size of a grain of rice in one of my breasts. I thought the unthinkable. It felt like a tiny blister, but it couldn't be waved away. I ran my fingers over it several times to confirm it wasn't an illusion. What the hell was it?

I looked at my sleeping partner and sneaked into the shower. There, it had disappeared – no, cunningly it had shifted beneath my skin. I needed to be alone. Then I considered the possibilities, which appeared meagre. A garden-variety benign cyst? I'd never had one. My mind exploded with questions. How had this invader mushroomed overnight? Or, if it hadn't, why hadn't I noticed it earlier? The feeling was surreal, an almost out-of-body experience. Suddenly isolated, I was seized by nagging anxiety and a sick feeling in the pit of my stomach.

But I waited a couple of days, hoping the tiny lump would vanish. When it didn't, I drove to Denpasar's Prima Medika

Hospital oncology unit for a mammogram and ultrasound tests. My oncologist Anda Tusta, a man generous of time and spirit, tried to soothe my anxiety, but the tests were inconclusive without a biopsy. Knowing the island's medical limitations, I ruled out having invasive procedures there. Tusta encouraged my return to Sydney, remarking on Bali's one-size-fits-all treatment. 'We only do bilateral mastectomies because women with breast cancer present in the last stage.' Why I was surprised, I don't know. I'd seen hundreds of villagers whose illnesses were untreatable because they were left too late.

Before I flew out, out of curiosity I consulted a shaman about my breast lump. My friend Puspa took me to the healer's putrid shack in Denpasar's backblocks, which I believed enhanced his authenticity. Not for me, some flashy charlatan.

When he gestured to a filthy bed behind a curtain, I lay down and removed my top, pointing to the tiny lump. Feigning professional attentiveness, the shrivelled old man, whose wife toiled out the back, squeezed, poked and touched my breast until I realised he was simply a depraved groper who may be causing the disease to spread, if it was malignant. He smiled and pronounced me healthy, telling Puspa the good news as she waited behind the curtain. I had joined the ranks of the vulnerable, wistfully clinging to the shaman's prognosis. I got his wandering hands as a bonus.

I mechanically packed a small suitcase and hopped on a plane to winter in Sydney.

Tusta's test results matched the Sydney ones. But the biopsy revealed I was indeed afflicted with the most common women's cancer.

Gripped with fear, I called my ex-partner; after all, we shared two children and twenty years. 'Don't blame me,' he retorted. I assumed he was referring to the deep stress I'd suffered from our separation and the scientific belief stress can contribute to cancer.

*

There is never a convenient time for illness. It seems to strike when we are at our busiest, so it's strange that we mutter stupidly to ourselves, 'Not *now*.'

Was I hurtling towards the end? What about my still-brimming bucket list? How would my children cope?

I was still young – well, relatively. At the time I'd been living on air with a boundless well of energy and good health, so I'd thought.

A team of Sydney specialists assembled. My surgeon at the Prince of Wales Hospital confirmed my invasive, stage 1, grade 3 tumour. The good news was, he said, stage 1 indicated the tumour hadn't metastasised and no lymph nodes were believed to be involved. The bad news, he continued grimly, was the grade 3 marker indicated it was aggressive and had a substantially higher risk of spreading than one of a lower grade. My tumour had been caught early, but this didn't rule out the chance of it running rogue.

A day after setting my luggage down, I embarked on the obligatory medical merry-go-round. The lump was removed but the risk remained it could have spread to the lymph nodes or breast tissue. More surgery ensued. I was on tenterhooks awaiting the crucial results.

Yet my diagnosis also left me oddly detached. I never focused on the thought I wouldn't pull through. My children, too, seemed unable to register the gravity. And although most friends were supportive, some vanished, possibly confronted by their own mortality. In any case, it is a journey done alone and I found myself buffeted by a wild tide.

When my doctor disclosed that the tumour was contained, I was euphoric. I could push the play button. Already I envisaged resuming my life and career in Indonesia. Plunged into the alien world of medical tests, surgery and hospital smells, I longed to return. Maybe I just needed radiotherapy?

But the oncologist had other ideas, warning of the dangers of omitting preventive treatments like chemotherapy, and factoring in my Jewish heritage, which rendered me susceptible to the BRCA gene. As my sister is BRCA1 positive, it was assumed I would be, too. I had to know my genetic status, as much for my children's sake as my own. When a positive result came back, it snapped at my heels. I worried about Jake and Ruby, in their twenties, who had a fifty-fifty chance of inheriting the BRCA1 gene from me.

Ruby has since found out she has inherited it, and she faces the daunting dilemma of taking proactive measures. Jake, if a carrier, is barely at greater risk of breast cancer than the general male population.

The statistics had been stacked against me: I'd been at least five times more likely to develop breast cancer during my lifetime compared to the general population.

Still, I fought the abhorrence of chemotherapy, choosing to wait for a second opinion from a renowned specialist on leave. My doctors calculated a two-month treatment delay was within safe parameters, which gave me a brief escape from acid hospital corridors and some breathing space after surgery. I returned to Bali on 1 October 2011, confident I was cancer-free, for now.

*

On 4 October, a dramatic story broke: a fourteen-year-old Australian schoolboy had been arrested in Bali for marijuana possession. Immediately, a huge, frenzied Australian media pack descended on the island. I was back in the thick of it.

Dubbed the Bali Boy, he was too young to be named under Indonesian law. The case drew massive coverage over the prospect of a minor imprisoned at the infamous Kerobokan jail with hardened criminals. Controversy grew with reports he was the victim of a police sting.

The boy, from Newcastle, New South Wales, had been holidaying with his parents and a friend in the upmarket Legian district when he was arrested after buying 3.6 grams from a Kuta street dealer. Police paraded him before the media, flanked by his lawyer Muhammad Rifan, and clad in a biker's mask, sunglasses and cap. The ghoulish Hannibal Lecter mask had nostril holes and pinholes over his mouth. 'Why is he wearing that weird mask?' asked Petra Rees on the Sydney newsdesk; normally officials used a balaclava to conceal an accused's identity. Finally, the chief prosecutor Gusti Gede Putu Atmaja admitted the mask had been his idea 'so no one can see his face. He has a good future. We feel sorry for him.'

The youth spent two months in custody, first at Polda – the Denpasar police headquarters – then at a room in a detention centre in Jimbaran Bay, about an hour south of Denpasar, his parents staying with him throughout the ordeal. There was no juvenile court system in the country, and the public image of a minor incarcerated and unprotected by law provoked a storm. Legal and diplomatic efforts from both countries escalated to secure the boy's release, with Canberra asking for leniency. Under Indonesia's stringent drug laws, the boy faced the maximum six years in jail as a juvenile. Tearful and distressed, he admitted to marijuana addiction – a confession that deals leniency – and remorsefully promised judges never to touch drugs again.

As someone with a seasoned Bali perspective, Australian expat photographer – and father – Jason Childs told me, 'It's a scary thing. You can't be with your children 24/7. In Australia there are laws to protect your kids. Here there aren't; they can be manipulated.'

As the first week dragged on, the media pack grew restless – any small detail was fodder. Cameras caught a pizza deliverer running upstairs to the boy's cell via a side entrance; the Bali Boy wasn't eating jail sludge. 'He is not suffering in terms of his diet,' reassured a source.

On the morning of 13 October, a major 6.8-magnitude quake struck a hundred kilometres south-west of the island, sending hundreds of police dashing into the courtyard. The boy was with drug squad investigators at the time, and he stayed inside Polda. This caused some consternation, although he was apparently about to be evacuated when the shaking subsided. Calls from the Sydney newsdesk ensued. 'It's all happening there,' laughed David King, *The Australian*'s then national chief-of-staff.

The controversial revelation that the boy's parents were on the verge of a lucrative deal with Channel 9 filled more column inches and airtime.

Finally, three weeks after the arrest, the case was registered for trial at the office of Chief Prosecutor Gusti Gede Putu Atmaja. I knew Atmaja through my years of court reporting; we were on good terms, and I had his mobile phone number. In contrast, the boy's lawyer, Muhammad Rifan, a veteran of high-profile Australian cases, including the Bali Nine, was easily accessible by media.

On 19 October, at the height of the drama, Atmaja abruptly suspended meetings about the boy for the following day because of a private event. Journalists vented their frustration and disbelief. When I called Atmaja for a comment, he explained his son's Balinese Hindu wedding was the next day. 'Would you like to join the reception at my Kerobokan home?'

'Thank you,' I replied. 'Could I come early for an interview?'

'No problem.'

The front of his home was elaborately adorned with flowers and palm leaves. The bride and groom welcomed me in colourful traditional costumes; then I found Atmaja waiting patiently on a white-tiled patio for my interview. The photos I shot portray the beaming chief prosecutor wearing a sarong, a batik *udeng* and a Harley-Davidson T-shirt. A packed reception area included Atmaja's childhood mates, all professional men who were his Harley-Davidson bike buddies. Herein lay the secret of the boy's biker mask.

In wonderment, I watched the entire uniformed staff from the prosecutor's office file in. I smiled to myself, thinking of the media pack irritated by Atmaja's delay.

A few days later, the Bali Boy emerged. He had a police escort and covered his face with a jacket, fighting his way through the media scrum for a formal interview at the prosecutor's office.

I had arrived early for a prime spot. When a TV cameraman hustled to push me back, I stood my ground.

'Look, we're trying to report this story,' he growled, brandishing his camera equipment like a weapon.

'What do you think I'm doing here?' I replied. 'Do you think I'm *not* covering the story?' He backed off.

I covered the Bali Boy until my return to Sydney for treatment on 27 October. I felt frustrated to leave at the climax of an unresolved case.

My colleague, Jakarta foreign correspondent Peter Alford, covered the boy's sentencing on 25 November. He was handed two months' jail backdated to his time already in custody. His release on 4 December brought another disorderly episode in the volatile Australia–Indonesia relationship to a timely close.

Lewis Mason didn't keep his promise. Five years later, he was back in an Australian court on cannabis charges.

*

'Can I book into a ward now?' I asked my surgeon. I was at the hospital, straight off the plane. There was a drainage problem after my surgery, but I had a room with an ensuite, a TV and plenty of painkillers.

The oncologist I'd waited to see unsurprisingly advised a chemotherapy regime, to which was later added radiotherapy and a laparoscopic operation.

I also needed a place to live. Accompanied by Bev, an old friend and neighbour, I traipsed through scores of gloomy flats, finally swooping on a bright little gem that would assuage my demons.

When I embarked on the initial chemotherapy session, a close friend and colleague from *The Australian*, Michael Johnston, virtually hand-held me to treatment. 'You'll be okay from here, won't you?' he asked at the threshold, squeamishly eyeing the infusion apparatus. As I watched the liquid empty into my body, I wondered if the process was overstated. I felt nothing. I was impervious to the effects.

Not for long.

My children were a comfort but they had difficulty understanding my enervated capacity and reduced independence – and the pain. Whoever first labelled breast cancer the 'sexy cancer' obviously never contracted it. During four months of treatment, I faced inexplicable brutal side effects that my oncologists downplayed or dismissed, such as the terrifying back pain that forced me to hospital emergency one midnight.

I later swore never to have chemotherapy again, but in retrospect you do whatever you can to save your life.

Superficial things upset me, like the temporary loss of my hair. Rationally, I knew physical changes should be the least of my worries – a mere sideshow to the main act of survival. I didn't have a long, silky mane, but my dark cropped hair was part of my identity. One morning as I blow-dried my hair, I watched in horror as thick clumps fell from my scalp. In preparation, I had bought a wig. Ruby told me I must wear only that; a scarf was a giveaway, she said. And she was right. No matter how elegant the scarf, people found it easy to distinguish the identically shrouded fashionista from the sick person. At the supermarket I was confronted by a woman shoving a bunch of basil in my face. She was so close I could smell her breath. The herb, she said, was the best source of antioxidants. Then she stared at me silently. Sandwiched between her and her partner, I felt flummoxed and vulnerable. Why did she think she could take such liberty in public?

There were more pressing concerns, such as the chronic fatigue and melancholy that grew cumulatively after multiple cycles of treatment. Trying to walk up a gentle hill – and failing – at the height of chemotherapy's blitz, I felt almost geriatric.

My unfinished Lombok feature was a welcome distraction. As I sat tapping out the final words in my small apartment, the equatorial island drifted back to me, its rugged terrain tainted with gold-rush madness. I finished the piece at my dining-room table, asking Jake to read it before I filed.

I loved having the children around, but as young adults they had their own lives, their partners and their independence. Sydney once again represented a tough, cold place where I spent months in survival mode – albeit in another context. I longed to return to Bali's cocoon and my correspondent work. On good days, I trudged into *The Australian*'s Surry Hills office, sat in a chair for seven hours and subedited while staring into a fluorescent screen.

For a break I flew to the Sunshine Coast in late January 2012 where I stayed at a surfside hotel and caught up with Bali Nine mother Vicki Czugaj. I arrived late and bedraggled in a storm, and the restaurant had closed, so we had a comical takeaway dinner and wine at a makeshift table in the lobby. Vicki told me, 'I don't know what this chemo does to your skin, but it looks fabulous.' She laughed kindly as she peered at my puffy face. A lead story on her son unexpectedly emerged from my impromptu getaway.

Writing my personal cancer story for *The Weekend Australian Magazine* during my treatment was cathartic. I handled it like any other assignment, researching assiduously and interviewing top oncologists. It kept my mind from wandering darkly, plus knowledge was a sort of balm. As a subjective participant, I felt fortunate to access the best brains on cancer when I had so many questions. Examining the cold hard facts made sense of them, and life retained a residue of order and purpose. But as I wrote the piece, probing my own mortality was neither comfortable nor avoidable.

For a distraction and to gauge 'normal' reactions, I interviewed my new-found pals, sadly all young mothers, in the cheery confines of the private hospital chemo ward, where upbeat nurses served tea and sandwiches. The mothers echoed my own insecurities and fears. We were battle-scarred, irradiated and fragile, and terrified by the possibility of a relapse.

One afternoon at News Limited, I was led downstairs to a makeup room. I was given a fantastic makeover before posing for pictures to accompany my cancer story. Dan Himbrechts, a wonderful cameraman who once tried to teach me the basic ropes, persuaded me to be photographed without my wig. It was the first time I had removed it at work, and I felt naked and exposed – but, of course, that was the story.

*

My instinct told me to keep moving. As much to prove my body still functioned as to rouse endorphins, I swam in Sydney's icy ocean – even as winter approached. It became a daily panacea, thrashing out laps, sometimes submerging in wild surf. My doctors, advising me to take baby steps, expressed amazement at this development. But it kept me sane.

All going to plan, my aim was to complete the requisite surgeries and treatment and return to my pre-cancer life. I had spent the best part of a gruelling year in the microcosm of the NSW health system.

But recovery wasn't so simple. At least another year passed before the chemo fog lifted completely and a semblance of normality returned. And as someone with a pernicious gene defect, I still assiduously jot appointments for annual cycles of tests, accepting my lot as a candidate for lifelong examination.

My *Weekend Australian* story had struck a chord in readerland, especially for those with the BRCA gene defect, and they wrote in to share their experiences and express thanks. The most gratifying feedback was from those who no longer felt isolated emotionally; they could explain to loved ones the complexity of their journey through my eyes, they said.

While my genetic fate remained beyond my control, the massive upheaval was behind me. One thing within my control was my return to Bali on 30 May 2012.

12

MURDER ON THE DANCE FLOOR

I was overjoyed to feel the sultry air on my skin after my life-changing health scare, though typically there was the conflicting sadness of leaving my children 4600 kilometres away.

The villa staff at the Seminyak compound I called home since late 2010, greeted me with wide smiles but strangely asked no questions about my lengthy absence. The Balinese are innately inquisitive, but the staff were also accustomed to my peripatetic lifestyle.

Within the week, I was reporting another Australian drug trial. Edward Myatt was arrested with over a kilo of hashish and four grams of *shabu* (methamphetamine). He was, according to expats I knew, a depressive hippy. Lucky to escape the death penalty, Myatt joined the burgeoning bunch of Western miscreants in Kerobokan jail, copping a relatively light eight-year sentence.

Approaching was the tenth anniversary of the catastrophic bombings that had ripped through Kuta on 12 October 2002, killing 202 and injuring 209, and leaving Bali economically devastated. The dead included eighty-eight Australians – the largest number of foreigners – and thirty-eight Indonesians. In the lead-up to the commemoration, I prepared stories about the Indonesian widows and widowers, the commemorative Bali Peace Park, which was to be built on the former Sari Club site but was hamstrung by the land's exorbitant sale price, and survivors and families of victims whom I'd known for years.

One Australian father, who'd lost his beloved daughter, explained it was a lifelong gaping wound. 'My life is divided into two parts: before Bali and after Bali.' Then there were those I met for the first time in 2012, whose stories also left a profound and lasting impact on me.

The morning of the anniversary on 12 October, my colleagues from *The Australian* in Jakarta and in Australia and I set off to the memorial service at 4 a.m. from Kuta, itself shrouded in dark, eerie quiet. We got lost; nerves rattled. A huge Australian press contingent was already there when we arrived, the camera crews jostling for plum positions at an apportioned platform. The hundreds of seats start filling. By 8 a.m. the unforgiving sun sent everyone scrambling for hats and bottled water.

The service was held in an amphitheatre at the cavernous Garuda Wisnu Kencana Cultural Park, in Jimbaran to the south of the island. As the sun rose, it revealed the strange magnificence of the gigantic limestone corridors. In the excavated space towered a sculpture of an eagle that helped Batara Wisnu, a god symbolising peace, to quell rage and conflict, according to Hindu beliefs.

Victims' loved ones and survivors sobbed and hugged one another, paid tribute with flowers and looked at rows of victims' photos posted on large boards. They shared raw outpourings of grief – and some relief on this milestone. In the currents of emotion, I found it impossible not to be swept along.

Victim's names were recited and candles representing each nation that lost citizens were lit in a pond. Under a blistering sun, people fanned themselves as they listened to speeches.

Queenslander Danny Hanley had lost two daughters: Renae Anderson, thirty-one, who was one of the first to die as she stood at the entrance to the Sari Club, and Simone Hanley, twenty-nine, who for fifty-eight days fought for her life in intensive care. Their mother, who had previously holidayed on the island, now shunned it. Simone was the eighty-eighth Australian victim and the mother of a four-year-old son, Noah.

Danny represented survivors and victims' loved ones, speaking with amazing dignity and composure. 'I felt honoured to speak on their behalf,' he told me at a commemorative service at Bali's Australian Consulate-General several years later.

He described the family's wrenching dilemma as one daughter battled for life. 'I had to send a relative over to look for our eldest daughter while we were in Perth caring for Simone.'

He hadn't envisaged returning after the tenth anniversary but found himself compelled on the hardest pilgrimage. 'I intend coming here every year as long as I can. I don't want to let my girls down.'

During the commemoration, counter-terrorist units were on the highest alert following the threat of another attack. It heightened anxieties.

A slew of VIPS attending would have been prime targets: John Howard, the Australian PM at the time of the blasts; the then prime minister, Julia Gillard; opposition leader Tony Abbott; Indonesian Foreign Minister Marty Natalegawa and dignitaries from twenty-one nations whose citizens were killed.

*

The night of the tenth anniversary, Felicity 'Flick' Boucher, an Australian, was sitting at a Kuta bar talking about the bombings with a married couple she'd met for the first time. Like everyone who'd come for the ceremony, the three were trying to process their emotions, and seek some closure.

Flick had tried to suppress searing memories that had plagued her for a decade. Haunting images had flooded back. They had sent her to psychological counselling and into alcohol-induced fogs. She had fought off the urge to suicide.

The previous day at the commemoration service, she had revealed her harrowing story for the first time to the parents of a young Australian man who had died in her arms in 2002.

She told me she had been in Bali on holiday for less than two hours when two explosions ripped through the two nightclubs, only a hundred metres from her Kuta hotel. She'd been walking towards the clubs, recommended by her travel agent, when all hell broke loose. Struck by flying debris, she became disorientated and faint; her ears rang. A mushroom-like cloud rose in the sky. 'It looked like an atomic bomb. I thought a plane had crashed. Then there was screaming and yelling, fire, it was carnage. I've never been in a world war but I guess it was like that.'

Fate had crossed her path earlier in the evening. In a slow crawl through gridlocked traffic, the taxi delivering her from the airport to her hotel passed the white explosive-loaded Mitsubishi van that was shortly to unleash a cataclysm. 'I remember this white van stuck out. It was oddly parked. Someone was looking after me because I should have been in the bar by then,' she told me.

After the attacks she had wandered into the dark apocalyptic landscape, instinctively drawn to a young man screaming for help. When she approached him, she didn't realise how critical he was. She knelt and cradled him in her arms. It was then she saw one of his legs had been blown away by the bombs.

He was aware of the severity of his injuries; he knew he was dying and that his time, like the blood from his body, was seeping away rapidly. He asked Flick to tell his parents how much he loved them and to reassure them he wasn't alone when he died.

In the minutes before he passed away in her arms, she promised to try to convey his dying wishes. But she knew neither his name nor his origins, and for the next decade she carried guilt over the unfulfilled vow. She needed to say, 'Your son did not spend his last minutes alone. I held him in my arms. I was in shock when he died, I was bawling. I didn't know what to do, or where to go.'

In the dark, she'd stumbled through a vision from Dante's *Inferno* to her hotel to be met by screaming burns victims seeking relief. Working through the night with other able-bodied guests, she submerged victims into the hotel swimming pool to cool them down.

'The next morning I walked up an alley on my way to a Balinese ceremony at Kuta beach [to make ritual offerings]. An Indonesian guy rode down the laneway on his motor scooter. As he drove past me he went "*boom*" and his face broke into a huge grin. That person was the so-called smiling assassin, Amrozi [one of the executed Bali bombers].' She later recognised his face with its toothy, sinister grin from a photo and reported the spooky encounter to police. 'The vision of his face will stay with me forever.'

Flick's unfulfilled promise had dogged her. She'd felt an overbearing sense of betrayal to the young man. To try to settle the matter, she'd returned for the landmark tenth anniversary and searched among the victims' photos pinned to one of the framed boards – poignant pictures chosen by families and friends, depicting happy times. She'd found the young man. Pressing a hand over his picture, she touched his face in an unguarded moment, sobbing, unaware his parents were behind her.

'Did you know our son?' they asked, puzzled.

'I knew your son, but not for long,' she replied.

'Did he die in your arms?' they asked. 'We heard someone was with him when he died.'

Relief washed over her. The weight lifted. 'I promised him I would tell you he had not died alone,' she told them, and then they hugged and graciously thanked her. Nothing more was needed.

In 2002, Flick had escaped the horror on the first plane out of Bali with the injured, only to be confronted by her own demons. She found herself in a surreal, barren place where she felt shunned and alienated. 'I had no one to talk to; people couldn't grasp the concept of it; they didn't want to hear it.' Or they'd offer piecemeal, hollow platitudes. 'Alcohol became a really, really paramount friend in my life. You just wanted to forget stuff, you wanted to die.'

It wasn't until she went back for the ten-year anniversary and met a couple in the bar that she turned a corner.

Richard and Gilana Poore, in their late forties from New Zealand and Australia respectively, chanced upon Flick; they had similar unresolved emotions, and, like Flick, they sought to exorcise the ghosts of Bali.

Flick had revealed her long-kept secret to the Poores. She vowed that would be her last visit. 'I'm pleased I went to the tenth anniversary because I really don't know what I'd be like now. If you can get through Bali you can get through anything.'

She had returned on the first anniversary but found it traumatic. 'I didn't want to leave Bali with this horrible image of people blaming the Balinese.'

The Poores had a parallel story. On 12 October 2002 they had been at the frontline, manning a makeshift triage unit for three days at Kuta's Bounty Hotel. They'd tended to hundreds of traumatised victims while coping with the carnage.

Our paths had first converged metres from ground zero – the Kuta memorial monument on which victims' names are inscribed – the day before the tenth anniversary. About five minutes after meeting the Poores, I was speaking to them in their air-conditioned room at the Bounty Hotel. We had wandered up the road away from the dense, noisy corridor of reporters and TV cameras. 'I know it seems odd we are staying at the Bounty,' said Gilana, 'but we actually feel safe here'. They were also fiercely loyal to the place.

I arranged to interview them again the day after the memorial service and it was then they told me about meeting Flick.

They had talked and cried with Flick into the small hours, drinking copious amounts of alcohol to dull their pain. Back in Auckland, where they coincidentally lived fifteen minutes apart, they later took comfort from one another, each suffering post-traumatic stress.

In 2002, the Poores had been celebrating their second honeymoon on their beloved island. A couple of days in, the explosions shattered their Hindu idyll.

A decade later, at the hotel they still considered a safe haven, the couple recounted chilling, courageous stories about lifesaving efforts that had earned them Orders of Australia.

Ten minutes before the Sari Club bomb exploded at 11.05 p.m., they had been at the club's doorstep with about three people queued before them. Boisterous laughter and chatter wafted in the balmy air, and they wondered if they could handle another heavy night of drinking with their new buddies from Sydney's Coogee Dolphins rugby team. They'd arranged to join the boys for drinks after meeting them at the Bounty where they were all staying near the most popular nightspot in Bali.

But they'd been partying hard together over the previous days, and the couple, who had two children back in New Zealand, on a whim decided they didn't have the stamina that evening. 'We actually heard them, they were drunk and really loud. Suddenly we thought, *We're too old for this*,' said Richard. 'They were all in their twenties, Gil and I are ten years older. We couldn't keep up with these guys. We thought, *We'll catch up with them tomorrow*.'

It was not to be. The Poores lost their six new mates, who had been celebrating the end-of-season sporting ritual.

The couple had just flopped onto their hotel bed when a suicide attack ricocheted from Paddy's Pub. A second ear-splitting explosion from the Sari Club threw everything into pitch-blackness as the power died. At first the couple didn't comprehend what had happened. 'We were tired,' said Richard. 'It had been a long day, we had just shut the door, we turned on the TV. An American drama was on. The windows blew out. We were beyond frightened, it's insane feelings that you have. We fell back. It felt like we had been physically punched. We actually thought a plane had crashed. But my first thought was to grab my camera equipment and go and see what had happened.' Richard had worked as a cameraman for Television NZ and Al Jazeera, and his powerful footage of the bombings was aired by Reuters, one of the first outlets on the scene. 'I still get a queasy feeling every time I see it on air,' he told me.

While Richard was filming in the darkness, a man had approached saying he believed the devastation was caused by a bomb. 'As he was speaking, I looked down and saw part of a foot still in a Nike shoe. I lost it. I stopped filming because I couldn't quite justify holding a camera. It was hard because that was my job. There were some others filming but not many ... it was chaotic. When I went out, I was in bare feet ... there was glass everywhere and there was still debris falling from the sky. The only light I could see was a massive bright yellow plume of smoke. I ran back into the hotel room to get some shoes. Gilana asked, "What's going on?" I said, "I've got no idea." People were starting to pour out of the wreckage, they were coming down the alleyway. Some were dirty and scuffed up. They were in hysterics and screaming. It wasn't until I got further down the road that I saw limbs missing from bodies and skin blown off, girls whose hair had been on fire. There were pieces blown out of people, parts of arms, chunks of flesh, missing. I vividly remember the acrid smell of burning flesh.'

Footage was limited initially – smartphones didn't exist yet. But the Poores' recollections were startling. An ominous irony was the music rumoured to have been heard before the explosions.

'What was it?' I asked Richard.

'"Murder on the Dancefloor", by Sophie Ellis-Bextor,' he flashed back. I could never confirm it but the hit song with its eerie lyrics was popular in 2002.

I speculated on why the couple hadn't gone the extra step through the Sari Club door. 'What are the odds of making that split decision?' I asked.

'It wasn't our time, that's the only way we can see it. We were obviously meant to help people because we did,' said Gilana.

'We went home and thought we didn't do enough,' Gilana said. 'I never felt lucky to survive it. There was remorse: why was I the lucky one?'

By the time Richard ran back to the Bounty Hotel, Gilana and a nurse had established the triage unit in the foyer. Processions of injured, shocked people flowed in to the Bounty – the only source of power nearby, with its own generator. They treated people for three days without sleep, living on Red Bull and adrenalin. 'It was so bizarre. People were on the floor. Blood and water and ripped sheets were everywhere,' said Gilana. 'It was weird, you could have heard a pin drop – there were no conversations, everyone was still in shock, it was dead quiet. Everyone was terrified there was going to be another bomb.'

They fielded phone calls from media, family and friends, and they started databases of survivors and the confirmed dead. Parents would call screaming over the phone, in fear for the safety of their children, and Richard had the grim task of telling a father of his son's death. 'Looking back, we wondered how the hell we kept it together.'

They returned to Auckland eight days after the bombings, immediately organising medical supplies and two burns nurses for a return trip to Bali, where they also treated injured locals unable to afford hospital care.

The Poores' love affair with Bali had begun on their first honeymoon in 1999. For three years they'd seen it as paradise before its sweetness and innocence were torn apart. 'We were so upset at seeing how [the bombings] affected Bali,' said Gilana. 'It was a beautiful paradise for us and to have it wrecked like that ...' Her voice trailed off.

'The grief doesn't lessen but you feel the people who passed away have been honoured,' Richard said after the anniversary service. It had conferred a little lightness at best, Richard and Gilana agreed; the word 'closure' didn't quite fit.

For the best part of two weeks, I stayed in the vortex of Kuta, embedded with Indonesian and Australian communities.

During this time there was a collective yearning for catharsis that transformed Kuta. Laid bare were outpourings of sorrow and unabashed camaraderie, the bonds shared by an unenviable club.

At the symbolic heart lay the site of the annihilated Sari Club.

Kuta's streets overflowed with Australians. At some point, the hyper-charged atmosphere assumed a bizarre carnival flavour. Stories of love and sudden loss intersected, each a haunting trajectory of retraced footsteps leading to the blasts. Inhibitions melted; people laughed and wept profusely. I had a perpetual lump in my throat. Tears welled as I listened to their recollections.

Barry Wallace, a father from New South Wales, told me of the surreal moment he arrived in the wake of the bombings to see his daughter Jodi's untouched hotel room, finding her stashed passport and other personal possessions. 'She hadn't even slept in her bed for one night,' he said, misty-eyed.

Jodi had been burnt beyond recognition. On her thirtieth birthday she was in the Bali morgue with her Sydney friend Charmaine Whitten. They had barely arrived in Bali when they dropped their luggage at their hotel and excitedly headed out to the

Sari Club. Their remains were among the last to be identified two months after the blasts, and then by DNA testing.

For Barry, the tenth anniversary was just a number. 'It's not a raw, yearning loss [as it was] but a part of you dies. It's still very poignant; pain and grief bubble to the surface. Time does help, but it doesn't heal. You learn to tolerate and try to manage your grief. At the end of the day, you have to survive.' The profound devastation had left many families broken; some turned to drugs or drink. 'I think we all drink more than we did in 2002.' Barry exemplified the sentiment of those enveloped in loss and anguish. 'I don't need to hear their stories, but this is one tribe we all belong to.'

Belonging had brought peripheral concerns. Barry was one fearing another attack after the warning of a potential strike.

'I do believe Bali will get hit again, at some point,' Barry said later, when we had relocated to the serene gardens of his Kuta hotel.

Most of Barry's extended family had flown in for the first time, and there were similar stories all over Bali. Many were confronting old wounds on a foreign island or revisiting them after years abroad because they couldn't stomach the place. It was a belated wake.

Conspiracy theories contradicting the Jemaah Islamiah-led attacks have always abounded. The strongest, partly based on the severity of victims' burns and the magnitude of the devastation, suggested the CIA had replaced the Sari Club bomb with a 'micro-nuclear' weapon. This theory was reiterated in 2006 by jailed firebrand cleric Abu Bakar Bashir, the bombers' spiritual mentor believed to be the mastermind behind the bombings, which he always denied. Numerous expats and witnesses to the aftermath expressed this theory.

Richard Poore, for one, was pilloried on the internet for his conspiracy views. Barry Wallace, one of the last Australians to brave annual pilgrimages, considered the theory possible.

Each year after the tenth anniversary, Barry and his second wife, Karmel, and I shared a few beers at a Kuta watering hole where he and his son Mark had sat every anniversary from 2003 to 2007. Back then, Barry had voiced his concern about future visits due to his advancing years – to which Mark, an arm around his father's shoulder, had replied, 'Don't worry, Dad, I will always be here for Jodi.' It was not to be. In 2008, Mark, then forty-two, died after receiving head injuries during a scuffle in Tweed Heads, New South Wales.

'Why do you keep attending the traumatic Bali commemorations?' I asked Barry.

'Many of us don't have any place to go to be with our kids in a spiritual sense except here. Many of our children aren't in a grave … I feel the loss of my daughter as though it was yesterday. It never goes away.'

In the days post-carnage, Barry had rummaged through wreckage with Mark, searching for his daughter amid charred bodies. 'I was in shock, it was surreal. I cannot begin to describe it.'

The bomb crater, the identity photos, the makeshift morgue, the rows of plain coffins randomly stacked, the waiting, the crying, the anger, the stench, the bodies covered with plastic and ice are immutable legacies of the horror.

Vaughan Hatch, a long-term New Zealand expat, didn't know about the bombs until the morning after. From his home in seaside Sanur, he rushed to donate blood at Denpasar's Sanglah Hospital, the largest victim base. 'It was chaotic, madness. Victims overflowed from wards; people were checking morgue lists trying to find missing loved ones. It was incredibly morbid.' The morgue was full, so bodies stacked with ice were outside in the sweltering heat. 'I was so overwhelmed, there were so many bodies, body bags, the smell was sickening. It was like something between a prison and an animal yard. Bloodied water and body bits were everywhere.'

Fluent in Bahasa Indonesia, Hatch was hived off to translate for an Adelaide doctor doing the rounds of three obscure hospitals where patients were clinging to life. The confronting scenes later pushed Hatch into a post-traumatic funk. To this day he battles the after-effects, with chronic aches and pains that still baffle doctors.

'Most of the people had third-degree burns,' he told me. 'They were all in a really bad way.' Most wouldn't make it, he thought at the time. 'One guy, a footballer wrapped in bandages from head to toe, looked like a mummy. You could only see part of his face. The doctor asked to inspect his burns; they were horrific. Patients were screaming and wailing and asking for help. The local doctors were out of their league and facilities were hopelessly inadequate. I was overwhelmed by how bad the hospitals were; the army hospital with green peeling paint was really Third World; there was a lot of trash, mosquitoes, and much of it was outdoors.'

The voices of Indonesian bomb survivors mingled with those of their Australian counterparts. Local victims with disfiguring burns and widows whose husbands had been killed in the atrocities told me their stories. A resilient group, they forged new lives by running a garment factory, Adopta Co-op, which churned out hundreds of online orders. Founded by an Australian couple, David and Moira Wedd, Adopta laid the financial foundation for the widows' path to self-sufficiency.

One of my most poignant interviews was with a widower whose Indonesian wife had been killed in the blasts. Raden Supriyo Laksono told me he'd since remarried and added two children to the two he'd had with Lilis Puspita. Considering he'd found new love and life, I thought this forty-six year old had fared better than the widows, but I was wrong: he remained deeply tormented. He explained that Lilis had left work to collect him from his hotel job opposite the Sari Club. Chaos erupted after the two explosions rocked the hotel, smashing glass and extinguishing electricity.

'People were running everywhere, crying, shouting, "It's a bomb."' In the pandemonium, it was 3 a.m. before he missed his wife. Panicked, he went to the hospitals 'where there were so many bodies they couldn't cope'. 'I couldn't find her. I was sure she was dead. I didn't go home for two days because I knew my children would ask, "Where's Mama?"' Tears rolled down his cheeks, and I was hard-pressed to keep my composure. Lilis had been pregnant when she died, he said.

A Muslim, Laksono retained deep hatred for the terrorists and fought overwhelming rage, incensed they had killed in the name of religion. And as Barry Wallace said, 'What did it achieve? Nothing. They've recruited others, and three bombers have been executed.'

Though the official number of Indonesian losses is thirty-eight, relief workers in Kuta at the time believed the figure was incorrect.

Many more who had no official IDs – such as sex workers and pimps who frequented Kuta's red-light district – were thought to be among the dead.

Ian Freestone, then Australian director of the International Friends of Compassion said at the time of the bombings in an online post, 'Body parts of eighty-five or so bomb victims were cremated here today. That caps the death toll at 307. Scores of society's rejects – beggars, prostitutes, drug pushers and others unworthy of official ID add to the unofficial tally.'

Australian Jakarta-based chaplain Jeff Hammond, who I knew well, had worked with churches assisting at hospitals, the morgue and other places where victims spilled. He helped Indonesian victims as Australians were airlifted out.

'Relief workers told me that the numbers of Indonesian deaths were probably a lot higher since the remains were not all identifiable and many were never reported missing; they may have been prostitutes from other islands whose parents never knew where they were or what happened to them.

'For positive identification they needed samples from relatives to be able to match them to samples they had.'

Al-Qaeda leader Osama Bin Laden had issued a fatwa in 1998 legitimising the bombings to fight Americans and their allies – and, as Australians soon found out, their favourite tourist destination was not immune.

Following the 2016 anniversary, I chanced upon Barry taking time out on the tiny island of Nusa Lembongan, just east of Bali. Deep in meditation, he was perched on rocks facing the beach – a forlorn figure looking out to sea, the senselessness of his daughter's death hitting him in waves all over again. I had caught him at a bad moment. Perhaps to conceal it, he turned his attention to the surf, a lifelong passion that sustained him. 'Surfing is the best therapy. You only have time to think about the next set. When it comes, you're either going to be exhilarated or crushed,' he said, gazing firmly at the horizon, determined to stay afloat.

*

Four years later, there were fears of further terror attacks in Bali. Indonesian counterterrorist police tried to keep it quiet, but their prevention of several suicide bomb plots in Java over the Christmas holidays made overseas headlines. Police revealed only that Islamic jihadists had planned strikes 'outside Java'. A few days before Christmas, I reported that the foiled Islamic State-inspired attacks had targeted Bali's golden triangle: the tourist hubs of Kuta, Legian, Seminyak and Ubud.

A nervous frisson swept through Bali residents whose sharp recall of the 2002 and 2005 bombings – in which twenty people were killed – invoked grotesque post-explosion imagery. And as a tourist destination, Bali could ill afford a third bombing: the crown jewel of Indonesia had lured tourists back a few years after 2005, by which time islanders were desperate for the income they relied upon. By 2017, five million foreigners were drawn annually, adding 75 per cent to the national economy.

Upgraded travel advisories circulated in 2016. When my intelligence source disclosed that a ten-kilogram bomb had been found, I omitted writing the scale of it for lack of verification.

On Christmas Day, I considered cancelling my plane ticket to Lombok, then reneged. A couple of nights previously I'd woken in a sweat from haunting, vivid dreams. I heard a voice saying, *There will be bombs but they won't be as bad as 2002 and 2005.* I later realised the prediction echoed one of my sources. Attack scenarios had been swimming in my mind since I'd heard about the thwarted plots.

Since 2011, I had reported Islamic extremism threats in Indonesia. Though police have had success in foiling terrorist plots since the Bali bombings, attacks persist – mainly targeting police in recent years.

13

CRIMES AND MISDEMEANOURS

A couple of weeks after the anniversary, I was back at the Denpasar District Court covering a complex drugs case for *The Times* of London. A UK cocaine-smuggling ring had been arrested, and the most serious verdict landed British grandmother Lindsay Sandiford on death row, where she remains.

Passing a squalid holding cell, I noticed a well-groomed Japanese teenager behind bars with a bunch of underage Indonesians. When I stopped to ask him why he was there, the seventeen-year-old courteously explained he was waiting to be sentenced for cannabis possession.

I'd heard that a few boys from Denpasar's international school had been busted with small amounts of marijuana. It had been reported in the local news, and mainly it whipped up panic and terror among expat parents of teenagers. The word was police were targeting wealthy families with joint-smoking kids for massive bribes. Fears also swirled of police planting drugs.

My mind strayed to a parallel case. What a difference a year made: exactly twelve months previously, in October 2011, I'd been among a media scrum reporting on the Bali Boy. Although he'd been in a similar position to this Japanese boy, he hadn't gone to jail for it. He'd served a couple of months in a detention centre in Jimbaran, where his parents had stayed with him. In contrast, the Japanese juvenile admitted to buying 2.6 grams of marijuana – a gram less than that which the Bali Boy had bought – and was sentenced to six months' jail for possession. Although his name was suppressed because he was underage, no one labelled him the Bali Boy.

When I was having dinner one night with a Dutch friend, she sternly warned her two adolescent boys to steer clear of drugs. In expat circles, it was known that some parents had paid up to $100,000 to keep their kids out of jail on minor drugs charges.

Expats began returning to their home countries when their children, raised by *pembantus* (housemaids) in the cloistered, colonial milieu, grew out of touch with reality and out of control, becoming easy marks for police. By the age of thirteen, some kids were obstreperous, spoiled and bored in the society that seemingly had no rules and didn't offer much stimulation outside school hours. Running amok, they rode motorbikes without licences, drank alcohol and smoked dope. I'd run into a few of these little gods.

The Japanese juvenile wasn't in that category. When I spoke to him, the tall, fragile-looking teen had already spent three months in the infamous Kerobokan jail. 'How are you coping?' I asked.

'It's pretty awful. I was sixteen when I was arrested and I had my seventeenth birthday in the jail. What a way to spend my birthday.' He sighed. 'I don't want to celebrate New Year in jail.' He didn't have a choice. He was freed in February 2013 and immediately deported.

Where the Bali Boy had been protected by his parents, the Japanese teenager was alone. Should he have known better, I wondered, having been raised in Bali by his mother and knowing the vicissitudes of the island? But he was still a minor, and his situation was sadly remarkable for the absence of family support. I felt sorry for him; he seemed like a nice boy on a rite-of-passage in the wrong place. His father, who lived in Japan, hadn't shown up at his arrest; neither had his mother.

'Will your parents come to court?' I asked.

Guests at the cremation ceremony of 83-year-old Anak Agung Ngurah Anom Mayun, the last king of Kerambitan, in Bali's south-west Tabanan Regency, in 2009.

At the cremation ceremony, with one of the king's twin cousins Prince Anak Agung Ngurah Rai Giri Gunadhi, the king's niece Princess Giri Putri and my friend and contact Asana Viebeke Lengkong.

The five wives of Anak Agung Ngurah Anom Mayun.

At the ninth-century Borobudur Temple in central Java, with Thai Buddhist monks, 2011.

Bali Nine's Renae Lawrence with female inmates at Kerobokan jail, 2010. (Photo: Made Nagi)

At Bali's Kerobokan jail in November 2013, interviewing prisoner Myuran Sukumaran, with my assistant Telly (Lia) Nathalia. (Photo: Jason Childs)

Scott Rush on his twenty-ninth birthday, in Karangasem jail, north-east Bali, 2014. (Photo: Made Nagi)

Caged man in Bali, 2015.

Interviewing an Islamic State follower at Jakarta's rebuilt Marriott Hotel, 2015.

Interviewing the then Indonesian chief of police, Tito Karnavian, and the last surviving member of the Bali bombers' inner circle, Ali Imron, at Jakarta's police headquarters, 2015.

At the end of the day, after interviewing Ali Imron, with the Singapore counter terrorism team headed by Rohan Gunaratna (in suit beside Tito Karnavian), 2015.

With powerful Indonesian tycoon Tomy Winata and villagers in Sumatra, 2016.

Balinese men on an odyssey to save Bali's Benoa Bay from reclamation, 2016.

On a boat in Benoa Bay, Balinese praying to their gods for salvation from the reclamation project, 2016.

Bali Nine lifer Matthew Norman in Kerobokan jail, Independence Day 2017.

Entrance to Nusa Kambangan penal island.

Celebrating the annual agricultural festival in Plaga, central Bali.

Preparing medicinal offerings in the midst of a busy upmarket Seminyak street.

Taking photos of students and teachers at Jakarta's only refugee school, Roshan ('Bright' in Farsi), April 2017.

Talking to refugees at Roshan.

A quiet moment: waiting for Schapelle Corby with Indonesian media outside Denpasar's parole office, 27 May 2017, before she returned to Australia.

Cadging a lift with Jakarta's Metro TV crew while covering the 2017 eruptions of Bali's sacred Mount Agung for *The Times* of London. Thousands were evacuated.

Passing rice paddies near Rendang's volcano-monitoring post, east Bali, during my coverage of Mount Agung's eruptions in 2017.

President Joko Widodo at the Klungkung sports centre, east Bali, distributing supplies to evacuees fleeing Mount Agung's 2017 eruptions.

With the senior editor of *The Jakarta Post*, Endy Bayuni, at the 2018 Ubud Writers and Readers Festival, Bali. (Photo: Priscilla Ziona Huwae)

With former Indonesian Minister for Foreign Affairs Marty Natalegawa and his wife, Sranya Bamrungphong, at the 2018 Ubud Writers and Readers Festival.

The Ogoh-ogoh parade in 2018, on the eve of Nyepi (Silent Day), the Balinese new year.

A Balinese ceremony, 2019.

Press card from the Indonesian Foreign Affairs Department.

With my children, Jake and Ruby.

The boy replied, 'They are not coming because they are in shock; they are ashamed because I am the only son. I can understand,' he murmured, without resentment.

Had they visited him since his arrest? 'No, they couldn't. They have lost face.'

His friend, arrested with a greater amount of drugs, had snitched on him. However, the youth didn't bear a grudge. 'That's what happens.' He smiled weakly. 'The police want names. But he's *really* in trouble – he's going to get at least five years because he's Indonesian and he has no money for a lawyer.'

I followed the lanky teen into court and watched him, rigid against a bare wooden chair, nervously listening to the judge. I couldn't help but admire him for holding his own. No one needed to translate; he spoke fluent Bahasa. But he was so alone, and again I thought how lucky the fourteen-year-old Bali Boy had been – perhaps mainly to be Australian.

*

In Indonesia, basic strategies lessened my chances of careless misadventure. One night when I should have taken a taxi instead of walking, I learnt that lesson. Returning home from dinner on a dark winding road, I noticed a young man on a motor scooter had stopped a few metres back to check his phone. That was the premise. As he idled past me, he paused to reach into my bra with a snake-like gesture for a quick breast grope. Then he zoomed off at breakneck speed – too fast for me to log his registration number.

These types of incidents – and worse – were reported ad infinitum on social media. Why was I surprised? I suppose I'd felt invincible. But now I felt violated – and infuriated that he had escaped with impunity. What had he got out of it? Had it been a dare? A quick thrill?

The crimes of Bali were as odd as they were veiled. Some were relegated to lore. Untouchable. The island has a history of recurring themes of missing people and mystery deaths. Weak law enforcement and entrenched corruption fed into the lawlessness that was the flip side of Bali's alluring lifestyle. Under media scrutiny for weeks or months, crime investigations suddenly shut down or were left pending; lab results went astray amid misinformation or no information.

From a tip-off in April 2013, I learnt of the violent death of an unidentified 54-year-old Australian woman. For two weeks her body had been laid out on a cold slab at Sanglah Hospital's mortuary. No one had come forward claiming a missing friend or family member. Her nationality was a mystery.

The story was painfully sad. Found bleeding one night beside a narrow Ungasan road, in the southern area of Jimbaran Bay, she was rushed to hospital but died the following day. This posed a conundrum to Denpasar's foreign embassies, none of which had heard about the death of a Western woman. I called the Australian Consulate-General, which after some days identified Linda Chilver as one of its citizens. A Victorian divorced mother of a teenage daughter, she had been discovered barely alive with no money or belongings, and wearing a pocketless sundress and sandals. How she'd come to be on that lonely stretch of road, away from tourist areas in the pitch-black night, was baffling.

An autopsy in Bali revealed internal injuries, brain damage and blunt force trauma to her body. Her family was told initially she had suffered a fall, with no suggestion of foul play. The forensics department chief at Denpasar's Sanglah Hospital, Dudut Rustyadi, told me her injuries pointed to a brutal bashing. Later he changed his mind, saying she had been hit by a speeding car.

As an aside, the small Denpasar morgue was Dudut's domain, one of my regular interview stops. Nine months after Chilver's death I'd arrived one afternoon to an animated huddle of reporters. I followed them into the rarely accessible inner sanctum, the cold storage area for corpses, unsure of what was unfolding. From two open cabinet doors, two pairs of stiff legs and feet protruded on body trays like white marble slabs. Name tags hung from the corpses' toes. It wasn't clear why the cubicle doors were open. Local TV crews milled about self-consciously as more reporters arrived. We all stood there in an awkward silence, surveying the macabre sight. The coroner, buoyed by the growing attentiveness, crossed nimbly from one cold room to another. 'Do you want to see this one?' he asked the TV crews enthusiastically, about to pull out another corpse. Mortified, they shook their heads, holding their hands aloft: 'No, don't.'

On the night I was tipped off about Linda Chilver's death, I drove to her hotel. A week before her death, she'd booked in alone to a hotel on the motorway heading south from Bali's airport. Probably her taxi driver had recommended it. When I entered the desolate white-tiled, mosquito-infested lobby, I felt I gleaned part of her life. Bali was the last leg of her holiday after a stay in Thailand. A vulnerable, divorced woman, estranged from her family, she had stepped out in the evening, apparently empty-handed, leaving her money, handbag and passport at the hotel. It didn't seem to make sense.

'She was always cheerful and polite,' the hotel manager replied after I inquired about Chilver's demeanour on the night of her disappearance. 'I mainly saw her at breakfast. She didn't say how long she would stay.' Yet she had been missing for two weeks and hadn't paid her hotel bill in advance.

'Where are Linda's personal effects?' I asked.

The manager surveyed me slowly. 'They're in her room. I will give them to the Australian consulate.' A local man watched on.

Apparently no one had noticed Chilver leaving the hotel that night, though she'd walked past the manager in the small, deserted lobby. She'd had no visitors, and no one collected her, although police suggested someone might have.

Chilver had been the only hotel guest at that hotel.

Police thought she may have drunk arak – the local backyard-brewed alcohol sometimes laced with deadly methanol – in a bar and gone wild, yet she'd carried no money and hadn't been spotted at any bar along that forbidding dark road. Ethanol and methanol had been found in her blood, but police denied she had died from ingesting a toxic drink. They didn't rule out foul play. There seemed to be so many loose ends.

Three witnesses were interviewed by police: the motorcyclist who'd found her, and two workers who had apparently seen her walking erratically earlier that night by the main road, 'babbling to herself and hugging a power pole'.

The mortician suggested *someone* may have moved her body from the main road, because the street in which she was found was too narrow for a speeding car. But after the autopsy, Chilver's death was officially noted as a hit-and-run.

*

A few months earlier, a similarly mysterious death of a Westerner in Bali had whipped up a media frenzy. On the morning of 30 November 2012, 33-year-old Australian Denni North was found unconscious by the pool of her villa north of Kuta. She was rushed to hospital but died on the way.

The vivacious blonde party girl had been in Bali less than six months, working as guest relations consultant at a trendy Seminyak beachfront bar, Cocoon Beach Club, not far from my home. She'd been a perfect fit for Cocoon, the glitzy sister club to Ku De Ta, both owned by the same wealthy businessman.

Media packs parachuted in from Australia, poking into the salacious details of North's private life. Sources said that bags of pills – GHB, also known as Fantasy and the 'date rape drug' due to its soporific effects – had been found in her villa after her death, and that the drugs had been removed from her villa before police arrived.

Police insisted no drugs or violence were involved, but no autopsy was carried out in Indonesia, at the request of her family.

North had been drinking in the early hours with three girlfriends. Two were Australian, one simply named Kelly and the other Felicity Bloom, while the third was a Frenchwoman, Agathe Ammeux, whom police called a *pacar*, the romantic term for boyfriend or girlfriend. When the Canggu police chief used this word, animated murmurs rippled through his office where I was being briefed with local reporters. The tragedy took on the hallmarks of a soap opera.

North had arrived home from work at 3 a.m. and her friends had gone to bed an hour later. Kelly had found her unconscious about 8 a.m. with her legs immersed in the swimming pool, said Kuta Utara police chief Aldi Alfa Faroqi.

When I checked out North's Batu Belig villa, north of Kuta, the only sign of life was a security man and the Balinese *pembantu* placing ritual offerings on the doorstep. She explained she was doing it for North and to cleanse the place, now an eerie shell.

As no autopsy was carried out in Indonesia, the investigation stopped when North's body was returned to Australia. What had happened in her final hours remained a mystery, and theories were still flying a week and a half after her death, when I, alone and unwelcome, attended her upbeat wake after Australian news crews flew home. About forty of North's best friends studiously avoided me at the hip Mantra bar in Petitenget – long closed – drinking copiously, the toilet a revolving door. Mantra had been North's favourite bar, and a private upstairs area was cordoned off for her memorial, an inebriated celebration of her short life. I sat on a high stool at the downstairs bar, listening to live music, biding my time. Eventually, loose-lipped, her friends joined me to talk effusively about the best friend they barely knew.

'An amazing girl,' a tall young Victorian man, Jesse Kirley, said repeatedly. 'We didn't really know Denni before her Bali experience ... but Bali's the sort of place that accelerates your friendship. She made an amazing impact, she was gregarious, energetic, she lived by the moment. It was hard to keep up with her. She was someone very special to me. There is a feeling of disbelief. We are still trying to come to terms with it.'

Felicity and Agathe moved through the gathering, tearfully hugging people. The so-called *pacar* more or less ignored me.

'How did Denni die?' I asked her.

'Denni died, that's what happened.'

Felicity, a slick blonde who pointedly mentioned that her parents were lawyers, insisted there was nothing suspicious about North's death – the media had blown it out of proportion. She didn't understand why confusion still surrounded North's death. 'I'm not going to talk about it,' she told me. 'It was a terrible accident. There's nothing more to it,' she added in a clipped, business-like tone.

Kelly, who had found North by the pool, couldn't be tracked down for a police interview. She was understood to have left Indonesia, but Bali police had continued to look for her, to no avail. 'Kelly has spoken to the family. The police know where she is,' Felicity said, without divulging the location. It remained unclear what happened in the early hours of that Sunday between when her friends went to bed and when North collapsed by the pool. Police had said they would reopen the case if more information came to light.

It was after midnight. Talk abruptly shifted to an afterparty wake at 'someone's' villa. As though a tornado had ripped through Mantra, the bar was suddenly empty. Outside, the street was unusually silent, it was so late. I drove home in my little rented car.

*

In January 2014, the sudden mystery deaths of a holidaying Queensland mother Noelene Bischoff and her teenage daughter Yvana sparked further alarm and another media circus. The pair had eaten seafood meals, become violently ill and died hours later in the early hours of the morning. Tourists told me that after hearing this story they'd almost cancelled their own trips, so paranoid were they about poor sanitation, bad food, tainted alcohol and inadequate health care.

The day the Bischoffs died I drove to their hotel, the Padang Bai Beach Resort in east Bali. The idyllic, palm-fringed seaside bay was almost desolate compared to the numbers I'd seen on previous visits, when I'd sometimes caught the ferry to the nearby Gili Island chain – which was exactly what the Bischoffs had in mind as part of their holiday.

In their small hotel room, then a crime scene, I ruminated on the pattern of vulnerable people whose situations turned pear-shaped in the poorly resourced eastern part of the island. The Bischoffs' first attempt to deal with their emergency had been to visit an inadequate local clinic.

Autopsy results in Australia found both Bischoffs had died from an allergic reaction after eating toxic fish, with asthma a contributing factor. An inquest was considered unnecessary. It was another tragedy with too many loose ends.

The deaths came weeks after a NSW teenager had been blinded in Bali after drinking a methanol-laced cocktail while on a schoolies trip.

*

Around this period, tourists faced a stark wake-up call. Violent robberies, unprovoked vicious attacks and batches of tainted alcohol tarnished Bali's rebuilt image. In response to the crimes and ineffective policing, expats turned to social media where they created a database of incidents and empowerment strategies. A Facebook page that registered crimes, 'Mugged in Bali', was created by long-term Perth expat Richard Flax and attracted hundreds of posts from foreigners.

At his Seminyak office, Flax told me that apart from CCTV there were no effective reporting processes in Bali. Victims came out of the woodwork, recounting horror stories of home invasions, muggings at knife point, being stopped and robbed while riding motorbikes, handbag thefts and countless scams. 'Some of these thieves are so good they can get a handphone out of closed clam shell,' said Flax. On 'Mugged in Bali', he moved quickly to identify crime hotspots and encourage alarm systems.

Canggu – a trendy foreign-resident enclave north of Kuta that had engulfed what was once a coastal strip of rice paddies and coconut groves – was at the epicentre of the deluge of crime, along with Kuta, Batu Belig and Legian. A building frenzy was a magnet for Indonesian migrant workers and scam artists blamed for a crime spike. Canggu's then police chief, Michael Risakotta, told me the development boom had lured Javanese organised crime syndicates to the area.

I interviewed many expats in palatial Canggu homes equipped with drivers and nannies, a lifestyle far beyond the realms of affordability in the West. Residents simply accommodated increased crime as the new normal and made some radical modifications. One family I interviewed had transformed their home into a small fortress after waking one night to the terrifying presence of knife-wielding Indonesian burglars who fled after much shrieking. I asked Australian Robyn Schonell if her home now felt like a prison, to which she replied in a clipped tone, 'You get used to it.'

Many crimes in the area went unreported in the media, such as one involving a single mum who returned hastily to Australia after a break-in at her Canggu home. Burglars had led the terrified woman at knifepoint to her safe, and she'd surrendered the contents.

Crime, chaos and unbridled development were undoubtedly damaging the reputation of the tropical idyll. As tourist numbers accelerated, with over three million foreign visitors in 2013 on an island the size of greater Sydney, so did crime.

14

TO CATCH A THIEF

One night in 2014 while driving into my villa's dimly lit carpark, I heard unidentifiable thuds. Dull, repetitive, hollow clunks. Like someone booting a flat football. It was 10 p.m. My eyes adjusted to a gruesome scene: Balinese thugs were beating an accused thief with unnerving relish. I watched as they booted the middle-aged man from one end of the carpark to the other.

Fear and trepidation pounded me – I had stumbled into the vortex of Bali's underbelly in my own villa complex on an otherwise peaceful, moonless night. I stood there, transfixed and repulsed, unsure what to do. I learnt that vigilant reception staff had apprehended the man from the adjoining *gang* (alley). Only one street back from Seminyak's fashionable shopping precinct, Bali's dark side was revealed.

Minutes before, the culprit had tried to steal a small purse from a young West Australian tourist. She and her boyfriend had been strolling back to their hotel after dinner when the Balinese man sidled up beside her on his motorbike and grabbed her purse. Because it was slung over both shoulders, the young woman was dragged alongside him for a moment – but she managed to escape, retaining the purse.

Shaken, the couple had related details to my reception staff who promptly ensured the application of disproportionate justice.

They phoned the *Banjar*: the traditional, semi-autonomous village council and local lawmakers. Scores of vigilantes joined the melee. Clad in T-shirts emblazoned with *Banjar*, they arrived on souped-up bikes, blue lights flashing in a mock police raid. They furiously texted, summoning their friends – heavily tattooed thugs with bulging biceps.

Now blood was gushing from the accused thief's mouth and ears; dark red pools soaked his torn clothing. Some of his teeth splattered to the bitumen, his eyes bulged, and his face swelled like a pufferfish. As I watched the vigilantes beat him, I felt impotent and numb. This poor man didn't have a chance. He didn't yelp or groan. He curled into a foetal position on the ground. Once he sat bolt upright and pleaded silently for mercy, his hands clasped in prayer. It didn't help. He slumped back motionless, legs splayed on the gravel, as he awaited death.

The Perth woman's eyes widened with fear. Her boyfriend urged her, 'Ash, let's go. Let's go, Ash. I don't want to see this.' His voice quivered. Then he asked me, tensely, 'Are they police?'

I shook my head. 'No.'

They were drawn into a dark web, encircled by thugs like trophy butterflies.

This wasn't in the glossy travel brochures. Any illusion these two tourists had of Bali as a purely gentle and peace-loving place unravelled that night. Finding themselves witness to 'justified' violence, the thugs ordered them to wait for police. They obeyed.

This was another vigilante attack undertaken with impunity, their antics witnessed with tacit police approval, the 'incident' to be duly noted in an official report. I had not witnessed such an attack before but they were well known and documented on social media.

Staff from my villa complex stood gawking, acquiescent and complicit. Skulking in the shadows was the owner of the complex, a married man with children. I had grown accustomed to ignoring his lewd remarks and the stream of simpering girls he took to vacant villas in the compound. His behaviour was an open joke among repeat customers; not so amusing were staff complaints of his failure to pay their wages.

Now he was emboldened by adrenalin-fuelled machismo, and his febrile face contorted into a ghoulish smile. 'Don't get involved,' he threatened me sternly, as I heard myself yelling instinctively into the void for the attack to stop.

What could I do? What idiot would interfere?

'These tourists are scared – I am going to drive them to their hotel,' I ventured feebly. My voice sounded like a disembodied echo. This was the villa compound I had called home for six years, the sanctuary I returned to after pursuing grim stories exposing humanity's ugly side. Yet the ground had shifted. No longer did it offer the security I'd previously felt. It had rearranged itself, assuming a new deranged face.

Silence. Then the owner changed tack. Still glued to the action, his eyes shining, he said lightly, 'We are not like your culture. On the other hand, look at the Yanks, look what they do at Guantanamo Bay.' As if by comparison, he conceded, 'The Balinese *do* like doing this. And killing them.'

When an effete uniformed police officer arrived, the spooked tourists barked, 'Who are you?' Looking vaguely amused, he confirmed his police status and attempted to calm them. Trying to maintain a degree of decorum, he straightened his slept-in uniform and stated that he required a witness statement. But we just stared silently at the dark, grimy yard and the man lying motionless in a pool of his own blood. The tourists resisted the officer's request and latched on to my offer of a lift. Their eyes darted from face to face. They pleaded to return to their hotel. The officer had to coax them gently. I lingered long enough to see him bundle the bloodied body of the Balinese accused and the tourists into his paddy wagon and drive off.

'Where is he taking the man?' I shouted at the goons.

'To the police station,' one of them said, smirking in the flickering shadows.

When the tourists were back home in Perth they would disassemble the Bali myth: the 'real Bali' – the term touts use to entice tourists on remote, beautiful tours through the island – was just a hackneyed adage.

The next morning I asked the hotel manager, Dewi, if she had heard about the ritualistic beating. 'Did he die?'

'I don't know,' she replied breezily, half-smiling. 'Agus [the security guard] said you were shouting for it to stop, otherwise the man would die. Why do you care? They deserve this.' Dewi's voice rose feverishly. 'They need to feel pain so they won't steal again; then others will hear what happened to him and be frightened. They will scare the tourists away if they keep stealing.'

'How about putting them in prison after a court trial?' I asked.

'Oh, that would be too comfortable,' Dewi said. They would just sit there all day and get free food and not have to work. Often they are killed,' she continued coolly. Indeed, only a lucky few survive such attacks. 'That's okay. It's a good lesson for others who want to steal from tourists.'

Such extrajudicial violence meted out for alleged thieving, traffic accidents, rapes and assaults is nothing new in Indonesia. Nicking a scrawny village chicken unleashes similar reprisals; Westerners, in the event they accidentally mow one down driving though, hightail it – invariably, masses of enraged villagers brandishing machetes and other lethal weapons converge. 'Don't stop; drive on,' expats advised.

Vigilantism is a dirty open secret ignored by mainstream media but disseminated on social media networks with graphic pictures.

On the streets of Bali in broad daylight, victims, more often than not, are beaten to death in a mob fervour. Two hungry, local teenagers narrowly escaped that fate in 2016 when they stole a few morsels from a food stall. Another accused thief wasn't so fortunate, and the horrific, brutal attack in seaside Sanur was promulgated on social media by expat witnesses. Why, asked expats, was no one brought to justice?

The deeply entrenched phenomenon has recently been increasing throughout Indonesia – according to the country's National Violence Monitoring System, which tracked a sharp rise between 2007 and 2014. But the vigilantism upsurge can be traced back to authoritarian state-building in Indonesia's young democracy that continues to lack transparency and accountability, wrote Sana Jaffrey in *New Mandala*, a 2017 South-East Asia online forum hosted by the Australian National University.

Having led the country's struggle for Independence in 1949, civilian militias played a central role during the 1965 communist killings in which up to a million people perished. But organised crime gangsters, *preman* (thugs for hire), went back to the pre-colonial era and colonial Dutch rule when, as agents of the state, they were given a fair degree of latitude. The New Order regime – a term coined by Suharto – not only continued to deploy these organisations for dissent control but also drew surveillance support from communities. In exchange, the state allowed communities some discretion in dealing with transgressions. But democratic reform after Suharto's fall in 1998 hasn't altered routine mob violence.

'In the majority of incidents against alleged criminal activity the suspect is a community outsider who is spontaneously punished by a citizen mob. In others, the accused is retrieved by ad-hoc search parties formed through text messages and social media,' Jaffrey wrote. Petty theft ranked as the major trigger. 'When the police are unable to dissuade vigilantes from conducting an attack, they legitimise the mob's demands by facilitating the raid.' As government agencies continued to groom old and new militia groups, incentives for tolerating vigilantism remained, despite violations of the legal code. 'Disgruntled citizens can take the law into their hands, while still enjoying impunity from investigation or arrest by state authorities.'

Yet I also knew some expats who, feeling impotent in the face of arcane laws and personal injustices – and acclimatised to cultural mores – bayed for blood. Whenever an expat reached that point, I believed it was time they left the country.

*

During a visit to the neighbouring island of Nusa Lembongan in 2016, I witnessed Indonesian collective aggression bearing similar traits.

One of three islands off Bali's south-east coast, Nusa Lembongan is under the jurisdiction of Bali's Klungkung Regency. One evening, villagers were celebrating the Hindu Nyepi Day (Day of Silence) under a full moon, the most holy day of the Balinese calendar. Hundreds of ceremonially clad locals traipsed across a bridge to the adjoining island of Nusa Ceningan to pray at the temple. The celebration, marked by fasting, meditation, demon-purging and a 24-hour island shutdown, was preparing for the new year the following day.

About 6 p.m. as locals crossed the connecting yellow suspension bridge accessible only by foot and motorbike, it collapsed under the heavy traffic. Eight locals fell to their deaths, seven motorbikes plunged to the sea, and scores were injured. The bridge had recently been repaired ineptly. An inspection preceding the collapse found it unfit to be used, and warning signs had been erected but ignored (not uncommon).

Distressed locals flocked with the injured to Nusa Lembongan's small, ill-equipped *puskesmas* (community health clinic). I went there too, trying to collate details for a news report. Hysterical crowds, irate over government negligence, sought to channel their frustration. They whipped themselves into a frenzy, the stifling air thick with aggression. The injured were trundled around precariously on medieval-style gurneys, with brown balloon-type drips and unplugged tubes trailing on the floor.

There was a brief power blackout. Agitated people roamed the narrow corridors, screaming and wailing, ramming those in their way; their eyes were glazed, their arms flailed. A straggle of Westerners accompanying Indonesian friends or family strode the corridors wild-eyed, seemingly infected by the frenzy. Caught in the eddy, I was shoved, manhandled and sandwiched between strapping local men. I imagined myself falling and subsequently being trampled in a stampede. The atmosphere was laced with primal madness. At that point, I fixed my eye on the front door and determined to reach it.

At the time of the disaster, I was visiting a friend, expat David Lewis. He'd shuddered as he dropped me a few streets from the *puskesmas*, before I'd gone in to investigate. 'I'm not going near the place.' He'd seen it all before.

*

Not long after my 2009 arrival in Bali, I'd met a fortyish, bespectacled Englishman, well versed in Indonesian law and language, named Alan. His older-style office was dim and gloomy, invoking a Raymond Chandler-like frisson of mystery.

I was seeking to clarify a point of law for a story. Indonesian law – a mishmash of existing precepts from Dutch colonisation in the sixteenth century, *adat* (customary law) and modern law – is arcane and mostly frustrating. Alan pointedly held aloft bulging law tomes with an air of resignation. Like many long-term Bali residents I met, he encapsulated a paranoia predicated on the volatile political climate. He wouldn't reveal his full name but offered sage advice about Bali's dark side, enriched with lurid examples. He leaned across his cluttered desk, his piercing blue eyes scrutinising my face. 'Scratch the surface and beneath the flimsy veneer of tourism, Bali is not a nice place at all. Be careful.'

That was the precursor to a story about a Western woman who survived an attack by four gangsters who had burst into her house and hit her repeatedly with a plank of wood until her skull split. Apparently this was the penalty for her refusal to pay several thousand dollars above an agreed annual house rental of $14,000 – which she had already paid. She left the island in a hurry. Authorities wouldn't help her without a further payout.

Bali is as much cowboy country as any other part of its nation but with a thin veneer of first-world respectability. The magnet that draws so many is freedom from the perceived shackles of Western society. Bali is a tourist bubble, imbued with affordable luxury and comforts. It's addictive. If you can live like a lord, pay like a pauper and escape rule-governed society, why live on Struggle Street in the West? Expats continually furnished me with upbeat tales of their lives. They ranged from retirees with helipads and live-in nurses to yummy mummies with Balinese nannies.

But during his twenty years in Bali, Australian expat photographer Jason Childs witnessed the fall from grace of foreigners trapped in a capricious, volatile system. 'A lot of people just come to Bali to party – you can be crazy and people just don't care. It's so cheap. Nowhere else in the world can you surf all day and party all night.' But the dream frequently turned into a nightmare.

Bali also draws Westerners down on their luck, living beyond their means despite the cheaper lifestyle.

One sunset, I was at an outside bar, since closed, in the salubrious Petitenget area, when I ran into my struggling hairdresser, an Australian who had been working in Bali for several years. He had lost his salon and could barely rub two pennies together. Unbeknown to me, the bar was a hangout for local gangsters and organised crime figures. My hairdresser had borrowed money from the bar owner, then failed to repay him. Once I grasped the situation – and recalling the vigilante scene at my villa – I asked in disbelief why he showed his face there. He grinned evasively, appearing cocky. Perhaps he was hoping for another loan.

As the last rays of light streaked across the sky, things turned ugly. I watched in dread as the diminutive hairdresser was set upon by several hulking bouncers. They pummelled him to the ground, and I was afraid they would kill him. His face was a bloody mess. One bouncer yelled at him to leave, but he couldn't stand.

No one – not one man – went to his aid. Perhaps, like me, they were too scared to get involved. Or they didn't care.

Mesmerised tourists snapped pictures on their phones. To them, it became a show. But this was my friend, and I felt a rising horror, guilt and discomfort that I was totally powerless to intervene.

Finally the goons kicked him down the street – like he was a piece of garbage – in front of passing traffic. He rolled down in a bloodied ball. I thought that was the end. But, after a few minutes, he picked himself up and limped home. When I called, he said he needed stitches but couldn't afford the hospital fees. Through the pain, he was surprisingly cheerful. 'I'm okay,' he insisted. It was hard to know why he persevered in Bali, or what to say. I suggested he return to Australia and go on the dole.

15

IN LIMBO

January 2013 marked a shift back to Java, where I waded into the escalating refugee crisis. Escaping Bali's tourist masses, I plunged into the harsh reality of those stranded in Indonesia awaiting resettlement to third countries.

Incessantly, I was besieged by refugees hoping I might be a bridge to a safer life. I like to think my stories helped some, but thousands languished in transit for years, some since 2000. Those I interviewed are etched in my memory: their pleas, their trauma and tears, the demise of their worlds. Some remain firm friends. Several whose stories I reported now live in Australia, New Zealand and the United States – though if my pieces had any impact on these outcomes, I don't know. After one piece, a father implored me to check on his case with the appropriate authorities; his family departed Indonesia shortly after in late 2018.

In early 2013 I initially hung around bustling Jalan Jaksa, a thriving backpackers' haunt and refugee networking street that was a short walk from my Central Jakarta hotel. Clusters of Iranian, Pakistani and Afghan asylum seekers flocked to cheap bars and food stalls, passing time, listening to music. 'Come and have a drink,' they called out to me, though they could barely afford a beer. In fact, their ears were pricked for news of imminent boat passages to Australia.

The air was thick with expectation, and I was captivated by the buzz. Most nights I was drawn there, trying to eavesdrop on clandestine phone conversations, fascinated by the people from Central and West Asian countries where I'd never been and perhaps never would venture, given the dangers.

Jalan Jaksa was one of two asylum-seeker hubs – the other was Bogor, West Java – where they swapped information on boats. Smugglers did a roaring trade, frequently from seedy drug- and gang-infested Jakarta nightclubs. The pecking order went like this: Iranian asylum seekers, clad in trendy sports gear, posed as tourists and could fly into Indonesia on tourist visas, while Pakistanis and Afghans – regarded as unstable nationalities – were denied visas. These two groups were typically dropped by smugglers into covert jungle points from where they headed to Jakarta's United Nations High Commissioner for Refugees, hoping to obtain asylum-seeker certificates. Thousands left professions in medicine, education, law and finance, quickly depleting their funds. Most lived in limbo for years in material and psychological destitution. Demoralised young men complained to me of jobless, undignified existences. But as a non-signatory to the 1951 Refugee Convention, Indonesia banned refugees from paid work, medical facilities and education. However, I knew many who flouted the rules.

Months after my forays to Jalan Jaksa, the street lost its asylum-seeker allure, becoming a virtual ghost town. The smugglers' business dried up in September 2013 after Australia implemented Operation Sovereign Borders, along with offshore detention, to stem illegal boat arrivals and drownings. The controversial boat tow-back policy under Tony Abbott's Coalition government was the final nail in the smugglers' coffin. But years later these measures didn't stop desperate attempts to reach Australia and even New Zealand on leaky wooden boats.

Returning one evening from Jalan Jaksa, I met a young Hazara Afghan asylum seeker, laptop in hand, availing the wi-fi encircling my hotel. Ali Nowroz was a 25-year-old former university student who was sick of immigrants' stories. Of his two years in Indonesia, sixteen months had been spent in detention in Bogor, West Java. Now he lived independently near Jalan Jaksa.

My interview with him at my hotel café the next morning developed into an ongoing friendship. Whenever I visited Jakarta, we discussed books, his aspiration to be a writer and the politics that kept him in limbo. A good-looking, serious fellow, he was determined to forge a better life. He had fled sectarian violence and persecution after receiving death threats in Quetta, Pakistan, where he was born. As a Shia-minority Hazara of Afghan origin, Ali had religious and ethnic roots that made him vulnerable to the Sunni Muslim-aligned Taliban insurgency. Being educated added further risk.

Like almost every asylum seeker I met, Ali had tried to reach Australia on a perilous sea passage, but his boat had disintegrated and many drowned on the 2011 journey from Surabaya, East Java. He told me, 'We were hanging in the water near Rote Island when Indonesian police picked us up.' During the long months in detention, his mental health deteriorated; eventually, he escaped. He did not reveal how.

Ali was my son's age. He had a good education and family, but, long subjugated, he lived by his wits. His aunt had been killed in Quetta when terrorists opened fire on her van and in 2004 he had narrowly escaped death while he walked in a Shia religious procession. About 80 people were killed in a suicide blast around him.

I pressed him to describe the scene. He became agitated as he recalled sickening flashbacks. 'I saw people carrying the dead bodies away. There were pieces of body, limbs, pieces of brain, people with bullets through their eyes. I was traumatised, shocked.

It's hell. How do you think we can live there while we are terrified of everybody? You've got an option: you get killed in Quetta or you move to Nauru – prison,' he said, aware of Australia's asylum-seeker policy. 'It's better than getting a mutilated body and shot in the head.' This strengthened his resolve to create a new life. 'I am desperate to find a shelter for my family and myself. I will never go back to that butcher house [Pakistan] again.'

After our first meeting in 2013, it took a couple of days for Ali to reveal his story to me. The Balochistan University student with easily identifiable Hazara features had been studying for an MBA and teaching English when he was forced to flee his home. 'The Taliban tried to kidnap me from the university. I received death threats about three times.' He didn't wait. On the well-worn asylum route from Karachi to Indonesia, he flew via Malaysia. His group travelled into the Kalimantan jungle, in Indonesian Borneo, where their provisions dried up. They slept in mosquito-infested wilderness and shuffled between a network of smugglers to whom Ali had paid US$6000.

When we met, Ali was renting a squalid *kost* (room) for A$50 a month and shared a bathroom with thirty others. He survived on a pittance from his family and could only afford one meal a day. 'I live in dire conditions, with not enough money to eat. I just survive. My monthly expenditure is under US$100.' He equated his bleak living conditions with going into the mines. 'It's never clean. I'm not used to living like this.' A proud man, he didn't mention the privations for some time, and he always appeared clean and neatly dressed. We drank coffee together but if I offered a meal he refused. As he was living independently, the Australian-funded International Organisation for Migration, which fed and accommodated detainees in overcrowded de facto processing centres, provided no assistance. There were plenty of others who slept rough near my hotel, outside the UNHCR building.

In 2014 Ali acquired refugee status. He was eventually accepted to the US. 'Congratulations,' I said, thrilled for him.

'I can't go yet, I'm waiting for my wife.' He revealed to me that he'd married his school sweetheart when they were very young in Quetta. They had a pact: she would follow him. Resettlement places were gold, and I worried Ali might miss out. But they resettled together in Philadelphia in 2016. They were some of the last before US President Donald Trump implemented his extreme vetting plan for refugees.

In 2017, Hazaras comprised half of Indonesia's 14,500 refugees and asylum seekers. But their resettlement prospects dimmed as the global refugee crisis blew out and Islamic State fell in the Middle East.

*

A month after meeting Ali, I wound my way up through the cool, mountainous West Java region of Cisarua, sixty-seven kilometres south of Jakarta. Narrow streets snaked off to villa compounds where refugees lived after assessments by the UNHCR. Among rabbit-warren lanes, one led to International Organisation of Migrants housing, tucked away from the world. Curious occupants emerged to speak with me.

'Do you think I can get a job in Australia? I would like to go to Melbourne and study to be a pharmacist,' Haidari, an Afghan Hazara refugee, implored me in halting English.

It was a familiar exhortation, and suddenly I was swamped by refugees from Myanmar, Sri Lanka, Afghanistan, Pakistan, Iran and Iraq inviting me into their modest houses for tea. Showing me UNHCR documentation, they summoned their children to translate. They recounted dangerous journeys that had left them in penury after they'd been duped by smugglers. Some, pleading with me to help, broke down, weeping and wailing. Amid crippling boredom and droning TV sets, it was their children who set an upbeat mood; parents relied on them not just for translation but emotional survival too.

Bogor's hilly, cool atmosphere appealed to refugees; it was cheaper than Jakarta, and from here they easily accessed leaky boats they hoped would ferry them to Australia. The IOM guesthouses I visited ranged from abysmally dilapidated to incongruous mountain retreats. The people were just as diverse. Some of the Iranian women were particularly striking, with their extraordinary almond-shaped dark eyes and luminous skin.

Around this time, simmering tensions flared in the community, triggering a government shutdown of Bogor's refugee shelters. Vehement local protests prompted a weeklong lockdown to protect immigrants from attacks. Haidari and fellow refugees were warned by the IOM to stay indoors.

'What happened?' I asked at each compound. I kept finding the same story.

'For one week we were not allowed to go outside, we stay at home because they want to beat and strike us,' Haidari told me. 'We scared, how long we stay when we finish the food? They don't like to have immigrant refugee in Cisarua.'

But beneath the hotbed of discontent lay a picture of locals emboldened by envy. Free housing and food was one thing, but when young immigrant men struck up relationships with local girls, tensions escalated. The local police chief complained of social unrest created by asylum seekers, accusing them of fighting with locals and stealing. Then there was a West Java MP, Gatot Subroto, who grumbled that immigrants simply used the area as a way station for passages to Australia.

Sitting in his office, my fixer Ronna and I were served bowls of *sop buah*, a popular sticky milk drink with fruit floaters. As I tried to sip it and juggle my notebook, it spilt down my front. Soaked in pink liquid, fruit blobs stuck to my blouse – it looked like I had vomited. Ronna and I erupted into hysterical laughter, grabbing wads of tissues from the MP's desk, picking the blobs from my chest. Undaunted and po-faced, the MP prattled on, seemingly oblivious of my mishap.

*

A couple of months later, I returned to Jakarta and West Java, exploring what officials called a dirty little secret. At the Muslim orphanage I had previously visited on Jakarta's outskirts, the offspring of terrorists mingled with stateless, mixed-race children of Middle Eastern descent. They were the progeny of Indonesian women or girls and asylum-seeker men, most of whom were now in Australia. Typically, the children were abandoned by their impoverished, ashamed Indonesian mothers, many of whom were among thousands of Javanese child prostitutes.

This problem wasn't the most pressing for Indonesia, but it was an underbelly authorities preferred to keep concealed. As immigrant numbers surged, the consequences of a parallel, oppressed subculture confined to society's margins demanded attention.

My contact, Seto Mulyadi, chairman of Indonesia's Commission for Child Protection advisory board, was concerned children would have no rights if mothers failed to register their births. But in poor *kampungs* (villages) the mainly illiterate mothers generally forgot the date of their child's birth. 'The fathers know [they are leaving children in Indonesia] but they don't care,' Seto said. The children of asylum seekers frequently were dispatched to relatives as well as orphanages. Their circumstances exposed them to violence, sexual exploitation and trafficking. 'When the girls don't want the babies they sell them through international commercial sex syndicates, mainly to Malaysia and China.' From there, children were commonly sold for cheap labour or body organs, Seto went on. In cahoots for a cut were village midwives who persuaded girls to sell their babies. But it was such a taboo subject that many officials refused to discuss it.

I was at the centre of an issue obfuscating organised crime that facilitated illegal, short-term contractual marriages, called *kawin kontraks*, and *nikah siri* (unregistered marriages) particular to the West Java-Puncak region. Thinly disguised as legitimate Muslim marriages, contracts enabled 'legal' adultery. These 'traveller's marriages' were popular among Middle Eastern tourists and asylum seekers blended into this underworld syndicate aligned to people smugglers. Authorities mainly turned a blind eye to illegal practices in Puncak, which drew holiday-makers, tourists and asylum seekers desperate for boats to Australia. It wasn't a priority for the overburdened country.

One evening, Ronna and I were dining out in Bogor's Puncak region, when we realised we were the only women in a Middle Eastern restaurant. Seated outdoors amid plumes of shisha pipe smoke and Saudis in long white tunics, we were the centre of attention. When I went inside to order, the owner asked what had brought me to the area. 'Sightseeing,' I said, though I saw no other Westerners around, which was odd because Puncak is a tourist spot. When I returned to the table Ronna was so unnerved by the staring eyes she asked for *bungkus* (takeaway food). Her instinct was spot-on, but though we were uncomfortable, I was riveted. It felt like we were in a bad movie.

We learnt the restaurant was part of a pick-up network. Outside, a convoy of *becak* (rickshaw tricycle) drivers waited. If you wanted a girl, you gave them a code word.

One who was concerned about the trade was Adrianus Meliala, an Indonesian criminologist and former national police commissioner. In a scathing rant about asylum seekers leaving a trail of fatherless children, he predicted a time-bomb scenario. 'We will have many Indonesians with West Asian faces, and having no citizenship,' he railed at Polda headquarters. 'The government is sweeping the issue under the carpet. Morally, they refuse to address it. It's too hard. It's actually disgusting ... I feel pity for the children.'

His outburst reminded me of an amusing quote by Vice-President Jusuf Kalla. In 2006 he'd copped flak when, as an adjunct to a tourism push, he was reported in the *Jakarta Post* as saying, 'If there are a lot of Middle East tourists travelling to Puncak to seek *janda* [a word for widows and divorcees] I think that it's OK. If the *janda* get modest homes, even if the tourists later leave them, then it's OK. The children resulting from these relationships will have good genes. There will be more television actors and actresses from these pretty boys and girls.'

When I raised this with Meliala, he conceded local women were spellbound by just such a prospect. 'The girls see it as a way to leverage their social status. They're using the contractual marriage as a way to gain social mobility.'

In impoverished Bogor villages, I saw no evidence of that. I was taken covertly to Cianjur to meet young mothers abandoned by asylum seekers. At the last moment, they pulled out, so ashamed and fearful were they of repercussions. But Annisa, an eighteen-year-old West Java woman, took me to a tiny house and spoke of her trauma after marrying a fifty-year-old Saudi man under a *kawin kontrak* when she was sixteen. Promised about A$600, she received A$100. The man disappeared after a week. 'He wanted a virgin,' she told me angrily. 'He would not marry anyone who was not a virgin.'

Poor parents encouraged the marriages or offered their daughters to syndicates. So covert was the subject that most child welfare agencies were frustratingly poor sources. But the chief of one, Lidya Indayani Umar, reeled off a price list like it was a spa menu. 'Typically the girl is sixteen to eighteen years old and paid between three million rupiah [A$300] and five million rupiah a month. If the girl is good-looking with a good body it will be more expensive. If the girl is a virgin she commands about IDR10 million [A$1000].' She recalled the case of a girl who, under a *kawin kontrak* arranged by a syndicate, married a man waiting for a boat to Australia in 2012. 'The contract was to last until he got on the boat.'

*

Intrinsic to many of my stories were two Iranian refugees, Mohammad and his wife Shirin, who took me to communities and translated from Farsi. Not only that, Mohammad picked me up at Jakarta's airport. It was comforting to see a friendly face in that shambolic city, especially that of one calling me 'sista'. Persecuted over their Christian faith, the couple and their young son, Ahoura, had lived in Indonesia since 2010, providing church services and care to refugees.

We became good friends. Once, Shirin asked me how I listed them as contacts in my phone. 'I hope you don't label us under "refugees".' They had their own story: each week at midnight they hit the airwaves broadcasting to thousands in Darwin and South-East Asia from the Indonesian capital. Through a church-sponsored program, they delivered news to refugees and offered help to those traumatised by dire circumstances and drownings of loved ones.

I went with the couple once to file a picture story. I hoped the coverage might push them up the resettlement queue. They were devastated to be rejected by Australia in 2015.

Over the years, Mohammad drove me all over Jakarta and Bogor for interviews – to strange areas I wouldn't otherwise have seen.

One afternoon we visited a South Jakarta IOM *kost* where painful memories and the discomfort of sharing cramped quarters – whole families squeezed into a single bed – took their toll. Among them, a couple's four-year-old child had drowned in 2012 while attempting a voyage to Australia, and almost everyone had attempted multiple boat passages. Some had nearly drowned. The smell of fear still lingered – fear they would be rejected for resettlement and of persecution if they had to return to their countries of origin.

It was here that this fear became tangible to me through another's voice.

A Pakistani Hazara refugee and freelance journalist, Syed Muhammad Hassan, was propped up on his single bed, his twelve-year-old son beside him. I perched at the end. Hassan spoke rapidly, in oddly inflected English. Depicting horrific scenes they had fled, he said, 'We have a different colour, different skins, we will be recognised that we are Hazaras, Muslim Shia; they [terrorists] just come up to you, and *BOOM*,' he bellowed, his arms flailing above his head. 'It's hell. You can't go to Karachi, you can't live in Islamabad. We are all psychotic, traumatised under these conditions. Yeah, we are psychos, you can't see that, it's hidden.' Then he spoke of his eternal gratitude for the privilege of being safe and alive. 'We are *so* lucky, we are *sooo* lucky,' he repeated over and over. His voice stuck in my head. 'And I'm thankful, deep in my heart, to IOM until I die, giving me food, accommodation. We have *everything*.'

Hassan, at forty-nine, shared the shoebox room and single bed with his son, Sheith Kazmi. It could have been a five-star hotel. In Pakistan, he'd made documentaries terrorists don't like – about widows and orphaned children after their husbands and fathers had been murdered, and about human trafficking and sex slavery. First targeted as an ethnic Hazara, the Lashkar-e-Jhangvi (an al-Qaeda-affiliated group), the Taliban and other terrorists tried to gag him in warning calls. 'They know me from TV, interviews. They said, "We know what time you leave, when you attend meetings. If you don't stop writing about these people, we will kill you." Once you get on to their list you're dead.'

The names of politicians, police generals, media, neighbours, relatives, friends and businessmen tripped off his tongue: 'All dead.'

'It's anarchy, different groups are killing people. You never know who is following on a motorbike. Sitting in a café outside, you hear the machine-gun fire.' He was soon to be resettled in the US but he was afraid to be photographed. 'They can do anything.' He shivered. 'I have nightmares every day. I don't want to die now.'

A compatriot, Liaquat Ali Changezi, whom I met a few years later in Bogor, fit the high-profile category so appealing to the Taliban. In Quetta, Changezi – with movie-star good looks – wore several hats. He was a famous TV actor, news, documentary and drama producer, and he'd started his own production house in 2003. He was also on the hit list.

Back in 2008, terrorists in Balochistan, Pakistan, were targeting people like Changezi amid daily massacres in the enclave of Hazara Town. He described the picture Hassan had painted. 'I had friends who were gunned down, point blank, in the street by Lashkar-e-Jhangvi.' One was the Hazara Democratic Party chairman Hussain Ali Yousafi, who was assassinated in 2009. Another, Pakistan's three-time Olympic boxer Abrar Hussain Hazara, was shot dead by unknown gunmen in 2011 in Quetta.

The Pakistani Hazara also received death threats by phone. He fled Quetta, leaving his family in a secure compound, to work in Kabul, Afghanistan. When he returned to Quetta in 2013, he found a genocide of monumental proportions. 'In one year they killed more than a thousand people. I decided there was no space for me.' After paying US$36,000 to people smugglers, the family landed in Indonesia in 2014.

I had met Changezi in Bogor at the school he'd opened in 2014 after finding none for his four children. Now a mecca for refugees, the Cisarua Refugee Learning Centre overflowed.

In 2018 the family resettled in New Zealand, a few months before the Christchurch mosque massacre – a coincidence not lost on them.

*

I wanted to interview unaccompanied refugee children, not often documented by journalists. Mohammad knew a South Jakarta shelter for minors, and one day we took four excitable Hazara boys out for their first pizza. The interviews evolved without the burden of undue bureaucracy, which wasn't uncommon in Indonesia – notwithstanding political sensitivities in areas such as West Papua and Aceh, at the northern tip of Sumatra.

The head of the all-male shelter, run by the Church World Service, granted me permission. I had one request: to interview the youngest boy, who was ten. I imagined him to have fewer inhibitions than the older children. They all eagerly piled into Mohammad's tiny *Mr Bean* car wearing their best donated clothes. But at the restaurant I felt the tension build. As a mother, I was particularly confronted by their harrowing experiences and solitary journeys from their home countries without a parent or guardian. I wanted to hug them.

Considered lucky to have a place at the shelter, the boys were among 643 unaccompanied minors registered with the UNHCR. Hadayad Ullah, the ten-year-old, exemplified the acute pain of each child. An angelic-looking boy, he had arrived from Afghanistan the month before. He was just a baby but his eyes portrayed the horror he had witnessed. As he sat toying with his pizza, he told me his father had been kidnapped by the Taliban and he had no idea where his mother was, or if she was even alive. His chocolate eyes watered. He pushed the uneaten pizza away. 'I'm so sad. They took my father. I thought maybe they will take me too. When I think about my mother and father I cry all night. I don't know if I'll see my mother again.' He stared out of a window, holding back tears.

In his short, turbulent life, Hadayad had learnt more about arbitrary persecution and murder than about how to read or write. The eldest of five children, he'd never attended school because his family feared firebombing by the Taliban. A family friend had paid an agent to fly him from Kabul to Jakarta. 'My life was in danger.'

'Didn't anyone ask why you were alone on the plane?' I asked.

'No, no one asked. I was scared and I felt sick.'

Arriving disoriented at Jakarta's airport, he had US$150 in his pocket. He'd connected with several asylum seekers on the same flight, and they took a taxi to Cisarua. There they dumped Hadayad unceremoniously by the side of the road.

'What did you do?' I asked.

'I was scared, I was crying. A person [an Afghan asylum seeker] saw me and took me to his house.'

The following day, Hadayad, with help from his new friend, registered at the UNHCR, enabling him to move to the shelter. He was lucky: many children ended up in squalid detention centres because there was nowhere else for them.

When my story was published in July 2014 in *The Guardian*, it drew hundreds of empathetic online comments. A few astounded me with conspiracy theories about Hadayad's photo – he was apparently too good-looking, too angelic and too well dressed; he had been plucked in a ploy to gain sympathy and appeal to readers. These were such farcical observations. Hadayad was incidentally photogenic, a beautiful child and the youngest. Did his face make his story more poignant to the newspaper's readers? If so, it could only be a good thing, I thought.

16

FREEDOM'S DOOR

Parallels and paradoxes could be drawn between the refugees and prisoners I visited: largely their absence of basic rights and protection. But each 17 August, Indonesia's Independence Day, Kerobokan jail inmates cast their woes aside. Amid music and dance, inmates displayed the fruits of their rehab programs. The Bali Nine showed paintings, screen-printed T-shirts and jewellery, and even participated in sport competitions, with journalists invited to appraise and mingle.

Most importantly, prisoners on set terms traditionally received sentence cuts. In 2013, all of the Bali Nine were still housed in Kerobokan, but only Renae Lawrence, serving twenty years, was eligible for a reduction. She and Schapelle Corby were generously rewarded for good behaviour, but that year the announcements were postponed.

This didn't dampen Lawrence's spirits. 'I'm happy,' she told me, smiling, 'as happy as I can be.'

With the usual pomp and pageantry for dignitaries over, journalists made a beeline for Bali Nine members. I had joined a small clutch around Lawrence. When reporters fanned out seeking other members, I remained chatting.

A UK correspondent approached us, inquiring after the welfare of Lindsay Sandiford. The British grandmother was known to be selective with reporters, and for her media silence. Lawrence firmly told the reporter that Sandiford, who never appeared on celebratory days, was off limits. When an Indonesian female inmate mumbled incoherently, Lawrence warned her to shut up. The UK journalist persisted. Lawrence reiterated authoritatively that *'no one'* would be discussing Sandiford. The female prisoner again muttered indecipherably, and the UK punter sauntered off.

From left field, a strapping female warden stepped in, swiping the inmate across her face with an open hand. The prisoner cringed and bowed her head. No one in the crowd seemed to have noticed. Stunned, I stopped mid-sentence to stare at the prisoner who'd just been bashed. Lawrence followed my gaze. After a brief silence, she explained nonchalantly that the woman had been 'speaking out of turn'.

Within the hierarchy of the jail, Lawrence wielded enormous power and was feared by many. She was known to have had a number of girlfriends among the inmates, and had been a leader, or *tamping*, entrusted by the jail governor and guards to uphold security within the women's block.

By the time of her release in November 2018, Lawrence had been transferred to Bangli prison in central Bali after allegedly plotting to kill a prison guard in Kerobokan jail in 2013 – which she denied.

*

The ties between Lawrence and Schapelle Corby were fickle and ambiguous. Lawrence's Indonesian lawyer Anggia Lubis Browne told me of jealousies, especially when Corby was granted parole. 'She is a bit jealous. She's upset, asking me to do something for her, and says, "It's not fair."'

The week preceding Corby's climactic parole release on 10 February 2014 from Kerobokan, Australian media packs parachuted into Bali for the spectacle of the decade. I had reported Corby's tumultuous course following her 2005 trial via the few permitted near the reclusive drug trafficker. But like most of the correspondents in Jakarta, I dreaded the unfolding media circus.

Amid a storm of controversy, in May 2012 Corby was granted five years' clemency on her twenty-year sentence by then-president Susilo Bambang Yudhoyono on humanitarian grounds for her deteriorating mental health. With accumulated remissions, she qualified for parole. Anticipating the convicted drug trafficker's first freedom steps, journalists staked out coveted positions around Kerobokan prison and Corby's proposed new home in Kuta.

Australia's then consul general to Bali, Brett Farmer, must have been relieved that his posting ended just before Corby's release. His final consular duty was a meeting with the Kerobokan jail governor Farid Junaedi before fronting hordes of journalists and flying out.

The week dragged on. Cameramen were so desperate they snapped anything in the prison yard, from parked dump trucks to barbed wire. Each afternoon when the prison governor went home, the media pounced. 'I'm waiting for the money shot,' freelance Queensland cameraman Nathan Richter whispered conspiratorially to me outside the jail. I gazed at the media throngs – bevies of Indonesians, local TV crews and Australian networks were occupied with that singular thought.

Richter's dogged enthusiasm finally got him deported when he was apprehended for working on a tourist visa near the Kuta home where Corby would stay with her sister and brother-in-law. Authorities denied the Corby family had requested his deportation. My source had seen Richter outside an office photographing Corby's sister Mercedes. Shortly after that, Richter got his marching orders along with a Network Ten reporter, also working on a tourist visa.

Then came a request from *Today Tonight* asking me, as an old Bali hand, for an interview about local and expatriate attitudes to

Corby. Was everyone on tenterhooks awaiting her release? From the locals' point of view, they were bemused by the fuss, while expats repeatedly, irritatingly, asked me if Corby had been released yet.

The excitement around her release reached fever pitch as she left Kerobokan in a police van for official processing. For three hours after she emerged – her face bizarrely obscured by a hat and scarf – from Kerobokan's gates through an obstacle course of officers and into a waiting van, she was in the eye of a rolling scrum of camera crews and reporters. They tailed the thirty-six-year-old on mopeds and in cars to her final destination: the Sentosa Luxury Villas in Seminyak. Only Corby's van and entourage of black SUVs – one carrying Channel Seven's veteran, semi-retired current affairs star, Michael Willesee, who planned to interview Corby for the *Sunday Night* program – eased inside the gates. Smiling broadly, Willesee would have been mightily disappointed. The exclusive paid interview, reportedly for about A$2 million, including spinoffs to the Seven Group's *New Idea* magazine, hit a wall: the Indonesian government threatened to revoke Corby's parole if it went ahead.

While Mercedes doubled down on negotiations, even flying to Jakarta to plead their case, Willesee strolled out of the bunker periodically to dine at the fashionable Petitenget restaurant across the road. Each time he ran the gauntlet of a media mob demanding to know what deal Seven had cut; the notion of a multimillion-dollar deal was just silly, he said.

The *Sunday Night* crew stayed in the Sentosa villa complex for three weeks with the Corby family, including Mercedes and their brother Michael, waiting in vain for a government backflip. It settled for an interview with Mercedes and a few still images of Corby.

When I called Australian Saxon Looker, owner of the Sentosa Seminyak where Corby was holed up, he seemed surprised a journalist had his mobile number. He declined to confirm Corby was a guest in the villa, which then cost up to US$1150 nightly. 'If she's there,' Looker said carefully, 'it's probably at the behest of some TV station. I can only imagine there's a big amount of money for an exclusive interview. The hotel is not part of a deal.' Looker had obviously forgotten my damning piece about his huge Canggu development, Sea Sentosa, that had decimated a beautiful coastal village.

Each day I drove to a café abutting Sentosa's gates where the media had set up office, waiting for a Schapelle appearance. News Limited, well represented, took a villa at the resort to get close to the Corbys. One night at a Sentosa drinks party, the entire Australian press corps was at the bar. Television networks and print journos huddled in groups, coordinating plans. We had made it to the inner sanctum but there was no sign of the Corbys, bunkered down in their villa cocoon.

We were running out of angles. During the hiatus, Fairfax correspondent Michael Bachelard threw a dinner party, ordering enough Balinese food for a jail. Ensconced in a magnificent compound in Batu Belig with other Fairfax reporters, the villas curved around an enormous centrepiece pool into which some plunged. No one got inebriated; they planned early morning starts and fresh tactics.

Meanwhile, journalists snapped up guesthouses in a laneway beside the Kuta family compound where Corby was expected to stay for her three-year parole with Mercedes, brother-in-law Wayan Widyartha and the couple's children. Television crews pointed cameras intrusively into the Corby compound.

The day before Corby's release I visited the Kuta family home, finding it eerily quiet, locked up with curtains drawn. Inside Wayan's compound, there was discord among the seven families about Corby living among them. She was an outsider who didn't belong in their Balinese Hindu tradition, they told me. Because of her history, they feared she would bring nasty spirits and bad karma. Nyoman, a priest as well as Wayan's uncle, stressed Corby couldn't live there. A cousin, Ayu, said, 'She cannot be brought here because her religion is different. She's not a member of the family.'

*

Mercedes, whose relationship with her husband had broken down in 2014, rented another Kuta house for her sister from which their brother Michael came and went. Mercedes relocated to the Gold Coast in 2015 with her children.

Corby's story had enthralled and appalled her compatriots since her arrest at Ngurah Rai airport on 8 October 2004. She'd been sentenced the following year to twenty years in jail for drug smuggling.

Since my first visit to Bali in 2006, Australian tourists had frequently added a Kerobokan jail visit to their list of Bali attractions. Corby was fair game before the Australian consulate in Denpasar within the next couple of years asked prison authorities to curtail the spectacle. Tourists then hoped for a glimpse of Corby during her rumoured day outings. At a beauty salon near the jail I heard an Australian woman ask, 'Does Schapelle Corby come in here?' The local hairdresser didn't know who Corby was.

The minutiae of her life – a new hairstyle, new best cell friend, her demeanour – was reported ad infinitum.

The frenetic build-up to her parole invited speculation on the media obsession over each nuance; Corby's future goldfish bowl existence in Kuta; how much dosh had been paid to the Corby industry, and on and on.

Then there was Network Nine's telefilm, *Schapelle*, which aired on 9 February, the week before her release. It was based on journalist Eamonn Duff's contentious book *Sins of the Father* to add oxygen to the feeding frenzy. But ratings didn't meet expectations – *Schapelle* was trounced by Seven Network's *INXS* mini-series on rock-star Michael Hutchence.

Aiding the Australian media scrutiny of the former Gold Coast beautician were the Indonesian newshounds and fixers employed to chase her. While other Australian drug offenders had tumbled into Kerobokan jail since Corby, notably the Bali Nine, none had her cachet. As an Australian consular official muttered, 'Watch the local media turn paparazzi when Corby is out.' What sort of freedom would it be? Certainly not free-range.

*

Back in 2008, Corby, animated and exceptionally well groomed, in a crisp white blouse and black pants, had sat on a groundsheet amid palls of acrid smoke, food wrappers and cigarette butts, chatting with Mercedes in the prison visiting yard.

One other prisoner matched her sartorial style that day: the Nigerian death-row inmate I was interviewing a few metres from her.

Pressed together in the stifling heat, inmates and visitors wiped sweat from their faces and carved out niches on the floor. As visiting ended, I picked my way through a sea of bodies to approach Corby. Mercedes, ever the eagle-eyed gatekeeper, jumped up to interject. She scrutinised my business card, listening to my request for an interview and promised to call. As soon as I'd turned my back, she screeched after me like an alley cat, 'S'cuse me, guard, there's a journalist in here.'

Media were generally vetted, and if anyone knew the rules, Mercedes did. Rarely did Corby venture into the visiting area, such was her dread of photos and media. I never received a call from her sister.

In June 2008, Corby was admitted to the international wing of Denpasar's Sanglah Hospital with severe depression. It was reportedly precipitated by the death of her father, Michael Corby, in January, along with the rejection of her final appeal against her twenty-year sentence.

She stayed in her private hospital room nearly three weeks, causing a flurry among reporters when she stepped out to a beauty salon for hair and nail treatments accompanied by an armed guard.

A year later, in May 2009, she returned to hospital again suffering depression. I went there with my friend from *The Bali Times*, William Furney, to try to catch a glimpse of her on her balcony.

Furney didn't have much time for Corby, writing scathingly about her in his paper. Schlapper, as he called her, got undeserved red-carpet treatment and he was sceptical she was mentally ill.

On 5 June 2009, a story appeared in *The Bali Times* headlined: Let's not Rain on Schlapper's Charade.

Furney wrote in part: 'I headed over to the international wing, now accompanied by an Australian journalist who was also on the scene. She had been caught by security, the previous day, wandering around the wing's gardens seeking signs of persons on balconies seeking rare peeks at the world. My friend and I approached the reception and told a flustered woman a family member was thinking about checking in for a procedure and that we had been sent ahead on a type of reconnaissance mission to check out the digs. What we wanted, we said, was a gawk around the rooms. (This was to give us an idea, and photos, of the accommodation of any celebrity patients). Fully booked, we were told, no room at this inn! Top-of-the-range comes in at IDR2.2 million (A\$220) a day, we were told. "It's about the same price as staying at a good hotel in Bali," my friend said. Hotel Sanglah? I ventured, casting my mind to a similarly themed facility in Kerobokan.'

Sanglah's chief psychiatrist, Nyoman Ratep, told me Corby was prescribed strong anti-depressants and psychotherapy. 'She has hallucinations, deep anxiety and insomnia.'

Another of her Indonesian psychiatrists, Denny Thong, whom I came to know well, told me she 'seemed not to be living in the real world; maybe that's best in her situation. Her thoughts are wild and fragmented.' He said she'd told him, 'I'm naughty.' *What did that mean?* we both pondered. He recommended her transfer to Bangli Mental Hospital, in central Bali, but her family wasn't keen. 'The best thing for her mental state would be for her to be set free,' Thong opined. When he treated Corby at the jail clinic in 2009, she arrived with Renae Lawrence who later dispensed anti-psychotic medication to Corby. 'She was escorted to the clinic by Renae. They were very close at the time and Renae was very concerned,' he told me. 'I asked Renae to give her the medication because Corby was being locked up early for misbehaviour.'

Thong later stood by his 2009 diagnosis, saying Corby was seriously mentally ill and hadn't feigned her condition, adding he hadn't been paid for his diagnosis.

In April 2014, Lawrence claimed Corby had one night confessed her guilt over the 2004 drug run that put her behind bars. In a secretly filmed interview aired by Network Ten, Lawrence said Corby admitted it was her fourth trip to Bali as a drug mule. 'She knew the marijuana was in the bag but that the person who was supposed to be at the airport at that time didn't show up for work ... and that's how she got caught,' Lawrence said. She also claimed Corby 'played crazy' to reduce her sentence.

I interviewed two of Corby's former prison wardens – Gusti Ngurah Wiranta and Siswanto (who went by one name) – in December 2013 before her paroled release. Their opinions of her differed widely from each other.

I met Siswanto, who was governor until early 2012, at a Starbucks in Denpasar. Clearly not a Corby fan, he had reported to his corrections superiors in late 2010 that she had feigned mental illness and was disobedient. 'If she really has mental illness why did she decline to be taken to a mental hospital?' he asked me. 'She thought that she is always right and she always wanted to win her stance. She really hated me because I don't like an inmate who wants to rule prison guards.'

On a media tour organised by Siswanto in January 2010, guards unexpectedly flung open cell doors in the women's unit, Block W. It was the first time I had seen the dormitory-like cells, which reminded me of my boarding-school days. A cosy atmosphere of stuffed animals on neatly made beds, personal photos, mementos and curios weren't what I had imagined.

While the local media pack rushed to Corby's cell, I found Lawrence sitting on her double bed, loquacious of spirit and glassy-eyed. For some time, my photographer Lauren Kelana and I were alone with Lawrence.

This was a crucial time for fellow courier Scott Rush in his final appeal against the death penalty, and Lawrence was expected to help him by testifying in court she had made several drug runs into Bali before her arrest. The confession would highlight inconsistencies in the sentencing of the Bali Nine. Lawrence had received a life sentence reduced to twenty years on appeal, yet Rush, who was a first-time courier, was sentenced to death. She denied reports she would return to court. 'I never said I would testify. I'm not going to court again. I've already been punished … I'm not stupid,' she told me. She would only provide a statement saying Rush was a courier, as she was.

Lauren continuously snapped pictures but Lawrence, unpeturbed by the camera, maintained a running commentary with me. Even when local fixers finally piled in, taping the interview, it was just me and Lawrence. The fixers, transmitting to their Australian bosses, had my exclusive.

Lawrence also denied she and Rush were close friends. Rather, she was closer to Corby, though that allegiance inevitably changed.

Sharing a ten-bed cell in the overcrowded block with 120 women, Corby, unlike Lawrence, wasn't happy to entertain the visiting media. Scurrying for cover, she locked herself in the bathroom, from where she threw buckets of water through a window at us. She didn't emerge that day, nor on any celebratory days when most inmates appeared. While almost every Australian seemed to have an opinion on her, she remained enigmatic and inaccessible despite the intense media coverage.

Corby was carefully managed by her family. Few others knew anything real about her beyond those visitors vetted by the family, her jailers, cellmates and occasional doctors and lawyers. Reported media deals and her deep paranoia of journalists generated an obsession for the Australian public, whipping the media into a frenzy at the mere hint of her name.

Impressions of Corby from good Samaritans – those providing rehabilitation programs and jail insiders – reflected her reclusive behaviour. Sydney expat Paula Gillham regularly visited the jail in a charitable role as part of the Bali International Women's Association, providing food, mattresses and social services to inmates. She said Corby typically ran and hid when they entered the women's block. 'That's how she responds to most people. She would hide in her room because she was told not to talk to anyone because she has exclusive magazine and TV contracts,' Gillham told me.

The BIWA past president Melly St Ange countered, 'What do you expect? She gets trauma, stress. Schapelle doesn't want to mingle with the crowd. I'm not surprised. Visitors, press, stare at her like she's in the circus, people calling out, "Schapelle, Schapelle."'

St Ange often took Australian tourists to the jail. 'Some want to see Corby, I say, "Don't bother her, she busy."' Corby, who had once aspired to open a beauty salon at the jail, passed time doing handicraft such as jewellery, beading and painting, rarely venturing outside her cell.

The campaigning for Corby's exoneration, particularly online, was well-drilled and intense: those who challenged her innocence could expect swift and fierce rebuttal. She was even compared to Lindy Chamberlain – eventually exonerated in the case of her daughter Azaria's death – who wrote to Corby in 2005, commiserating about her guilty verdict and declaring, 'My heart bleeds for you.'

When Patrick Scott, a New Zealand expat, met Corby in 2007 during a Rotary visit to improve sanitation in Block W, Mercedes – whom Scott didn't know – phoned to ask if he believed Corby was innocent or guilty. 'I said, "I don't know,"' Scott recalled. 'It was irrelevant to me.' But Mercedes seemed satisfied. 'She may well have rung to see if I had another agenda, if I was going to go to the papers,' he told me. He was 'pleasantly surprised' by the encounter. '[Corby] was caring of the other female inmates. She looked well groomed, clean and well dressed. I liked her personality.' If she was depressed, it wasn't obvious to him. 'She was bright, she was very together. I thought she was brave.'

After Corby's hospitalisations for depression, her family arranged, with the backing of *New Idea*, for an assessment by psychiatrist Jonathan Phillips. In August 2009 the former president of the Royal Australian and New Zealand College of Psychiatrists warned that Corby's mental health was very fragile and likely to get worse, and urged that she be transferred as a prisoner to Australia and be hospitalised. The effect was explosive in Australia, with then prime minister Kevin Rudd coming under pressure to somehow arrange her repatriation.

But Kerobokan guards were sceptical, according to Bali psychiatrist Lely Setyawati. 'I would not say she was insane,' Lely told me. However, after a consultation sixteen months previously, she said Corby had suffered 'mixed schizophrenia and affective disorders or bipolar disorder' and might be unable to cope in the glare of public and media attention outside jail. 'It will not magically dissolve.'

During parole preparations, I also spoke to Sanglah Hospital psychiatrist Sri Diniari, who diagnosed Corby with mild depression and said she was not psychotic. 'She has normal behaviour ... but she is irritable,' Diniari told me.

Corby's sentence reduction triggered a barrage of local condemnation. GRANAT, the National Movement Against Narcotics, tried to overturn the clemency grant, and at least one Indonesian MP accused the Yudhoyono administration of doing a secret deal with Australia. What further raised Indonesian eyebrows was that in obtaining presidential clemency, Corby hadn't conceded guilt for the crime in her parole application, though the law demands this along with 'justice collaboration' – implicating others involved in the crime. This apparent partiality didn't apply to Corby because the law hadn't been in place when she was convicted, said Justice Minister Amir Syamsuddin at the time.

The balance of Australian public opinion about Corby's guilt shifted against her across time, though the overwhelming view was that she had done enough prison time. There are still those who found it galling she'd attained a form of celebrity-through-suffering, and there were rumours that some members of the Corby family had benefited financially from her crime and punishment (rumours which were denied by her family). Paula Gillham told me disdainfully, 'She and her family give the rest of the Australians here [in Bali] such a bad name. I'm not against her getting out early, but I am against the family benefiting from her crime.'

Succeeding Corby's prison governor Siswanto was Ngurah Gusti Wiratna, whom I interviewed at his Denpasar restaurant in December 2013. Before he retired the previous month, he approved her application to seek parole.

Wiratna found her initially difficult and introverted. But her attitude and behaviour improved 'after I opened communications. I advised her to be more patient and pray, she became more communicative and not that exclusive. I was thinking maybe it's because she hopes for processing of her parole, so she is changed, but we cannot have bad thought like that.'

Wiratna had been appointed to Kerobokan in February 2012, after rioting inmates burnt down a large section of the severely overcrowded prison: built for three hundred inmates, it was then holding more than a thousand. He described Corby as essentially a 'good person', careful in her friendships and traumatised by fear of media intrusion.

Dubbed 'ganja queen' by the Indonesian media, as the celebrity prisoner walked free on parole, speculation over her guilt or innocence was no less impassioned than when she was arrested.

But as the parole process edged forward, Corby was on tenterhooks, especially during negative jail incidents such as the detection of a drugs party in the women's block a few months previously in 2013.

'She [Corby] is afraid to get her hopes up,' a jail insider told me. 'She's nervous. She says, "Until I walk out of here I don't believe it will happen."'

A soap opera from the start, her journey was also an extraordinary political saga that strained bilateral relations between Australia and Indonesia. Parole left Corby anchored to the island of her arrest for three years, free to roam in a *Truman Show*-like setting. Local media snapped her swimming, running, larking with boyfriend Ben Panangian (a former inmate she'd met in jail), eating and attending monthly parole check-ups. When she gained weight, it was assumed she was pregnant. But she wasn't – and she blamed the weight gain on the heckling media. How could she exercise outdoors in private?

On 27 May 2017, she was deported, again drawing frenzied media packs – in which I was knocked to the ground but suffered only shock. The public appetite is not what it was but she has a large social media following. She lives with her mother Rosleigh Rose on the Gold Coast, regularly posting Instagram updates of herself. At the time of writing, the then 42-year-old had no job and was giving a series of Australian media interviews to promote her updated autobiography first published in 2006.

Most importantly, her departure from Indonesia eased pressure on bilateral relations.

17

POSTER BOY

'Some people get human rights, some people die. It depends on how much money you have, right.'

— Scott Rush, Bali Nine courier

Amid the roar and kerfuffle of the Schapelle Corby media circus, Scott Rush, a despondent figure, was one of the forgotten Australian inmates in Bali. Suspended in the shadows of the convicted trafficker's spotlight, he was particularly alone. Isolated in Karangasem jail, in remote east Bali at his request, he was at the end of his tether after enduring a prison hell for almost a decade. He frequently spoke to me about death as his only way out.

Since 2006, I had interviewed most of the Bali Nine gang. Rush I'd spoken with countless times, sometimes by phone but usually at Kerobokan jail. He had quietly slipped away from the prison amid the Corby commotion before her release on parole. 'I didn't tell anyone I was going, no one knew, not even the rest of the Bali Nine,' he said with a vague smile.

It was my first visit to the bucolic jail. Three hours from the southern hub, it appeared from the outside more serene retreat than dystopian penitentiary. Leaning in to the thick iron bars separating us in the visiting area, Rush eagerly consumed details of Corby's release. He seemed to harbour no malice, rather surprise over the furore she'd sparked regarding an alleged A$2 million tell-all TV interview – and to hear she was ensconced in a luxury villa. Eyes bulging, he craved minutiae of a sumptuousness he may never know. He wasn't jealous, though he conceded that plenty of Australian inmates would be. 'Good on her,' he said. 'She's lost ten years of her life – she should be compensated. We should all get compensation when we get out.'

*

A month later, in March 2014, I watched Rush approach the visiting area hand-in-hand with an Indonesian inmate. At the entrance, they split up. It isn't unusual for same-sex Indonesians to walk arm-in-arm or hold hands, but this wasn't typical behaviour for Rush. The twenty-eight-year-old had changed, shedding the bloated appearance of the past couple of years that had made him almost unrecognisable from earlier days. His latest dramatic physical transformation returned him to the uncanny poster boy image of his 2005 arrest.

'Who's your new friend?' I asked.

'Just another prisoner,' Rush replied airily.

He'd been so long immersed in the culture, perhaps it was an Indonesian habit he had adopted, I mused.

On his transfer from Kerobokan jail the previous month, Rush had been the only foreigner among 157 mostly male Indonesian inmates. Then Australian drug trafficker Michael Sacatides had arrived; he was serving eighteen years. 'I don't speak to him,' Rush told me. 'He's derogatory [sic] to the people here and he's kind of counter-productive to the whole system.' I didn't ask if Rush considered himself productive. At times, he wistfully voiced ambitions to start rehab programs to make a difference 'the way they do at Kerobokan', but he never did.

Wearing a checked shirt and board shorts, his hair floppy, Rush walked mechanically into the visiting cage. If this was humiliating for him, it didn't show. I squeezed onto a narrow bench with about fifty local visitors. Prisoners jostled to light Rush's cigarettes and fuss over him. 'Why the attention?' I asked.

He smirked. 'It's only for what they think they can get out of me.'

Visitors were few, excluding his Balinese 'foster family', living near Karangasem jail, and he admitted he was lonely, though he didn't miss Kerobokan. 'I didn't socialise. I had to leave,' he told me without elaborating.

Long institutionalised, Rush had been living by his wits for nearly a decade. Inmates variously irritated or angered him, stole from him and harmed him, he said. But it didn't worry him that they crowded him at visiting time, taking the food and cigarettes I brought. 'That's how they are,' he said and shrugged. Yet if he were whisked from his prison hell, he would happily call Bali home as much as Australia. 'I love the place, the people. It's just jail that I don't like. The culture's very rich and interesting – from what I've read.'

Rush had reportedly owed drug debts when he left Kerobokan, a jail awash with hard drugs controlled by local gangs. Yet he denied the reports and scoffed at comments he'd moved to resist temptation. Still, he revealed, 'If I stayed another six months I might have died.' He was afraid for himself and of those who might harm him.

In January 2014, just before he was transferred, a photograph of Rush purportedly smoking crack cocaine in his cell went viral. A source named Bali Nine courier Martin Stephens as the informant.

Rush told me the Australians all mulled the real possibility of dying in prison. Since that conversation, a third member of the gang has died. Tan Duc Thanh Nguyen died in May 2018 from stomach cancer.

'No one knows Tan,' Rush told me after I'd visited Nguyen on 8 April 2015 at Malang's jail in east Java. Nguyen, once nominated third-in-command of the drug-smuggling ring, had recruited Rush in 2005, who in turn signed up Michael Czugaj.

Recalling the fateful day of the group's arrest, 17 April 2005, Rush said Renae Lawrence had turned to him in terror, asking, 'Are they going to shoot us now?'

'I said, "Yeah, probably." Everyone was crying. I wasn't. I was in shock. I just wanted to go home.'

A decade on, he dreamt of how things might have been, admitting he desperately wanted a wife and children and to lead a normal life. 'I don't want to be on a life sentence. But I really don't know what I would do [on the outside]. I'm a good person gone bad.' At the time of his arrest, Rush had applied to enter the Royal Australian Air Force. 'I had just finished an exam … I was about to go on my first mission.'

Now freedom existed in a fantasy.

Vicki Czugaj told me, 'They don't know what goes on in the real world anymore. [If Michael were released] he'd need some sort of rehabilitation, to learn all over again what life's about. You think this sort of thing only happens in movies but, holy hell, this is real life.' She scraped together the money to visit her son annually until he was transferred in 2016 to the remote Madiun prison in East Java. Indonesian authorities claimed he was addicted to ice and said he'd been separated from suppliers. Later they inexplicably attributed the shift to overcrowding in Kerobokan jail.

How, I asked Rush, did he cope waking up each morning to his prison nightmare? He stared at me blankly. 'It's surreal. I have nightmares all the time. I don't give a shit. I just don't care much anymore. I don't have hope.'

Prone to destructive tendencies, he was plagued by suicidal thoughts and self-harm. Labelling his malaise 'environmental depression' expressed through paranoia, he asserted, 'It's hard to even trust my own instincts. Part of the problem is being treated like I am already dead. You can go crazy and stab someone in the eye; it's better to mess myself up.' In colourful voice recordings and texts to me, Rush lurched from despair and rage to mad rants to money-making schemes and pleas to help him resurrect soured love affairs with girlfriends. Indeed, an Australian lawyer who had represented him, Robert Welfare, marvelled at Rush's Don Juan trysts behind bars.

Rush spoke frequently of suicide as his only way out, and once I received a text supposedly from his cellmate that Rush had tried to hang himself four times that week. 'I'm not going to be able to survive here,' he said. 'I wish I was dead. I'm trying to figure out a way to do it that's moral. It's a coward's way out, but I can't put up with this shit any more. I'll never get out. I will be taken away from here in a box.' A year later, in March 2015, on a brighter note, he said effusively. 'I've always been lucky in life, I'm religious and I like being a gentleman and I have principles and that's how I win people over, and that's why I have an angel sitting on my shoulder. I trust in God.' He was full of rough charm and contradictions.

As a source, Rush peppered apocryphal accounts with truth – and vice versa. Not all of my visits generated stories. We built an unusual rapport. He spoke of family and jail problems, drugs and impossible love, while wistfully dreaming of freedom.

The highpoint of 2014 was his whirlwind romance with glamorous London lawyer Nikki Butler, a mother of two who worked for a large investment bank. 'She's a positive influence. She gives me somewhere to belong. You can see the change in me, can't you? I can see the change in me.' Apparently they'd declared their undying love for each other. 'I would never want to be with anyone else, I adore her,' Rush told me. Would I write the story? The Sydney newsdesk deemed it un-newsworthy. But then it popped up on *60 Minutes* in August 2014, piquing intrigue. It seemed improbable that a successful lawyer with small children would ditch her London life for someone doing life in a foreign slammer.

Yet his demons were never far away. He relied on a methadone program; when left without it for three days, he called me complaining of loneliness. He continued to be haunted by his five-year death-row ordeal and 'dreamt' about an imagined journey accompanying Andrew Chan to Nusa Kambangan to execution island: 'the last bus stop'. 'I was affected massively. That's why I'm messed up all the time.' While he was on death row, it was overwhelming. 'I couldn't sleep, I felt hopeless.'

*

Back in December 2014, Nikki had returned to Bali from London for Rush's twenty-ninth birthday. It was her seventh visit that year. There was heightened interest about the couple's curious long-distance relationship, which had blossomed several months earlier. I would do a piece covering the birthday celebration, the teaser to the main event in which the smitten couple were to marry the following year. It was unclear how such a relationship would work.

I met Nikki at a coastal hotel in Candi Dasa, forty minutes south from the jail. Returning from visiting Rush, she swept into the lobby like a flustered film star. She wore a long cream gown and perfect makeup, her brown hair cascading over her shoulders. Emotional and weepy, she described the nastiness of a new prison guard during her visit to Rush. Then she switched to chatting about the birthday preparations. Suddenly she turned around, showing me a muddy splodge on the back of her strapless dress, explaining she had sat in something. 'It looks like I've shat myself,' she blurted in an East London accent. 'Give me half an hour, I need to change and de-stress. Then come over.'

Dusk was falling when I made my way to her capacious villa. Cocktail in hand, she opened the front door to an opulent room strewn with clothes, underwear and wads of red IDR100,000 notes that she referred to as tens. In the massive bathroom, mountains of makeup, hairpieces and chocolate bars spilled out, even into handbasins.

Over wine and room-service pizza, she explained an undying infatuation with Rush after running into him in Ubud the day before his arrest in 2005. She and a girlfriend were holidaying in Bali. Nikki knew the island, but it was her friend's first visit. 'I just wanted to party, to get pissed. My friend wanted to do all the touristy stuff, see the temples and go to Ubud.' Which is where they wound up. Her friend gravitated to bed linen, Nikki to a bar across the road. 'It was about eleven in the morning and I thought, *Fuck this*. I walked outside and I saw this guy smiling at me from a bar. I thought, *He's quite hot*. He beckoned me over and we spent the next five hours snogging. We didn't really talk. My friend came back with the bed linen and I'm dry humping Scott. She was so embarrassed, she dragged me away. I was absolutely hammered.' Rush was nineteen and told Nikki he was twenty-three. She was in fact ten years his senior and finalising a divorce. 'Scott said he had to return to Sydney for a bit of business and that he'd call. I never heard from him again.' Rush was arrested the following day.

During UK media coverage of the 2012 arrest of Lindsay Sandiford in Bali, Nikki had recognised an image of Rush on TV. She'd had no idea about his incarceration and soon contacted him through his father, Lee.

On 3 December 2014, Nikki, immaculately dressed and made up, loaded an SUV with lavish gifts, a picnic basket and birthday cake. My cameraman Made Nagi waited at Karangasem jail.

Several supportive friends trooped in to wish Rush, who was standing in his cage, many happy returns. It was the oddest birthday party I'd ever attended. The cake, candles smouldering, was served on paper plates and passed through thick iron bars. Nikki's gift-wrapped parcels followed suit. Rush was allowed 'out' for a photo shoot with his fiancée, but guards suddenly stopped the frivolity, banishing Rush back to his cage. Unperturbed, Made Nagi pointed his lens through an outside window and resumed snapping in view of the guards. The fact that Rush was sucking Nikki's toes through the bars wasn't an issue – as long as lockup rules were observed.

Rush's marriage proposal had elicited immediate acceptance. 'I just adore him,' Nikki said. 'Did you ever touch anyone and feel that sizzle? I don't want to be with anyone else. I have no interest in other men. For us, it works perfectly.' But canoodling through jail bars isn't most people's idea of romance, and Nikki joked that even her mother was stumped, asking, 'Are you doing a reality show?' And Lee Rush also had his concerns. Nikki told me, 'He thinks I'm trying to use Scott for money, for media, for publicity, which I'm not. I love Scott. I don't want to be with anybody else.'

As Rush opened his gifts, a small, symbolic key – with an encrusted diamond – struck him the most. 'Hopefully, it's a magic key,' he said, looping its leather band around his neck while he beamed inside his cage. Bemused, we watched him open many other gifts from Nikki: expensive cologne and clothes, including a hat; an everyman's prison kit. But the buoyancy of what was apparently new love didn't help Rush's crippling depression, for which Nikki was determined to get him medical assistance. 'No one seems to care. They're never going to let him out so they may as well just shoot him. It's the humane thing to do,' she cried.

Nearly a decade on from his arrest, he was drowning, he told me. 'Today feels one step closer to not knowing when I'm going to get out. I feel terrible, it's the mental anguish I have to go through,' he said while scoffing cake and unwrapping gifts.

The wedding was planned for the following August. Then what? The prospect of a prolonged separation – perhaps three years, Nikki surmised – didn't faze her. 'We're going to be under one roof soon, and that's our hope.' She would give up her high-flying lifestyle and perhaps write a book with Rush.

It seems she was reading my mind when she stated the relationship was not a hoax. Some saw her as a publicity seeker; others inferred she enjoyed exerting power over a jailed man. But according to Nikki, the couple were simply besotted with one another. 'He's got nothing to offer me, [but] he's the hottest guy ever. He makes me laugh; he's slightly psychotic and a bit naughty. I've got a reputation for going out with bad boys. I will do everything I can to help him get out of jail. He does not deserve to be still in there, he's not a criminal. We believe in blessings and karma. You've got to believe in a miracle.'

After voicing her concerns about Rush's mental health and his self-harm, she said she wouldn't tolerate his drug use. 'I just want to keep him alive. I don't know if I can save Scott. He is more lonely than anyone I know. He's probably got another two years if he doesn't have help to get out,' she said, breaking down.

Whatever had driven him to be circumcised – in a 2010 covert operation by members of an Islamic group at Kerobokan jail – remained nebulous. The procedure frequently precedes conversion to Islam, but he vowed he was still devoutly Catholic. 'I don't want to go to hell. I pray every day, I feel bad when I don't and if I forget I ask to be forgiven,' he said when I inquired about the operation. If he had been coerced, he wouldn't say. Later he opined that the Christian church was judgmental. The circumcision had provided a catalyst for 'a deeper study into religion' through Islam. 'I'm not sorry I did it. It's about me finding spirituality, trying to understand fellow human beings. Religion helps massively inside a jail.'

Nikki also asserted he hadn't been brainwashed by the Islamic group. 'There was no anaesthetic. They just came and lopped it off. I can confirm he's got no scars, it looks fine. They did a good job on it.' She had been astonished, in fact, at his appearance laid bare.

'Well, how do you manage conjugal visits?' I found myself asking.

'They won't let him out of the cage anymore. The windows at the side used to be blacked out – it used to be private – and they used to occasionally let people out of the cage. Nobody should have ever seen anything.' She was talking about the window my cameraman used for the toe-sucking shots. 'Then there's a corner around the back, and now you can't do that anymore. Then there was an incident,' she continued delicately, 'when they decided to take the black off [covering the windows]. It's not possible now, unless you have a private room.' The lascivious images I conjured of a couple rolling about a filthy prison floor weren't exactly erotic.

It was midday, visiting was over. We decamped to a seminal restaurant with unimpeded views to Mount Agung and toasted the happy couple with tropical cocktails. Nikki was radiant despite the absence of her other half who was eating rice in the gulag.

I then returned to the hotel to file a story, Nikki to the jail.

Over the next couple of days she told me about her life – including her two ex-husbands. Her first was a millionaire who 'wanted me to be a Princes Diana trophy wife' and paid for her to have elocution and acting lessons. 'Have you seen the TV show *The Only Way is Essex?*' She mimicked the broad dialect spoken in the aspirational British reality series. 'That's the way I used to talk,' she said with a laugh.

Nikki's dream was always to be a lawyer, but her then-husband wouldn't have a bar of it. So she packed her bags and did it alone, working two jobs.

The second husband, with whom she'd had her children, was a 'trader' and didn't get much of a mention, except that he was away a lot and they were divorcing.

As I prepared to return to Seminyak, Nikki insisted I stay another night. We would drive down together the following day. Returning from her final jail visit overwrought, she described an altercation with guards as they stopped her and Rush from sharing a last embrace. 'It's hard because they won't let him out of the cage and it's like a rugby scrum because you've got hundreds of these Indonesian visitors who come all the time and I can only come a few times a year.'

Guards had injured her leg, she claimed, but the evidence was barely visible and so she thought about applying makeup to feign bruising. Her relationship with Bali's Australian Consulate-General, which oversaw her jail visits, was wearing thin.

Life then got a little stranger – Nikki told me that Rush needed 'medication' and a transfer to the Bangli prison in central Bali to access facilities at Bangli Mental Hospital. Could we pop in to see psychiatrist Denny Thong at his Denpasar hospital office? He had treated Bali Nine members, including Rush, as well as Schapelle Corby.

Clearly overwhelmed by the attractive Londoner, Thong listened attentively to her concerns for Rush. A letter was fired off recommending Rush's transfer, along with scripts for Xanax (an anti-anxiety medication) for Rush and herself. The letter was delivered to the Australian Consulate-General. On 5 December, Dr Thong wrote, in part: 'It is quite evident that he [Rush] needs a rehabilitation program from opiate dependency which is complicated by psychotic features, and [he] has strong suicidal ideations. Based on that, I strongly advise him to be moved to the jail in Bangli, which is very close to the psychiatric institute, as soon as possible to commence professional treatment.' Dr Thong, who died in early

2018, was the founding director of Bangli Mental Hospital. His advice for Rush was based on numerous consultations, and Rush was transferred to a narcotics prison in Bangli, central Bali, in September the same year. Doubtless, Nikki's entreaties helped.

Back in Seminyak, she suggested a sunset drink on the beach. Sinking into a beanbag facing the surf, she was in high spirits. 'This is Scott's dream, to sit on the beach with a couple of Bintangs [a brand of beer] with our feet in the sand and watch the sunset.'

I didn't see her again, but for a while she texted regularly about Rush.

A year later, in 2016, Rush phoned me with a 'proposition' alleging some illegal operations out of Kerobokan jail. Rush asked me for A$15,000 in exchange for abstruse information – he promised to reveal all once I paid up.

During this call, Rush also spoke to me about Nikki Butler. When I asked if he'd ever intended to marry her, he emphatically replied, '*No*. You'd have to be fucked up to marry someone who's been divorced two times. But honestly, it doesn't matter to me, I've got nothing better to do.'

This was my concern: that he had infinite amounts of time and finite ways to amuse himself.

18

THE GODS, THE CHICKEN AND
THE WATER

On Friday evenings, I often attended a progressive Jewish Shabbat service in Bali. I had stumbled on this improbable expat community in 2009 via word-of-mouth. Part of an entrenched Israeli diaspora, Liat Solomon had opened her Seminyak house for twenty years, serving meals and a sense of belonging, tradition – and chutzpah. Judaism is not one of Indonesia's six sanctioned religions.

Religious freedom is a mainstay of the Indonesian constitution, but in its contrariness the government recognises only six religions: Islam, Protestantism, Catholicism, Hinduism, Buddhism and Confucianism. A tiny percentage of citizens fall outside these faiths. For safety, most identify under an official religion.

When a 'competing' French Chabad couple, A and S, started Friday Sabbaths in the same area, incorporating table-thumping and raucous singing, I rarely attended. It seemed foolhardy to draw attention to a faith neither liked nor legal in Indonesia.

Once, an Indonesian woman I met at one of these Friday Sabbaths said she had received threatening messages. She didn't know from whom but the sender knew her routine and where she practised. When the hosts became aware, they were unconcerned, which I thought was indicative of a complacency often assumed by expats in Bali.

In my early days, I went to services with a sense of derring-do. On Ramadan, as calls to prayer resounded across the land, I stood in a makeshift synagogue surrounded by tropical palms to the age-old blast of the shofar and chanting from the Torah on Rosh Hashanah (New Year). I was spellbound.

But the following year, it was different.

Reflecting on bewildering events that befell the community in 2010, Liat Solomon, a restaurateur, told me a story years later in 2017 she branded 'the eleventh plague'.

A Singaporean rabbi had offered to help with the service for Passover – the festival of freedom commemorating the ten plagues sent to liberate enslaved Israelites from the ancient Egyptians – as Liat was then heavily pregnant. Both Singapore and New York Chabad communities joined the Bali crowd. Liat found a rental villa for them over the eight-day holiday. 'But the New York people insisted on one on the beach,' she said. A stunning grotto-style villa on Seminyak Beach was found.

When Liat's Balinese staff checked the villa's suitability, they reported back it would first need a Hindu cleansing ceremony to exorcise evil spirits. Three months earlier, a Frenchwoman had hanged herself in the living room and the house had remained vacant since because no one had paid for the ritual. 'I told the Chabad group we had to do a cleansing ceremony,' said Liat. 'Their reaction was to laugh; they mocked me. Then they said, "Oh Hashem ['God' in Hebrew] cleans and takes care of everything."'

Liat, like many expats, particularly those employing Balinese as she did, undertook a range of ceremonies subsumed in daily life. They are the bedrock of the Hindu-Balinese tenet: *Sekala* and *Niskala*, the seen and the unseen – or the tangible and the mystical. They were interwoven; one could not exist without the other in the

Balinese animist universe. If cleansing rituals and offerings were neglected, 'sickness, death and all sorts of unimaginably bad things may result', wrote Fred B. Eiseman Jr in *Bali: Sekala and Niskala*. Liat explained to the group the risk of ignoring Bali's beliefs.

She told me, 'People here live in a different realm. If you are on this island, you have to respect the spiritual rules. They believe in black magic and spirits. They want to live in peace and harmony with the spirits.'

The suicide and spurned spiritual purification were a secret within that Jewish inner circle. I only learnt about it seven years later.

The Chabad group went about their duty, slaughtering chickens according to kosher Jewish law; they were pre-cooked for consumption on the holiday. Three days later, I sat with 110 people around long tables on the eve of Passover. The feast was eaten on a shimmering evening; we gazed out over rolling surf illuminated by a full moon. That night I eschewed water for wine, simply because the wine bottle was within reach, the water jug was not.

The next day, I returned to a lunch table of a few people. A was one. 'Where is everyone?' I asked him.

'They are seriously ill in hospital.'

Liat contracted typhus, while others were diagnosed with E. coli, salmonella and kidney failure. Some collapsed – on the verge of death – even messaging their last thoughts, though all survived. Many were evacuated to Singapore, including the rabbi. 'I was having contractions.' Liat told me. But she couldn't distinguish between the typhus pain and labour contractions. She delivered a healthy baby boy a few days later.

A theory circulated blaming anti-Semitic Muslim locals for water poisoning. Others concluded that the chicken was contaminated. This was reasonable: there was insufficient refrigeration for so much chicken, and a vast amount sat on benches in the open. 'They had no idea how to cook in the tropics for so many people, or apply safety precautions,' said Liat, seven years on.

But here was a conundrum: I hadn't drunk the water that came in sealed gallon containers and was served in jugs. But I'd eaten the chicken; possibly, I'd eaten a refrigerated portion. A had also drunk wine only. I heard years later that he too had fallen ill several days after the others. At the time, we ruminated about the water, but he, aware of the whole story, kept schtum about the suicide.

'We're never going to know what happened,' said Liat, sitting in her office.

Whether the gods were vengeful, the chicken was contaminated or the water was poisoned remains a mystery. The eleventh plague is now lore, if only it had a name.

*

One Friday evening several years later, Indonesian Yaakov Baruch attended Liat's sabbath meal. The de facto rabbi and descendant of Dutch Jews wore the Orthodox garb and broad-brimmed hat of Chabad-Lubavitch devotees. Intrigued, I asked him about his background, the upshot being that I felt compelled to visit him in Manado, at the tip of North Sulawesi, where he was born and led a small synagogue.

Baruch wasn't the only Indonesian Jew to turn up at Liat's Shabbats. There were Jews from small, cautious communities in Jakarta, Surabaya in East Java, Manado and a few in Bali – about two hundred through the archipelago. That disregarded those who had intermarried or converted to other religions.

Baruch, who was raised a Presbyterian, wanted to perpetuate his Jewish faith, he said, as we drove thirty minutes inland from Manado airport through thickly rainforested North Minahasa where he lived. He'd changed his name, his faith and his life about fifteen years earlier, after learning from his material great-aunt that he was the great-grandson of a nineteenth-century Dutch Jewish immigrant called Elias van Beugen. 'I made a strong decision to keep the Jewish faith.' He was named Toar Pallingin, after his father, who was raised a Protestant. His late mother was Muslim, and Baruch's birth name remained on his ID card. Father and son taught law at Manado's Sam Ratulangi University. Completing the circle, Pallingin, then fifty-three, had discovered three years before I visited that his maternal great-grandmother was German Jewish.

Manado is a curious outpost lying directly south of the Philippines; the majority 70 per cent Christian population embraces Judaism, even incorporating Jewish liturgy into some worship. This community is also tolerant of the Muslims in their midst.

Baruch wore Orthodox clothing with impunity here. Though few in Manado knew the significance of the garb, 'everyone here knows I'm Jewish', he said. 'I want to keep Judaism and Hebrew existing in this country.' His Islamic wife had also converted, and they were raising their toddler son to be a Jew.

I was amazed to see Jewish concepts embedded in Manado's Christian community. Based on the monotheistic concept, evangelical and charismatic Christians, tagged born-again Jews, strangely promoted common ties with Judaism. It was during the colonial era of the Dutch East Indies in the nineteenth century that several thousand Dutch and some Iraqi Jews were drawn mainly to the spice trade and missionary work. Others fled Nazi persecution in Europe.

I learnt Judaism thrived in West Papua. Some Jewish traders on the Spice Island route had settled in a village in Bonggo, according to the *Jerusalem Post*. Others, after being persecuted during the Spanish Inquisition in the fifteenth century, made their way to Peru only to be met with further oppression. They landed in Papua after fleeing in boats via Japan.

I was fascinated by this diaspora. My own heritage is Dutch and Polish, and I was raised in an observant Jewish household. The stirring traditions, songs and prayers are in my DNA. A source of familiar comfort and belonging, it embodies the principles of my childhood, despite the fact I am secular. As much as it would ease my anxieties to believe in a God, I am sceptical. My mother, stalwart keeper of the faith for our family, surprised us on her deathbed by impatiently waving away the rabbi come to ease her into the next world – or oblivion. Perhaps he personified the Grim Reaper.

My background is steeped in long, proud tradition. On the matrilineal side, my Dutch great-grandfather, Herman van Staveren, a philanthropist, was New Zealand's first rabbi in 1877. A tall, august man with a long, flowing beard, he and his English wife Miriam had sailed from London, making Wellington their home. They, too, opened their doors to the masses on Friday Sabbaths. When Herman died, he was feted with a state funeral and people lining the streets.

The descendants of their thirteen children are scattered around the globe. When I lived in London in my early twenties, I spent Sabbaths with one of Herman's granddaughters, my diminutive 97-year-old great-aunt Sally, in affluent St John's Wood. We were virtually next-door neighbours.

'Is it a squat, then?' Sally asked bluntly one day, not so much in the spirit of a caring relative, I thought.

Like a rabbit in the spotlight, I nodded. 'Yes.'

'I don't approve,' she clucked primly, before sinking into a post-prandial armchair slumber.

In those days, it was almost a badge of honour to live in a squat under Margaret Thatcher's recessed Britain. Like many, we were a bunch of university-educated unemployed. Respected journalist colleagues were even on the scrapheap, I consoled myself. When we were about to be chucked out of the squat, my Kiwi friend Noel

Crawford suggested we move into the Hebrew school up the road. Savouring my shocked reaction, he quipped, 'It's all right for you, you can stay with your great-aunt.'

But my heritage helped to land me my first Sydney job, as media adviser at the Israeli Consulate while I moonlighted at the *Sydney Morning Herald* as a sub-editor. It was 1982, during the Israel–Lebanon conflict. My most vivid memories are of streams of anti-Israel calls to my desk. 'How do you feel now, you murdering bastards?' was one that still rings in my ears. The other memorable event was in December of that year, when the consulate was bombed, injuring the elderly tea lady, who already shook so much that teacups were half empty on delivery. I had long gone by the time cost-cutting measures closed the consulate in 2002.

*

On my first night in north Minahasa at Baruch's home, he led the Friday night's Sabbath in the time-honoured tradition as the sun set. For us, the universal language was Hebrew. His was the tiniest Sabbath table I had seen; I joined one regular, his Presbyterian grandmother. Baruch's wife and son were away, and his father was indisposed.

Amid a diminished but determined Jewish community, Manado locals were enamoured of Judaism and Israel. Surprising public displays of its symbolism substantiated it. Against Indonesia's fragile religious balance, it seemed one of the most unlikely places to see Israeli flags, Stars of David and Mossad stickers on cars and taxis; batik shirts emblazoned with Hebrew; the world's largest menorah; a shop named Purim selling Judaic items; and the only synagogue in the country.

Pushing open the door to the Purim shop, I asked the Christian owner the reason for the dedicated shop. 'Jesus was a Jew. Judaism is part of the Christian faith,' she replied, adding that the items sold well. This was the most sensible misconception I'd heard while I was in Manado. Reasons for people's partiality to Judaism ranged widely.

But over the preceding few years, about ten prominent Indonesian Jewish families had either died out or moved to Jakarta and other areas in Java, leaving Manado almost bereft of Jews. But Baruch, at thirty-one, had been resurrecting his roots with gusto. He was optimistic of a revival. Who would guess this was the most populous Muslim nation on earth?

Manado officials make it clear Jews are welcome. The local government had paid for a makeover of the ten-year-old Shaar Hashamayim Synagogue (Hebrew for 'Gate of Heaven'), an hour to the north from the centre of Minahasa, where I spent an inordinate amount of time snapping the ornate interior. Officials had also forked out A$150,000 for the world's tallest – at nineteen metres – menorah, built on a mountain-top facing Manado. Not to be outdone, a property developer built a 31-metre-tall statue of Jesus perched atop another outlook, channelling Rio de Janeiro's Jesus.

This was a region of contradictions with few polarising influences – and that was how politicians wanted it to stay. Indonesia had no diplomatic ties with Israel, but tourism – mainly pilgrims visiting Israel – and trade links through the Israel-Indonesia Chamber of Commerce were curiously robust.

In Manado, support appeared more emblematic of religious freedom and was often seen as a counter to extremism. Officials such as Wenny Warouw, former head of BIN (the state intelligence agency) in north Sulawesi, trumpeted his endorsement.

I discovered this while driving past his house with Baruch. Encircling the house was a fence interwoven with giant Stars of David. 'Stop!' I blurted, after discovering who he was. I rapped on his door.

Warouw was bemused by my interest in his fence. 'They are symbols of prosperity,' he said. More practically, he added, 'Minahasa people like Jewish people; they think they are a foil against terrorists. Muslim people here are very peaceful and anti-extremist.' Undoubtedly wary after inter-religious violence had plagued Poso in Central Sulawesi for years, Warouw said the threat was from outside. 'We are very close to the southern Philippines where extremists train.' Indicating that Manado was a well-trodden transit point for terrorists, he said one of the Bali bombers had stayed there after training in the Philippines. Amrozi, who was executed in 2008, had two one-way plane tickets to Manado after the atrocities and was thought to be on his way to the Philippines.

Of the Christian stronghold and Jewish sanctuary, Warouw proclaimed correctly, 'People are only friendly to Jews in Manado.' His comments came after Islamic fundamentalists closed the country's only other synagogue – in Surabaya, East Java – in 2009 while protesting against the war in the Gaza Strip. After the incident, the synagogue was heritage-listed.

But this didn't save it. I learnt later that in May 2013 it was reduced to rubble, with the land allegedly sold by the Dutch Jewish caretaker to an unknown private investor. A police report was filed by David Mussry, the 83-year-old Iraqi president of the Indonesian Jewish community, and David Abraham, an Iraqi Jewish lawyer representing the community, whose family had fled to Surabaya after persecution in 1914.

When I'd met Abraham in Bali, he told me the Dutch Jewish caretaker allegedly sold the land for US$4.5 million. In 2011 Joseph Sayers had argued in court that he was the only Jewish person left in Surabaya, making the use of a synagogue obsolete and entitling him to buy the land from the government. Abraham, who was openly Jewish and wore a small gold Torah around his neck, was outraged. 'The sale was done quietly. It's a pure criminal act perpetrated by a Jew.' That was part of the problem: the community was ashamed Sayers was Jewish and wanted it hushed up. 'That's rubbish,' he scoffed of their embarrassment. 'I feel it's a slap in the face,' Abraham said angrily. 'I'm going after him. We will do everything possible to get the land back and restore the building.'

Sadly, the synagogue was superseded by a huge hotel in 2018 and I was told Sayers fled to Israel. Though the community broke up, Surabaya was still home to about 15 Jews in 2018, David Mussry told me.

News of the synagogue's demise spread through Jewish communities in Australia and internationally, but the circumstances were vague. I asked Jeremy Jones, the director of International and Community Affairs of the Australia/Israel & Jewish Affairs Council, if he was aware of the details – he was not. Most in the Jewish communities, including Jones, assumed there had been Islamic fundamentalist involvement.

The outward display of Jewish acceptance made Manado generally a safe haven for people such as Baruch. It wasn't the same in Jakarta, where his life had been threatened by Islamic youths demanding he remove his kippah (the Hebrew word for a skullcap or head covering). 'Outside Manado I have to keep a low profile. Here I am free to fight back and take a stand,' he said doggedly. Fluent in Hebrew, Baruch had visited Israel six times – but, incredibly, he'd gleaned most of his religious knowledge from the internet. 'Google and YouTube taught me how to be a Jew.'

His great-aunt had told him of ten other Dutch Jewish descendants in Manado. Among them was a renowned Dutch Jewish descendant family called Bollegraf. I met Oral Bollegraf over an animated dinner one night with his Pentecostal wife, Ma Lan.

Bollegraf had been raised a Pentecostal Christian but knew his grandfather had maintained the family home as Manado's only synagogue. His great-grandfather Abraham was a Dutch Jew who'd married twice, the second time to an Indonesian. 'I knew about my heritage when I was very young but we didn't talk about it for safety reasons,' he said.

Baruch said their parents had been forbidden to say they were Jewish. 'It was World War II and the Jews were being taken to Japanese internment camps just as they were by the Germans,' Baruch explained.

Now Bollegraf revelled in his religious freedom; his son had even had a bar mitzvah. Yet the threat of reprisal was never far away. Baruch and his fellow Jewish descendants in Jakarta and Surabaya were fearful, and some asked not to be identified.

'We live in a jungle,' Baruch said. 'We don't have any protection. It's like we live during the time of Hitler. Nobody guarantees our life.'

After Indonesia's independence from the Netherlands in 1945, most descendants had converted to Christianity or Islam for protection.

*

My children were raised as secular Jews. Their non-Jewish father was a disinterested, occasional participant in such things as my son's bar mitzvah.

But Ruby chose to settle in Israel in 2013. She was in a different jungle: she watched rocket attacks in Jerusalem near her home, witnessed the state teetering on the brink of war and had a brush with terrorists in Tel Aviv.

Having lived in Israel myself, I knew people acclimatised to high anxiety and elevated periods of risk. But did my daughter have to?

The dangers might have conspired to change her course. On the contrary, she found it a vibrant, mesmerising culture. She was home there, connecting to the history of her ancestors. 'There are things I get here ... one is a sense of belonging.'

It has come full circle. 'For me, having a Jewish partner is important because I want my descendants to be Jewish. I want to raise my children in a Jewish home, and I want their children to be raised in a Jewish home. Personally, I think being Jewish is special.'

When I first arrived in Israel to spend a year there in my twenties, the immigration man startled me when he exclaimed, 'Ah, Devorah, you have come home.'

My daughter is living that sentiment, continuing my family's precious traditions and heritage.

19

TILL DEATH DO US PART

A shocking murder in October 2014 reminded me of the closeness between my social and professional connections in tiny Bali. By association, I knew several people who'd been friends with Robert Ellis, a sixty-year-old Australian-British businessman whose Indonesian wife masterminded his grisly murder.

Bob's body was pulled from a ditch running alongside a paddy field about twenty-five kilometres north of Denpasar. The body was bound and wrapped in plastic. His hands and legs were tied and he was bruised and beaten, his throat slashed. That's what he got for twenty-five years of marriage.

His Javanese wife, Julaikah Noor Aini, known as Noor Ellis, had plotted the murder of her wealthy husband, hiring five hitmen to carry out a cold-blooded A$15,000 contract execution. They killed him in the kitchen of the couple's luxury villa in seaside Sanur, thirty minutes east of Denpasar, as Noor sat in another room, waiting for it to be over. She and the hitmen then drove to dump her husband's body in the rice paddy.

'It was all about money,' a neighbour told me, describing the ostentatious jewellery Noor wore.

Bali is no stranger to sensational stories of money, greed and gruesome murder, but this was different. Beneath the couple's seemingly staid, well-heeled lives bubbled a calculating Lady

Macbeth figure, who even attempted to bribe her two sons for court evidence to fast-track her jail release.

This perplexing story became clearer after I found a group of Bob's expat male friends who, I was told, gathered each evening for a beer at an unnamed beachside *warung* in Sanur. They were easy to pick: stony-faced middle-aged men huddled round a table in a corner. When I approached, they appeared shell-shocked, fearful and surprised to be found. But they wanted to speak out. They were trying to make sense of the murder of their respected, well-liked friend.

The couple's marriage had been foundering, said Richard (not his real name). Bob had been confident the rocky patch would pass, reasoning his marital problems were attributed to his wife suffering perimenopausal symptoms. But strange events unfolded involving money. Bob told his friends Noor had stolen A$250,000 from their joint bank account while he was holidaying with their sons in New Zealand; confronted, she simply told him to take out a loan to replace the money.

By the time Noor was sentenced to twelve years' jail for the premeditated murder of her husband in June 2015, large amounts of Bob's wealth had disappeared, with Noor's lawyer arguing he had kept her in penury. She was found to have financial motives for killing her husband, while she blamed his womanising for her bitterness.

Bob's friends dismissed her claim as ridiculous. 'He was loving and generous to Noor and he wasn't interested in other women,' they concurred.

What is known is that Bob had vast financial interests. In a bid to protect his fortune, which was in Noor's name, he had sought Indonesian citizenship to transfer assets to his own. Under Indonesian law, foreigners are forbidden from owning property, and so he tried to establish trust accounts for his four children: two sons with Noor, who have since disowned their mother, and a son and daughter from his previous marriage.

At the *warung*, gazing out to sea, his friends shuddered about a good life snuffed out ruthlessly, brutally – for just A$15,000. 'You can see what people are willing to do for such a small amount. If Noor had just asked for a divorce she could have walked away a wealthy woman,' said Richard.

After my piece ran, the friends went to ground. Running scared over their ties to Bob, they felt vulnerable to possible police or other corrupt involvement. They changed their details and their habits, and cut contact with me.

Then, one afternoon, as I stood on a footpath in Sanur covering the ongoing murder story, I received an overseas call imparting a personal crisis. My eldest sister was in a coma.

My surroundings fell away in a dreamlike sequence.

My sister was in New Zealand. Her life hung in the balance.

Everything around me dissolved: the furious sun belting down, the busyness, the beat of the street. I was in remote-control mode. I don't recall leaving Sanur, only that I made frantic calls, still on the footpath, trying to check updates of my sister's condition.

'Come now,' I was told. My brother had already flown from Sydney.

Securing a direct flight to New Zealand proved difficult at first, but with my emergency status established everything was expedited. Beyond that it's a blur.

Thankfully my sister came through it.

*

On my return to Indonesia a few weeks later, I decided to explore a social issue that had piqued my interest since I'd first settled in Bali: the romantic dynamic between Western men and Indonesian women. The rules seemed basic: men were providers, women subordinate. In reality, it was like a poker game – if you play, be prepared to get burnt.

When I met Australian property developer Stuart Smith, a tanned, fit and energetic fifty-four-year-old, he was sitting in his Seminyak resort office eating *nasi goreng* and juggling business decisions on the phone. He abruptly turned his attention to me. 'It's hard to see an old, out-of-shape, fat guy with absolutely nothing to offer anyone in the West, or here, with a very young girl,' he began. 'Sure, I had those feelings; that's off, it's not right, there's something wrong with that scene, isn't there? Is that what you think?'

'It doesn't look good,' I conceded.

'It looks good to him though,' he said with a belly laugh. 'I've been an Asian fan for years – you don't just see it here, you see it in Thailand, all over Asia. These girls are looking for a way out, they're uneducated and come from a poor background, as my wife does.' But she was different, he insisted; she hadn't attempted to flee that life.

In 1998, as the riots that toppled dictator Suharto had raged through Indonesia, Smith had been holidaying in Bali. Strolling through Seminyak, the Melburnian stopped at a gift shop where a girl called Made was earning money to send home to her family in a poor east Bali village. He was instantly besotted. She was seventeen; he was thirty-seven. 'She was drop-dead gorgeous, the classical, old-school Balinese beauty. I made quite a few stops at that shop,' Smith recalled. But she wouldn't go out with him.

When he later moved to Bali to pursue business opportunities and for the lifestyle, he asked her again. Two years after they first met, Made finally consented to have dinner with him. On the first date, three of her brothers turned up as chaperones, and Smith was under strict instructions to have her home by 8.30 p.m. Thereafter it was a slow courtship, with some hiccups. When he invited her to his house, 'she wouldn't come in because I didn't have a [Hindu] temple. I said, "All right, can you organise one for me?" Which she did.'

Fifteen years later, the temple still adjoined what was their marital home. Smith was uncommitted to a faith; nevertheless, he embraced Balinese Hindu values and believed they imbued their sons Shelby, then ten, and Jet, eleven, with a deep sense of morality.

Made's journey into Western culture, including periods in Australia and extensive travel, was, she told me, 'a steep learning curve'. She felt the envy of other Indonesian women eyeing her lifestyle, her husband and her home. 'It's not an easy life, with all the differences,' the 34-year-old beauty confided at the couple's dazzling Kerobokan home. Yet over time 'we have become so much more understanding towards each other. Stuart speaks my language fluently and more importantly, understands and respects the way of the Balinese. Our children have benefited from a cross culture [influence] and better schooling.'

I had driven over to Smith's house. Jason Childs was to meet me there for a photo shoot of the family. When he walked through the door, Smith asked him, 'Have you crossed the bamboo bridge too?' I'd heard the expression many times. They laughed.

'No, mate.' Childs explained he had an Australian wife and family.

I was focused on Australian men who were drawn irresistibly not only to local women but also to the country's patriarchal sensibilities. If there's a corner of the earth where men can still be king, it's here.

Smith expanded on the beguiling world that Western men enter when they come to Bali. 'You have to understand the dynamics of an Indonesian or Balinese relationship. The men are the power. Women are totally subservient. The boys are born into that egotistical world. I see it a lot. It was really prevalent when I went to Made's village all those years ago.'

While Smith's marriage had stood the test of time, he knew of scores that unravelled not just because of infidelity but also because men underestimated the effect of cultural and religious differences, of ethical, familial and financial expectations, and even the widespread belief in sorcery.

On a practical level, divorce can be particularly harsh for foreigners: Indonesian law forbids them from buying property, so a local partner, wife or nominee is usually the only name on title deeds. Countless men fell into a trap.

Melbourne landscape gardener Warren was one. In my email exchange with the sixty-three-year-old, he told me he was living in penury in the wake of his failed marriage to an Indonesian woman. When they met in Sulawesi in 2006, he was on an adventure to see traditional *pinisi* yachts and plan a sailing trip. Instead he became entranced with a nurse ten years his junior – despite having a girlfriend in Australia – and within five months the couple had married in Melbourne, returning to Sulawesi for a traditional Muslim wedding. Two years later they moved to Australia after Warren's wife was granted a spouse visa. In Melbourne, she worked in aged care. 'For the first year, things were okay,' he told me. 'But the relationship deteriorated and one day she walked out, taking all our savings and the title to a beautiful piece of land in Sulawesi – in her name, but paid for by me. I was left with nothing but a broken heart and no finances.'

Despite the risks, the attraction of Indonesian women remained a potent force, heightened by a view among many foreign men I interviewed that Western women were overbearing. 'I know many expats here who say "never again" with a Western woman,' said Dean Keddell, a softly spoken Victorian expat, and part owner and chef at a popular restaurant in upmarket Oberoi. 'It's because of the independence, the nagging – they're high maintenance. It's much easier with an Asian girl, if you can find an honest one.' He was happily settled in Kerobokan with his Indonesian wife Baya, thirty-five, and two-year-old son Jackson.

After numerous relationships in Australia, Smith was of a similar mind to Keddell. 'I was always with really domineering women,' he said. 'I don't think it was ever going to work for me.'

I consulted Malcolm (not is real name), a long-time expat in his late sixties who played father confessor to male denizens and didn't mince words. 'Western women are ball-breakers; older guys start losing their self-esteem. Here they regain it, with Asian women, generally. The men feel wanted, attractive, happier. They're vital again. When a fifty-something man meets a twenty-five to thirty-year-old Asian girl, he finds the fountain of youth. Asian women treat men like men. You might call them subservient, but I don't go for that. They're looking for a guy who has substance. They want to be taken care of; the man provides.' Decades of sweeping women's progress had slipped him by. The guy was a '50s relic, I thought. I sat listening to him, as he proudly described the men he counselled. Usually they were at rock bottom, about to lose their properties to vengeful wives they'd betrayed.

It was a common expat theme. But just who was exploiting whom was frequently opaque in a high-stakes game possibly involving the custody of children, probably involving assets.

Malcolm moved on to sex, describing explicitly how malleable a petite girl was, and how much fun he had.

How about having a conversation? I asked.

Malcolm contemplated the idea. 'I just want to have sex,' he said, 'share a few jokes and have fun together. I don't want the girls around.'

They were like sex toys; he could put them away afterwards.

*

At sixty-six my Kiwi friend, architect Ross Franklin, had been twice married to Indonesian women. With his second wife, Ardriani, thirty-eight, he had a seven-year-old daughter, Alexi.

'What is the attraction in such relationships?' I asked him over coffee.

'In cross-racial and ethnic marriages you're diving more into the unknown but there is fascination for that,' he said. 'It's more exciting, it's crossing a border.' He went on, 'That men are led by physical attraction as much as women are by financial security is a fundamental biological imperative.' In Franklin, I got unabashed pith. Usually prone to rambling, on this Franklin was unequivocal. The men I interviewed for this story largely agreed with Franklin.

I sought a psychologist. Fiona Paton had counselled couples in cross-cultural marriages in Bali for five years, and in an email exchange she cautiously opined such partnerships worked better for a Western man and Indonesian woman than vice versa. 'Maybe because the former conforms to more traditional gender role stereotypes that work for both partners.' She cautiously wrote it was too easy to peg female stereotypes as subservient or to assert cultural mores as the root of problems. Beyond that, there was polygamy and prostitution in Indonesia where men enjoyed more legal rights and higher socio-economic status. 'Women who are not financially independent may sometimes tolerate male infidelity if the alternative of losing their home and children is too hard.'

But the distinction between acceptable and taboo behaviour was blurred, as far I saw. Men, I learnt, have a free rein in marriages. In my interviews I was told infidelity was quite rampant. Wives generally turned a blind eye unless they lost face with their Indonesian peers who found out and gossiped.

One morning, an expat I know arrived home after staying out all night to be asked sweetly by his partner what he fancied for breakfast before he went to sleep. 'She didn't say, "Where have you been?"' he told me. 'She ignored it.'

*

On the Australian Consulate-General's tally of Bali residents, twelve thousand were Australians on various visas in 2014. They included hundreds of fly-in fly-out (FIFO) workers and those employed at mines throughout the archipelago. I had written articles about FIFO workers, but at that time had no knowledge of the double lives many led.

It was through a coincidental meeting in Bali with a young mother, Robyn (not her real name), that I was enlightened. She was married to a Victorian FIFO worker based in Kalimantan and the couple had two young daughters. She described a 'sliding doors' phenomenon as men moved seamlessly between families in Indonesia and Australia, unbeknown to the Australian family. Robyn is the product of such a marriage, the daughter of a West Timorese mother and an American father who also had two sons with a woman from Bougainville, Papua New Guinea, where he ran a cattle station. At the time, the difference between them and most others in this situation was that Robyn's mother left when she was a baby, taking her from West Timor to live in Darwin where she was raised. Since then, Robyn had never tried to contact her father.

Her husband's work environment was accepting of the endemic Indonesian practice of polygamy, in which a man can legally have more than one wife. Robyn knew Australian men with two sets of families, a practice her husband said was rampant. She became concerned when he confessed to a one-night stand with an Indonesian woman. 'It was a honey trap. The girl had got his mobile number and the family was threatening him, saying, "You've defiled her so are you going to marry her?" They knew he was married with two kids.'

Robyn told them to back off. She moved to Bali with the children to protect her marriage, and her husband changed his roster from six to three weeks on. 'If I'd continued to live in Australia and my husband was in Indonesia for six weeks at a time, there was no way he would not get involved in a relationship. And I make a conscious effort to visit the workplace so the women know he's married with children.'

At a barbecue in Seminyak, Robyn was charmed by the children of another FIFO worker and asked him if he had others. 'He said, "These are from my Indonesian wife."' His 'first' wife and adult children were in Australia. 'When the husband goes back to Australia the Indonesian wife doesn't question it, because she's being financially supported. The men don't see anything morally wrong with it. They lose all sight of normality. They know the two worlds won't collide and if the Indonesian wife doesn't speak much English it's better because she won't connect with the Australian family.'

Among a group of Australian early retiree expats in Bali there were similar principles. 'The expat community in Bali is very much how Darwin used to be in the 1970s and '80s: the men were men and the women were just there. It's a time warp.' While women were consigned to the kitchen preparing dinner, men were at the bar flirting with young girls or out with the boys. 'The expat wives aren't going to complain, they've got home help with cooking and cleaning, book club and mahjong, lunches with girlfriends and the spa. They're in domestic bliss. They turn a blind eye.'

For scores of other FIFO workers and retirees, bliss was at the end of a laneway in Sanur, at the budget Bali Senia Hotel, a convivial hub that was a home away from home. Perched on bar stools, with a steady diet of TV football, pool and beer, the men forged solid friendships. I watched young Indonesian women gravitating there; they sought a ticket out of poverty. The retirees, men in their sixties and seventies, were 'in heaven', co-owner and Victorian expat Peter Pearson remarked earnestly, as we sat at the bar watching a passing parade of women. 'They have families down there in Australia but they don't see them much.'

Pearson had hosted six weddings at the Senia. None of the marriages survived. One bride was visibly pregnant; her ex-boyfriend was the best man, and the groom had had a vasectomy. Pleased as punch, the groom deadpanned on his wedding day, 'It's a miracle, isn't it?' A lot of the girls had Indonesian husbands or boyfriends. But although many romances failed, the 55-year-old Pearson knew plenty that worked, his own included. Like many I interviewed, he was never involved in a long-term relationship in Australia. He met his wife Deni, twenty-nine, in Lombok and married in her village on the island of Sumbawa eight years before. He married into the Muslim faith, adhering to Indonesian law that stipulates couples must be the same religion. His conversion was a mere formality; neither he nor Deni are religious.

Pearson had been a Bahasa Indonesia teacher in Uluru in the Northern Territory and in Lombok, and his fluency demolished the language barrier on which many mixed couples foundered. Their son, Ray, eight, was bilingual.

In an email interview, I asked Deni what the advantages were for her in marrying a foreigner.

'I prefer being with a Western partner as I feel more secure financially and socially,' she replied.

As Pearson and I chatted, a constant stream of young women visited the men. Neither group could speak the other's language, and male hopes of reconstructing a suburban Australian 1950s dream added further distance. 'The men want a villa and a girl who stays at home to cook and clean, and go out to dinner with sometimes,' Pearson continued. 'But that's culturally foreign to the women, who are used to socialising in their villages. They're looking to support themselves and their families. That's the only reason they're involved. The men don't see that – they see it as a nice, happy relationship.'

Lonely men looking for love and companionship were often easy marks. Some visited Bali only a few times a year but continued to support girlfriends who did sex work, unaware of the duplicity. 'The men use me as mediator. They transfer huge amounts of money to the girls through my bank account, often about A$1000 a month. They buy them iPhones, iPads, motorbikes.' Then the girls claimed the goods had been stolen, and the men bought a second lot – all to be sold on the black market.

Before he'd met Baya, Dean Keddell told me, he'd had such an experience. Eighteen months passed before he realised his Javanese fiancée was an upmarket hooker and that each time he returned to Australia she was hustling. 'It was stupid – I've heard this story billions of times. She was sending me messages, "I miss you, I love you." It's just a bad experience but I never lost a house or car.' He had, however, paid a year's house rental.

Such 'good-time girls', as Keddell described them, party hard while feigning serious relationships, sometimes several simultaneously, before moving on.

Many seek help from *dukuns* to try to nail their targets, inserting *susuk*, or charm needles, beneath the skin anywhere in the body including the vagina and face, as talismans. *Susuk* are usually made of gold, silver, copper or other metals on which a spell has been cast. Popular in south-east Asia, *susuk* are believed to enhance or preserve beauty, youth, charisma, strength, health or prosperity.

Betrayal was a two-way street. 'A lot of expat men married to local women pick up hookers at every opportunity,' Keddell affirmed. 'If you lived in Australia and you were sleeping with hookers every night, your wife would kill you. But I know a lot of so-called respected expats and this is what they do. There are no restraints, no laws; this is the Wild West.'

Smith's and Keddell's marriages benefited from their determination to overcome the differences in backgrounds. Keddell, who had lived in Bali for eight years and was inured to the customs, maintained a novice would be alarmed. 'If you came here straight from Australia and you married a year later, you'd get the fright of your life. It is a culture shock.' According to Asian values, he provides for Baya's family, on a needs basis, particularly as she, at his request, stopped working. 'I don't give them a salary though a lot [of men] do.'

The couple had also contended with discrimination in Bali. 'I'm with a *bule* [foreigner], I must be after the money,' Baya said simply.

I knew many Indonesian women saw in Western men opportunities for their children that otherwise would be unattainable, and Baya told me optimistically, 'Our son will grow up with wide eyes and a big heart. He will be able to understand both cultures and speak a few languages; he will be at peace with everyone.'

Smith's love story hadn't always been easy either, but life was good. Facing the family property in Kerobokan was a lush rice paddy, an anomaly in the overdeveloped heart of the island for which people pay a premium. Smith had bought it to retain the view – and because he could. Just as he could afford the daily domestic help and nannies that helped iron out marital crinkles. 'We don't have financial problems, we don't have a lot of pressure like they do in the West,' he said. But he credited Made with the relationship's success. 'Made was an old wise soul in a young person's body and she still is. She has something very special that's kept us together.'

20

SILENCE OF THE DAMNED

In a realm that relied on *balians* for advice and guidance to solve life's problems, so many things could go wrong, so much was left to the deities and karma. Impoverished and uneducated villagers, susceptible to supernatural beliefs, are deeply suspicious the mentally ill are conduits for evil spirits and bad karma. It is usually in remote Bali – and elsewhere in Indonesia – that such people use the egregious practice of *pasung*: the shackling and caging of Bali's mentally ill.

Where did these pariahs fit in to Bali's long-feted paradise? Beneath a highly developed tourism industry, silent victims languished, tethered, imprisoned and hidden away by their families for decades.

It was with a sense of dread and disbelief that I embarked on this assignment. I wasn't sure why I wanted to see the victims – perhaps as undeniable proof of their existence. Undoubtedly, this was a compelling and traumatic story, and few got this close to it. That tourists stayed a few kilometres away from *pasung* victims, revelling in sun and surf, padding about plush hotels, intensified my sense of the surreal.

In late 2014 I drove with Rudi Waisnawa, a photographic documenter of *pasung* victims, to Klungkung regency, several hours north of Denpasar. Our visit to a 'suburban' address was organised by Bali psychiatrist Luh Ketut Suryani, whom I had known for some years. We picked our way up a garden path, bracing for the worst. At first glance, nothing was awry: cheerful family members gathered in a typical Balinese setting. The TV burbled in the background. Sticks of incense smouldered in the morning sun, and chatter filled a white-tiled courtyard, competing with the incessant yapping of a caged dog as the family anticipated a Hindu cleansing ceremony.

Where would a restrained man be? Turning a corner, we suddenly came upon him. The bizarre image of the forlorn figure of Kadek, chained to his bed, his feet in wooden stocks, in a room just metres from the courtyard hub, shattered the illusion of normalcy. I could barely process this vision. He sat facing a paneless window with a permanent view of half a tree and the dog. The 47-year-old's sporadic, guttural guffaws punctuated the household's routine. But he wasn't part of it. The family ignored him.

Kadek's body was misshapen, gnome-like, and his skinny legs were bare, his only clothing a filthy, torn shirt. Empty banana leaves, which served as a plate, lay on the bed beside a jar filled with coconut water. A bucket under the bed was his toilet, and a crude hole had been cut in the coarse bamboo bed – dispensing of the need to move him. His family had disposed of his faeces but the stench of caked filth and urine was overpowering.

He was a grey, withered shadow of a man. His left eye was permanently closed, and he had lost the ability to walk. Sometimes he made eye contact; mostly he was lost in a desolate world.

That morning his ninety-year-old mother entered the fetid room, Kadek's jail-home for almost a decade. Arm outstretched, he silently sought a reassuring touch, but she remained just out of reach, ignoring his entreaties. She had emerged from her adjoining bedroom in a pale-pink lace *kebaya* and a scruffy sarong, wondering why Kadek was the object of attention. Strands of white hair fell from a bun at the nape of her neck. Stooped, she carried a crude walking stick, moving cautiously into the room. Glancing at us wordlessly, she turned to Kadek, locked in his gaze.

For Rudi and me, this was a spine-chilling venture into no-man's land. He had snapped Kadek from every angle. Now the dynamics between mother and son entered a secret dark corner from the past. She was impossible to read. Was it shame, remorse, guilt, anger, or simply love for a long-lost son that she felt? In a split second, Kadek segued from hope to despair. He withdrew his arm as if stung. His face shut down. His mother retired to her room. No words passed between them.

Kadek had schizophrenia and a tendency towards aggression. I sat with the family on the tiled floor. 'Why is Kadek shackled and in stocks?' I asked.

His cousin-in-law, Anggraeni, a woman of twenty-eight, replied breezily that Kadek's propensity to attack people and steal would be unmanageable were he free. She was one of ten relatives, including three young children, Kadek's brother and elderly mother, sharing the compound. 'This is horrible and sad, the chains, but Kadek is with mental illness,' Anggraeni told me, adding the stocks were backup security should he break the heavy chains. 'If he was free he would make trouble for the neighbours.' She went on, 'Before [he was restrained] the family was scared of him. He was always disturbed. If people didn't give him money or food he attacked them.' Apart from a brief taste of freedom during a 2012 hospital stay for tuberculosis, Kadek had remained shackled.

'Does he complain of discomfort or pain?' I asked.

'He never says he is in pain,' Anggraeni replied. 'Normally, people with mental illness have strong antibodies. He never has colds or flu. When mosquitoes bite, he doesn't complain; when the weather is cold, he doesn't ask for a blanket.'

Neither did Kadek wish for freedom. '*No*,' he told me emphatically when I inquired, one of the few words he uttered.

His life was one of regret and hopelessness. On the walls of his room, he had twice pencilled a plea to God: *Awuloh (Allah) ampunilah hidupku* (God forgive my life). He didn't recall when he'd written it, and we couldn't see any writing tools. The daily Muslim prayers that rang out from a nearby mosque were his only sensory stimulation as he sat imprisoned in the Hindu compound. There was nothing to suggest any semblance of a life amid the deprivation.

Kadek had been twenty-six when the hallucinations began. At high school he'd studied religion, going on to teach it at a primary school. Proficient in English and possessing good social skills, his goal was to be a tour guide. But his first episode of mental illness was the forerunner to numerous stays at Bali's Bangli Mental Hospital. On returning home, Kadek was shackled. He couldn't walk, but the family still feared he would 'run amok', stealing, assaulting neighbours and destroying property, as he had before being tethered.

The family, now dressed in ceremonial costume, prepared for the cleansing ritual at the local temple. As we started to leave, Kadek suddenly became animated and requested sweets and cake, which we bought at the corner *warung*. His cousin laughed gaily, saying he had a sweet tooth. Chewing hungrily, he obviously craved more than cake. His mother reappeared, planted herself in a chair and watched, sphinx-like, as her son received the attention she could not or would not provide. A child of about ten came out to wave goodbye. Kadek, in his stocks and chains, smiled shyly and thanked me in English for the food.

On the drive back, Rudi and I stopped at Keramas Beach, a wild, black sand stretch and surfing idyll in Denpasar. We sat at a *warung* eating nasi goreng and drinking bitter black coffee, lost in thought. The beach was deserted. Surging waves rolled in to shore, and a blustery wind that I'd never before felt in Bali swept over us like a cleansing balm.

Rudi's searing images formed part of an acclaimed 2014 photo exhibition depicting *pasung* patients, called *Tears in Paradise: Photographing the Tyranny of Mental Illness in Bali*.

A couple of years later, a Bali government program provided new housing to impoverished families of *pasung* patients. Kadek's family qualified but they confined him to a locked room.

His case isn't uncommon, though there is headway. Numbers have dropped in Indonesia to about 12,800 in mid-2018 from the last reported figure of nearly 18,800, according to government data. It's estimated there are 350 *pasung* victims in Bali. Even though the practice has been outlawed since 1977, it is widespread among poor Indonesian families who resort to iron shackles, wooden stocks, ropes, cages and locked rooms. The custom extends to most Asian and African countries, but it is neglected by researchers and intermittently it re-emerges as news.

*

An anti-*pasung* program was launched in 2011 and more than five thousand restrained people were freed. The then national director of mental health, Eka Viora, had optimistically predicted a *pasung*-free program for 2015–19, although it was unclear how violators would be penalised. There remained substantial obstacles to eradicating the practice, not least the severe shortage of mental health facilities, psychiatrists and families' lack of education and financial means.

Mental health attracts a tiny percentage of the national budget. The 2015 health budget was a paltry 1.5 per cent of the total, government data shows. Of forty-eight mental health hospitals, more than half are in only four of Indonesia's thirty-four provinces, Human Rights Watch reported in 2016.

At Bali's only state psychiatric institution, the Bangli Mental Hospital, at least fifty previously shackled patients were still admitted annually in 2018. Most were recurring patients – like a disoriented elderly woman I encountered there, who was muttering incoherently. Staff described her as delusional, with memory loss. She had been chained at the ankle by her family for months after wandering off and stealing from neighbours. After exhausting her medication she had relapsed, was rechained and reported by the community.

Just as diseases like leprosy and HIV/AIDS, which I had covered in Bali, were stigmatised in Indonesia, so too were *pasung* patients. 'Most are schizophrenic with hallucinations. Families isolate them because they are ashamed and embarrassed,' said the head of services at Bangli Mental Hospital, Dewa Gede Basudew Dewa, when we first met in 2014 and he showed me the brightly lit hospital wards. 'The patients have many long-term problems. Some cannot walk or have atrophy. Some have been in chains for twenty years. They have infections, tuberculosis, malnutrition. We want to find *pasung* people, prevent them from being rechained and stop them being chained in the first place.'

Enter psychiatrist Luh Ketut Suryani. Leading the push to eradicate the imprisonment of the mentally ill, the indefatigable crusader worked with her psychiatrist colleague – who was also her son – Cokorda Bagus Jaya Lesmana. The seventy-year-old, silver-haired, feisty grandmother and former head of psychiatry at Bali's Udayana University had discovered the *pasung* phenomenon while researching a spike in suicides after the 2002 Bali bombings. Among her patients she had treated seventy-nine chained victims, but her energy had diminished along with her caseloads. 'I am old now,' she told me, though she retained her striking good looks and upright figure. Despite thoughts of easing into retirement, she'd been coaxed back by Italian businessman and photographer Luciano Checco, who had come across horrifying images of *pasung* victims and pledged to support them. Checco largely sponsored *Tears in Paradise*, collated by Suryani and Lesmana.

I'd first met Suryani in 2010 through her groundbreaking work on foreign paedophile networks and her Committee Against Sexual Abuse. Her name had become synonymous with a movement against Bali's underbelly and fiery attempts to prod the provincial government into action.

Armed with intravenous anti-psychotic drugs, Suryani took me on some of her monthly home visits in 2014 to administer medication, tracking patients' behavioural and physical changes. Most were well enough to be freed within several months, but if families kept them shackled she refused further treatment – as was Kadek's fate. Based on her holistic approach, she offered meditation and hypnosis if patients recovered sufficiently. Suryani had found that 31 per cent of shackled patients recovered with ongoing treatment. Those who relapsed generally returned to restraints or confinement as many families resisted interference. Balinese psychiatrist Denny Thong told me, 'They are ashamed of a mentally ill family member. They don't say they have a mental illness, they say they are possessed.'

A decade earlier Suryani had successfully appealed to the former governor for funding that went to the Suryani Institute for Mental Health. She claimed almost all of her treated *pasung* patients remained free that year. But it was a one-off subsidy. Officials questioned Suryani's methods of 'meditation and singing sessions'. 'They said, "She gets a lot of money just for teaching meditation and relaxation,"' Suryani scoffed as we sat in her clinic. A strong advocate of religious beliefs and traditional healing, she contended, '[In Balinese Hindu culture] the purification ceremony throws out the evil spirit influence. It will make patients quickly recover and maintain mental health. I say, "Please do practise beliefs."' Suryani and Lesmana relied on donations; when they dried up, Suryani dug into her own pocket.

Thong, the founding director of Bangli Mental Hospital, similarly advocated treating *pasung* patients with a mix of Eastern and Western psychiatry. He knew Suryani from Bali's Udayana University in the 1970s when he'd been studying psychiatry. 'She was different from other Balinese women,' he recalled. He described her as a force to be reckoned with; a charismatic, ambitious woman who bucked social strictures and alienated people. 'Bali women are more submissive and subservient. She's headstrong and outspoken. She wants things done her way.' He smiled wryly.

Reasons for using restraints are primarily financial; families in remote villages regard it as the best option if mentally ill relatives are aggressive and disturb the peace. Most would prefer to consult nearby traditional healers rather than pay for travel to free facilities. There is also the stigmatisation. 'The families generally believe mental illness is caused by curses, black magic or karma,' said Lesmana.

Early one morning, I joined Suryani and Lesmana on a trip to Gianyar, an hour north-east from the tourist hub. The IV anti-psychotic drugs would tide patients over until Suryani's return.

We had a grim start to the day: Suryani and Lesmana assessed a caged man following an alert from a charity organisation. It was a confronting scene. Flanking a deserted house where Made, a 43-year-old man suffering schizophrenia, had once lived with his wife and two sons, was a custom-built cage, his home of two years. Shirtless and heavily tattooed, Made hung his head and stood, occasionally groaning as he pressed against padlocked iron bars. The room behind him was putrid, with no toilet facilities or running water. The smell of excrement was nauseating, exacerbated by the fact Made had a prolapsed rectum. His skin was ashen, his body emaciated.

In a twenty-year history of mental illness, the former labourer had spun out of control in 2004 when his wife had married and had a child with his father. 'He ran amok with a knife,' said Suryani. 'His family sent him to Bangli [mental hospital]. He wanted to kill the father and wife. The family and neighbours were scared of him.' Frequent stints at Bangli were unsuccessful, and in 2012 the *Banjar* (local council) built the caged room and locked him in.

Suddenly Made turned, stripped off his clothes and lay naked on a foul mattress on the dirt floor. His teenage sons – Made, fifteen, and Wayan, eighteen – sat silently outside in despair amid mounds of rubbish. Both had been tormented and bullied over their 'crazy' father. They were the only visitors, delivering daily water and food rations bought by Made's mother.

Suryani furiously worked the phones, appealing to a parliamentarian and hospital for Made's immediate release and proffering her own money to make it happen. 'Many people know about this but nobody wants to take action. Everyone worries he will be aggressive,' said Suryani, adding that the *Banjar*'s edict wasn't easily nullified.

Two paramedics arrived in an ambulance, but the key to the padlock was missing. They hacked at it with knives until it broke. Dazed, Made stumbled out, so weak he needed help to the ambulance. We followed him to the hospital, where doctors diagnosed him with anaemia and said he needed an operation for his rectal prolapse. He was shifted between various hospitals because no one wanted a psychiatric patient, and he ended up back in his caged room. But with ongoing treatment he ventured out more frequently. A few months later the charity Solemen renovated the dilapidated house adjoining the caged room – which was demolished – and paid for his medication. Living with his mother in the house, he picked up simple work.

Further on, we visited two women patients Suryani had treated for a year. Wayan lay on her bed, agitated, while her mother stroked her arms, attempting to calm her. The thirty-eight-year-old was catatonic and unable to walk after twenty years of being chained at her ankles in a locked room she shared with chickens. At fifteen she'd developed severe psychosis with hallucinations and started damaging the family home. During her turmoil she'd frequently run away – sometimes naked, screaming – disrupting the village. So her family had locked her up. After Wayan's father died the year before, Suryani had begun treating her. She was moved to an open room where her mother slept alongside her on the floor.

'The mothers love their children but they are hopeless and uneducated,' said Suryani. 'And they fear their child's antisocial behaviour will provoke vicious attacks from neighbours who might beat or kill them.' Wayan's family rejected further treatment or aid.

Suryani's next patient, Nyoman, was twirling a flower in her hand. Fixated, she was far away in the threadbare grasp of her own strange reality. Her mother kept a watchful eye. By all accounts, the forty-three-year-old woman had been a pretty and clever schoolgirl with numerous friends. But at sixteen she'd been assaulted by a man and something snapped. She had become painfully thin, and suffered schizophrenia and violent mood disorders. 'She ran amok, cut up her clothes and bedding and destroyed her room,' said Suryani, who'd first seen Nyoman in a room rank with excrement and urine. 'She was harmful to herself, not others.' For more than twenty years, Nyoman had been confined to a room. Her mother was her constant companion, even sleeping amid the putrid conditions.

Since Suryani had begun treating Nyoman, she was no longer confined. But, though improved, she was still clearly traumatised.

'She doesn't know anything – we must try to make her brain active again,' Suryani muttered. I have stayed in touch with Suryani and Lesmana, who update me about their patients. The initial abhorrence and disbelief I felt on seeing these victims remain. To see humans at this level is beyond comprehension, an aberration and stain on humanity, in which beauty, goodness and tenderness are voided.

21

LAST THOUGHTS FROM DEATH ROW

The beginning of 2015 jolted Bali into the darkest of places. Foreboding leached into the air as Indonesia's state-sanctioned executions cranked up after a four-year hiatus. The horror story with which I'd become intimately connected proved the most challenging and chilling of my career. It was a personal story. I'd followed the legal cases of death-row inmates Myuran Sukumaran and Andrew Chan since my first visits to Bali in 2006. If I didn't interview them on my numerous prison visits I frequently saw them and exchanged greetings.

On 17 January, hours before five foreign drug convicts and one Indonesian were executed by firing squad, I became the unwitting confidante of Myuran Sukumaran. As one of the Bali Nine ringleaders, he knew the resumption of executions was an ominous portent. He and his co-conspirator, Andrew Chan, were slated for a second imminent wave. So began the final stretch of their nightmare roller-coaster.

That weekend, I was coincidentally scheduled to interview Sukumaran and Archibald Prize-winning artist Ben Quilty for an arts piece inside Kerobokan jail. A year earlier, I had approached Quilty at the Ubud Writers & Readers Festival. He had spoken about his exhibition *After Afghanistan*, the result of his tenure as official war artist in 2011, and the synchronicity between it and his work with Sukumaran. The story was immediately obvious: I wanted to examine the unique relationship between Quilty, the art tutor, and Sukumaran, his inmate student. Both were enthusiastic.

But as news spread that January day in 2015, the tenor of the piece catapulted into a chilling front-page news story, and the prison went into lockdown. From his exhibition in Hong Kong, Quilty raced over to support his friend in Bali. After some difficulty, he was permitted into the jail to give an art class, taking his cousin – and Gold Walkley-winning photographer – Andrew Quilty as his 'assistant'.

The forty-one-year-old Quilty had mentored Sukumaran for three years, paying regular visits to the jail. It had been home to the condemned duo since they were arrested in 2005, then sentenced to death the following year for plotting to smuggle 8.3 kilograms of heroin from Bali to Australia.

In the art studio, Sukumaran's sanctuary, they spent a harried day, lurching from art work to panic, horror and despair. Andrew Quilty's haunting photos bear testimony.

After their jail visit, I whipped over to the Quiltys' hotel for an interview. Everything was rushed because the cousins were flying out of Bali that night.

That same evening I spoke with Sukumaran on the phone as he sat alone in his cell, hours before the first executions. It was one of his last interviews after the president's rejection of his clemency bid on 30 December 2014. With Chan's denial of clemency confirmed on 22 January, the fate of the two men was sealed as they were to be executed together. An interview published at that time would have jeopardised their legal cases and fragile bids for mercy, so my words could not then be told.

I knew Sukumaran better than Chan. To me, they were very different people sharing similar tough backgrounds and likeminded redemptive goals – and violent deaths. While Chan, who had become an ordained Christian pastor in jail, had been instrumental in inspiring scores of inmates to give up drugs and take up religion, Sukumaran had enlightened the moribund prison with his arts programs, miraculously creating a school behind jail walls, one that engaged and reformed dozens. From his studio, the impassioned novice emerged a talent after three years, drawing strength and dignity through his art until the night he and Chan were tethered to stakes and shot dead side by side, with six fellow inmates in Indonesia's steamy jungle. At the eleventh hour 30-year-old Filipina migrant worker and mother of two Mary Jane Veloso was spared after her alleged recruiter surrendered to police.

On 17 January – the night the Quiltys left Bali – Sukumaran confided during our phone interview he was terrified he and Chan would be next. They were confirmed for execution on 2 February.

For the past week Sukumaran had been consumed by panic and dread, unable to put brush to paper. In his final year of a fine arts degree through Curtin University, he lost the will to concentrate. (Two months before his execution, his dream was realised: he was awarded an associate fine arts degree.)

Earlier that evening I'd sat in Quilty's hotel garden listening to him describe Sukumaran's reaction to his likely impending execution. 'I was very worried about Myuran and how he would be, but he just wanted to get back to work.' Mostly, Quilty had braced himself to discuss the subject of execution. 'We discussed how he feels about it, really the nitty-gritty of what it means to be executed.' He said his friend was shutting down. 'It's good timing for me to be there because he needs something to do.'

'Will you come back to support him if he isn't spared?' I asked.

'Absolutely, I will come back, I will be there for him. I love him, he's my mate, he's my friend,' said Quilty. When it happened, though, he was in Australia, deeply disturbed and upset. He'd said goodbye on the phone. He had been told he would not be permitted into the prison. In the final hours, authorities allowed only the pair's families and spiritual counsellors inside.

Doubtless, Sukumaran's soul-saving, redemptive art that served him until the bitter end was largely influenced by Quilty, who had campaigned tirelessly for mercy for both condemned men. When Sukumaran complained he couldn't focus on his painting that day, Quilty would urge him to pick up his brushes. 'What else are you going to do?' he'd ask. And Sukumaran did. As long as he had life in him, he painted feverishly, sharing his terror and grief from Nusa Kambangan, the island of his execution. One of his last paintings depicted the Indonesian flag dripping blood, forever stained.

'We talked a lot about art,' Sukumaran told me that evening on the phone after Quilty's visit. 'It was one of the better days I've had recently.' Through the earpiece, as we discussed his probable fate, Sukumaran's soft voice revealed a gamut of emotions: shock, terror, desperation, grief, regret and incomprehension. Facing his demons, racked with anguish and confronting his mortality, he said, 'I'm cracking up. I walk around crying. I usually never cry. I can't stop it. I don't know what to do.'

Trying to gather my wits, I floundered. I could only listen; he was so alone.

He'd been sleeping fitfully, waiting for the footsteps of his executioners. 'I keep waking up, and if I hear voices I think it's someone coming to take me at night.'

The duo's transfer to Nusa Kambangan island off Cilacap in Central Java would be under cover of darkness, with prisoners in lockdown to prevent riots.

I was in alien territory. What consolation or hope could I – or any psychologist, for that matter – offer someone in line for the firing squad? I grappled for apposite words.

There was only one person who could truly understand Sukumaran: that was Andrew Chan. When I feebly asked Sukumaran if it helped that Chan was in the same boat, he joked, 'It's better than going down by yourself, I guess.'

Their solid friendship withstood their ten-year ordeal. The pair kept each other's spirits up, while simultaneously respecting each other's privacy.

Quilty had painted Chan that same January day. 'He's a great guy. His Ocker accent … a huge Panthers [rugby] supporter. All he's worried about is that the Panthers beat Melbourne this year in the Grand Final.' Chan wore his Penrith Panthers rugby league jersey at his execution. He had smiled his way through a bittersweet wedding ceremony with his fiancée Febyanti Herewila, also a Christian pastor, the day before.

After Ben Quilty left Bali on the Saturday night of my interview, I found it difficult to contact him because he was in high demand from journalists. But as the story raged, I needed to maintain well-connected sources.

Melbourne artist Matt Sleeth was one. He'd conducted Kerobokan jail workshops with Quilty, and I could rely on him on deadline. Where most key figures pussyfooted around Indonesia, Sleeth bristled with rage and indignation, and I admired his outspokenness. He verbalised what many Australians thought after all our country's urgent pleading failed. 'Let's not be so dainty and polite … it's the height of barbarity, brutality and cowardice,' he said. 'I can't believe they are going to take them to a dark beach in the middle of the night, tie them to a pole and shoot them through the chest in cold blood. It's starting to feel less to do with justice and a lot more to do with political theatre.'

As a mother, I found it excruciating to watch the families' nightmare jail vigils. Particularly gruelling was the torment of Sukumaran's mother, Raji, who, utterly broken, begged for her son's life. How President Joko Widodo remained deaf to her, I don't know.

Back in 2010 I had covered the duo's judicial appeals – the final appeal known as a PK (*Peninjauan Kembali*), or case review. Raji, along with Sukumaran's brother Chinthu and sister Brintha, and Chan's brother Michael had all watched the proceedings with little expression. When I'd asked Raji afterwards if she felt confident, she'd smiled and shrugged as though she didn't trust herself to speak.

Australians vented outrage at Indonesia for condemning rehabilitated prisoners, the platform on which the pair's lawyers had repeatedly appealed. A Twitter hashtag Boycottindonesia gained traction and in one day before their deaths Australians had posted 150,000 tweets condemning the executions.

Widodo's hardline stance on drug convicts baffled Sukumaran: he couldn't understand this sudden bloodlust. Elected in October 2014 on a platform of clean governance and human rights, Widodo had also pledged to be tough on drug offenders. Two months later, in a populist move to lift his support base, he'd declared the nation in the grip of a 'drugs emergency', vowing no drug convicts on death row would be spared. The data for his cherry-picked figures was later discredited.

Widodo shored up the domestic support he'd sought: 85 per cent of Indonesians agreed with the death penalty.

A substantial rump in Australia also opined Sukumaran and Chan were odious criminals who deserved to die. As Quilty remarked, it was easy for people to sit back in their homes in a first-world country and say that. 'Myuran is a good man. He has reformed. I think compassion is the keystone of a healthy society, and I think compassion is often missing in Australia.'

*

The news coverage and media presence of the executions were unprecedented in my time in Bali. Journalists lined the roads around the jail, fixers and photographers keeping watch there round the clock. A daily revolving door of stony-faced lawyers, along with family, friends and religious figures came and went. International opprobrium and diplomatic ructions snowballed; members of the European Parliament wrote to Widodo requesting him to call off the executions, UN Secretary General Ban Ki-moon appealed to Indonesia to spare the group, and foreign ambassadors in Jakarta were recalled in protest. Widodo's standard response was to warn Australia – and the other countries whose citizens faced execution – not to interfere: Indonesia was protecting its political and judicial sovereignty. Until the eleventh hour, Australia's then prime minister Tony Abbott and foreign minister Julie Bishop sought clemency, with Abbott raising heated bilateral tensions. Widodo remained unmoved.

In the mid-January phone call when I asked Sukumaran if he had thoughts of escape, he replied without a hint of irony, 'Yeah, but don't write that, it would get me into a lot of trouble. That would probably get me shot.'

Yet flickers of hope prevailed that night.

'It's scary, but I feel God's there,' said Sukumaran, although by his own admission he wasn't particularly religious. 'I've been in jail for ten years and a lot of stuff has happened to me – that should have gone bad. But it feels like somebody has been watching over me, protecting me.' The freshness of his ordeal was overwhelming. 'I do have hope; the situation is so surreal. But I don't even know how I should be preparing, getting my affairs in order, my personal things, the project leadership.' He worried his rehabilitation programs would collapse without him. I was lost for words when he said, 'Just yesterday I heard news that I'm going to be executed by the end of the month. I thought, "Jeez, what can I do? What do I say to my family? What do I say?" I just don't know how I should be.' Articulating his torment, he tried to shield the bleak reality from his family. 'I try to avoid talking to them as much as possible,' he said – his mother, Raji, particularly. 'I rely on my brother to slowly break the news to my mum.'

His fellow inmates avoided him. 'How do you ask someone in that position how they are?' said Michael Czugaj.

Matthew Norman said what I thought: 'It seems like it cannot happen.' He went on, 'Everyone's devastated. You'd have to be a scum-like person if you don't show any emotion. No one is really talking about it.'

Dejected and confused, Sukumaran was alone in a cell after Martin Stephens had been transferred to an East Javanese jail. 'A lot of people have been avoiding me – guards and prisoners,' he said. 'Nobody really knows what to say to me in this situation. I can understand that. So far I don't know how to be.' With the creeping stench of death came an emptiness he tried to quell with food. 'I'm just eating everything I can find, till I feel sick, almost, binge eating.'

When I tentatively broached the subject of life after death, to my surprise he replied enthusiastically. 'I really, really hope there is, to get a second chance to improve. I was never good at anything. When I was at school, I had no interest. I didn't know you could have a career in art or study it at university. If someone had put pencils and paper in front of me, my life probably would have turned out differently.' He'd been revisiting his boyhood and teen years. 'I've been thinking a lot about memories with my family – the good days and the bad.' But there were blanks, spaces that he couldn't fill in, and this bothered him enormously. Though a future remained tangible that night, his words made me uneasy. 'I still paint like Ben but in a year or two I will have my own style.'

Of course he regretted gambling with his life, but he repeated what many say – that the follies of youth had simply gone too far. 'I knew about Indonesia's death penalty for drugs but I was only twenty-three, and I just didn't think. I felt invincible.' Wryly, he ruminated on how to prepare for execution while maintaining a degree of control and decorum – something he achieved in his final days, although not without a torturous journey. 'It's really hard. They're talking about the way it's going to be done.' He had researched his fate on the internet, and he described the last choice he would make before a hail of bullets would cut his life short. 'I'm allowed three choices: I can lie down, sit or stand,' he told me stoically. 'You can have a blindfold ... I hear all these stories now. We have had to research what happens. Everything is happening so fast. It's happening before they notify us. And everyone – the media – seems to know what's happening before we do.'

It was true. I cringed when the Indonesian authorities, by turns impassive and excitable, shared the most personal and macabre details – including a 'countdown' schedule – with the media. The condemned duo were the last to know what the world had already consumed.

Sukumaran almost whispered that he'd heard he would be kept naked for three days before execution – this turned out to be false. But bizarre official comments did not escape him. He smarted from a farcical aside by Indonesia's Attorney-General Muhammad Prasetyo: 'Myuran will have to wait for his turn.' He meant until Chan received the presidential decision on his clemency application. Sukumaran's plea had already been rejected on 7 January and it was expected Chan's would follow suit. If that were the case, the pair were to be executed together.

'It's a public spectacle, the way that they're talking about it ... it's like a joke,' Sukumaran went on.

More bewildered than bitter, Sukumaran mused on the meaning of the rehabilitation he and Chan had achieved while transforming the prison that had housed them for ten years. He saw it as a conundrum that their clemency bids had been refused. 'They [authorities] don't take our rehabilitation into account,' he said.

As his Australian barrister Julian McMahon said, 'Why kill what you have fixed? Why encourage the men to rehabilitate, then kill them when it happens?' This was the second time McMahon endured the excruciating task of watching his clients face execution, after the 2005 hanging in Singapore of Australian drug trafficker Van Tuong Nguyen. How McMahon coped with these harrowing experiences was unimaginable.

*

The shock waves of the impending executions reverberated through the scattered Bali Nine members. In early April, I flew to Malang, East Java, where couriers Tan Duc Thanh Nguyen and Martin Stephens, the eldest of the gang at forty-two, were transferred from Kerobokan in 2014 after violating prison rules.

Malang, a pretty colonial city with wide, tree-lined boulevards, had a shockingly overcrowded all-male jail. Nguyen appeared stunned when I showed up. Looking for a space to sit in the open-air visiting area, we squeezed onto a bench, the pungent smell of bad *bungkus* (takeaway food) in our faces. I watched Stephens picking his way through the crowds with his mother in tow on her precious annual visit.

Nguyen, a Brisbanite of Vietnamese descent, had been working out at the gym, his muscular torso the result of endless empty hours whiled away pumping iron. When I reminded him that a decade had passed since his arrest, Nguyen seemed dumbfounded. 'Ten years, already. It's a long time,' he muttered. He'd endured a two-year stint on death row, and he now spoke of his despair facing a life term. He hoped to launch his sixth appeal for a fixed term. 'It's a punishment. We can't do nothing. Since 2010, we have all been trying to apply for fixed terms. It's our right,' he said vehemently.

A month before the executions, I received a tormented letter from Stephens in which he feared rotting behind jail bars. 'It is more humane to just take me out the back and shoot me like Andrew and Myuran.'

Nguyen messaged me after the executions, saying he had followed the horror on TV. 'I couldn't believe it was happening. Step by step I watched it unfold. I will never forget what happened and the events leading up to it. Can't believe they are gone.'

Three years later, Nguyen was dead from stomach cancer.

*

Sukumaran lamented, 'After ten years I thought they'd give us a second chance. I thought, honestly, I would get clemency before. Now it's being taken away. I don't understand because I've been rehabilitated.'

Rehabilitation was pivotal to the duo's clemency bid. Every legal avenue was explored. The men's team, led by McMahon and Indonesian human rights lawyer Todung Mulya Lubis, lodged unprecedented second judicial reviews on 30 January 2015 in a last-ditch bid to save the pair. Their first 2011 reviews had failed to have their death sentences commuted.

The basis of the new application was that Indonesia's Supreme Court overlooked Chan's and Sukumaran's rehabilitation during their decade in prison. It was rejected due to a lack of new evidence.

Lubis was based in Jakarta, so his hectic schedule involved commutes between the capital and Bali. Notwithstanding interview bytes at the prison gates amid a sea of journalists, I found it increasingly difficult to pin him down. When he agreed to meet me after a jail visit to Chan and Sukumaran, I was delighted. Mysteriously, he told me over the phone he would apprise me of the location once his driver was on the way.

Several phone calls later, I taxied to the Sababay Winery in Gianyar, over an hour north of Kuta. In a tasting room, Lubis sat at a long table surrounded by staff and dozens of half-filled wine glasses. Smiling, he asked if I would like to sample the wine.

After two hours with his clients, Lubis clearly relished getting some distance from them. It allowed him to reflect on their impossible situation. The only legal recourse left, he told me, was the second judicial appeal.

Desperately, he considered the other remaining options: human rights appeals, an emphatic plea for greater Australian diplomatic action (*could I ramp it up?* he seemed to suggest) and the invocation of international law declaring the sanctity of life. Lubis knew the PKs were shaky and he was nervous.

He argued that at the very least, the condemned men were entitled to know the reasons for their clemency denial – which, he said, had never been provided.

Lubis looked tired. 'Myuran and Andrew expect to be given a second chance, to prove they are better people. They hope for a miracle. So many things are beyond our control.' He sighed. 'There's no certainty. It is extremely difficult. I tried to explain [to them] the legal reality – what the rules are and what the reality is. You come away [from the jail] thinking it may be the last time you see them. It's devastating, I've known them for a long time.'

When the second PKs were rejected on 4 February, Lubis and McMahon scrambled for further legal avenues. One was pending at the time of the executions – an Indonesia Constitutional Court challenge questioning the president's process of refusing clemency, and his obligation to consider the cases based on Chan's and

243

Sukumaran's rehabilitation. But it was not within the court's power to alter the death sentences.

On 28 April, the day before the executions, Lubis tweeted, 'I failed, I lost.' Then, on 29 April, 'I'm sorry.'

A year later, Lubis told me he remained deeply troubled by the executions. 'They [Sukumaran and Chan] had completely changed. I did everything I could as far as fighting under our legal system in Indonesia. But I don't have the power to stop the executions … I still find it hard to accept. I knew Myuran and Andrew very well, since 2008.'

Sukumaran's dream of being free to train under Quilty – a tantalising open offer – had been too good to be true. But in the end, he had painstakingly attained the control and decorum of a humble man. By all accounts, he achieved an inner peace in his final days. He was executed twelve days after his thirty-fourth birthday.

The last wishes of Chan and Sukumaran were for the global abolition of the death penalty.

*

For some respite during those months of intensive reporting, as I drove to interviews around Bali I listened to cheap CD copies of my favourite songs until they jammed and died. I was a sight, crying at the steering wheel. My tinted windows insulated me against tourist clatter – and some expats (themselves drug users) who spouted appalling invective about the condemned pair. I honed my playlist to the dulcet tones of Nick Drake and turned up the volume. I couldn't register that the two men's lives were about to end in such a barbaric and pointless fashion. Who could?

My friend Russell Darnley – an Australian author and an Indonesia watcher – later asked me if journalists had been offered counselling for post-traumatic stress disorder by employers. I hadn't thought about it but it was a fair question. Like everyone, I had reacted to a breaking story. But for me it had become an unhealthy obsession.

I was consumed by the story as it unfolded in a surreal, macabre sequence. For four months I thought about nothing else. Day after day I would go to bed with the thought of the executions ringing in my head, wake in the night obsessed with them and unsure of my bearings, then immerse myself from early morning. While I bashed out copy, sometimes still in my pyjamas at midday, media outlets in Australia periodically called to ask me to go on air. I was always too busy.

About 2.30 a.m. on 4 March, the duo's transfer began from Kerobokan jail in a farcical display of military force. Riot police and elite paramilitary police known as Brimob (the Mobile Brigade Corps) were deployed outside the jail. In chaotic scenes, Chan and Sukumaran were loaded into a Barracuda armoured vehicle and taken to Bali's airport, where they boarded a chartered commercial plane to Cilacap at 7 a.m., tailed by two Sukhoi fighter jets.

Bizarre photos starting leaking in local and international media around 10 a.m. on 4 March. My heart sank when I saw police chief Djoko Hari Utomo grinning out of a macabre photo. He was standing in the plane's aisle, his arm draped around Chan's shoulder; the ashen-faced Chan had a catatonic stare, and he was surrounded by paramilitary officers in balaclavas. In another photo, Sukumaran was pictured talking to the chief cop, whose arm rested casually on the condemned man's shoulder. Djoko's happy snaps drew international outrage and amplified the diplomatic storm between Australia and Indonesia.

The photos had been shot by guards and leaked to fixers who'd sold them as exclusives for up to A$600 each. They'd first landed on Indonesian media websites through intermediaries. I'd been offered two photos for A$500. I was sent one, via various channels, of Chan in his seat looking as though he was about to break down. Djoko had his back to the camera while another officer was smiling broadly in the background. Another showed Chan in handcuffs on the tarmac in Cilacap, now a well-publicised picture. I was told they were exclusives, so I sent them to *The Australian*'s picture editor Milan Scepanovic, who was keen to buy them. But I sensed something was wrong, the source was not one I trusted. When Milan discovered News Corp had already bought the photos, he was miffed. I suggest you tell them to jump, he emailed. It was nauseating to discover there was horse-trading over Chan's and Sukumaran's lives.

I later visited Djoko at Bali's police headquarters amid irate calls for his head. Clad in an Islamic tunic and prayer cap, He was praying at the police *musholla* (prayer room). 'I am really sad about the Bali Nine. I really have a feeling to make them happy,' he told me, looking fatigued. 'It was not a selfie. It was taken for police documentation.' When I asked if his job was compromised, he said he didn't know, but added that he'd received a reprimand from his superiors. It turned out that he was finished in Bali, his career besmirched. He was quietly moved to another island, I later heard. That was the end of my reliable tip-offs.

But this didn't weigh heavily on my mind. My thoughts were on Sukumaran and Chan. They had arrived on Cilacap's tarmac haggard, manacled and shackled. After being photographed amid masked security guards, they'd been hustled on to another armoured vehicle amid the pandemonium of more police and military vehicles, and ferried across the strait to Death Island. They would be there in isolation for nearly two months before their execution.

On 4 March I worked through the night during their transfer, and by lunchtime the next day I told the newsdesk I needed a couple of hours' sleep.

Though I stayed in Bali while my colleague Peter Alford was in Cilacap, off Nusa Kambangan, I had sources on the penal island.

One described the growing stench of fear as condemned death-row inmates waited for Sukumaran and Chan to arrive.

'Everybody is waiting for the Bali Nine. When the Bali Nine [pair] arrive, they know execution is a reality. It's going to happen,' my source said.

In the seventy-two hours before their executions, Chan and Sukumaran consoled the other little-known condemned, relating their stories to the outside world while escalating a relentless campaign to end the death penalty from their isolation cells.

From the maximum-security Besi prison, Sukumaran painted haunting self-portraits in his isolation cell, which were ferried across a two-kilometre narrow strait and displayed to journalists on Cilacap's Wijaya Pura dock.

Just after midnight on 29 April, amid outpourings of grief and vigils in Cilacap and in Australia, Sukumaran and Chan were executed by firing squad.

Chan had led the prisoners in prayer and effusive song while tied to stakes. In their final moments, they sang 'Amazing Grace' and 'Bless the Lord O My Soul', silenced by bullets mid-song. They had eschewed blindfolds to stare down their executioners.

*

Shortly before the two batches of 2015 executions, elite police honed their target skills at a new firing range near the water's edge, behind a police station, close to Nusa Kambangan's port entrance.

The range, replacing a hilly execution site, was erected by Sumatran engineers and had an official opening ceremony in November 2014, a month after President Widodo was first sworn in.

A banner at the site declared: *peresmian lapangan tembak* (inauguration of a firing range). It even had a name: *Tunggal Panaluan*, meaning magic staff.

A *tunggal panaluan* is used by shamans of the ethnic Batak people in north Sumatra's highlands to ward off disaster. The staff is traditionally made from wood carved with human figures, adorned with horsehair and cooked human brains from sacrificial victims.

During an assignment on Indonesia's death penalty, in 2017, I had glimpsed the range, mostly obscured by thick jungle, from a fishing boat off the restricted island.

The island's seven-prison super-max complex houses drug convicts, terrorists, murderers and graft inmates. Those executed, mainly drug felons, were returned to Cilacap by ambulance and placed in coffins, made while they were still alive, with their names, dates of birth and death already inscribed.

Locals were haunted by the ghosts of the executed. They feared unanchored ghosts had flown off the cliffs.

'If you don't have something hard behind the person being shot (a wall or bank), the bullets go through them and can go anywhere. Locals are afraid of spirits knocking around,' the resident Cilacap Catholic priest, Father Charlie Burrows, told me.

Burrows had lived in Cilacap since 1973. The 74-year-old, a spiritual counsellor to Nusa Kambangan's death-row inmates, was also deeply involved with the local community.

When ten of fourteen drug felons bound for the firing squad were spared at the last minute in July 2016, the reason wasn't clear. Violent lightning and thunderstorms that lashed Nusa Kambangan that night had blown up the electricity transformer, and ten remained in their cells.

It was also a sacred, auspicious night in the Javanese calendar: *Malam Jumat Kliwon* (the night before Friday), when the Javanese fear evil spirits wreak havoc. The locals attributed the storm causing the blackout to a supernatural event. 'They saw it as a sign the spirits were not happy about the executions,' said Burrows.

*

It was no small matter either that evil spirits and ghosts of hundreds of communist sympathisers roamed the island. Many had died of hunger or been killed and buried in mass graves on Nusa Kambangan during Indonesia's 1965–66 anti-communist purges. The massacres had been hushed up and the location of the graves, engulfed by jungle, was hazy; the incarcerated had simply disappeared, an island insider disclosed. But eleven island executions have been publicly listed as 'subversion, (politics, 1965 cases)'.

Dutch colonialists in the sixteenth century found the island ideal for a fortress before developing secure prisons.

In its current incarnation, locals believe the past is merged, and that their ancestors were reincarnated as panthers, leopards, monkeys, snakes and other animals.

A land clearer told Burrows he had seen locals 'running up trees like monkeys and slithering around the ground like snakes and other creatures'.

Though Bali was not seriously considered for the 2015 executions, the then governor, Made Mangku Pastika, strongly rejected the possibility. He was afraid evil spirits and karma would curse Bali and drive away the lucrative tourist trade.

*

For four months from 17 January until 29 April I'd been out of circulation, speaking only with my children and those involved in this gruesome, surreal story: my colleague, *The Australian's* Jakarta correspondent, Peter Alford; my fixer, Firdia Lisnawati; my photographer, Sonny Tumbelaka; the Sydney newsdesk; and my sources. The bright sunny world of normality had ceased to exist.

22

NEST OF VIPERS

After the executions, an eerie lull settled over Bali. Intense months-long coverage in Indonesia abated; foreign journalists went home, and the roar of outrage dimmed. In the emptiness, grief and a belated sense of shock gripped Kerobokan inmates. They were gutted. For a while, Myuran Sukumaran's studio remained deserted. The six surviving Bali Nine members on life terms lay low, terrified and morose. No one broached the prospect of an appeal. They would wait until things calmed, they told me.

In early May, on my visit to Scott Rush at Karangasem jail, I wondered how he was coping. Sitting in his visiting cage, he told me he hadn't watched TV coverage of the executions and detached himself from the final moments before Sukumaran and Chan were shot. 'It was overwhelming,' he said. 'It's been on my mind a lot. It makes me feel sick … Why do they deserve to be killed?' The executions had revived his fears from five years of living under the shadow of his own death, and for the past fortnight he had been severely depressed, hiding out in his cell to avoid talking to other inmates.

It was then that he suddenly dropped a bombshell, retracting his decade-long court testimony that Chan had threatened him to participate in the smuggling plot despite alleging this at his 2005 trial. Rush's timing was poignant, given my story was published the day of Sukumaran's funeral on 9 May.

'I lied in court,' Rush told me. 'I wrote a letter [later] to try and clear Andrew's name and say that I wasn't threatened by him. Even till now, I feel guilty about it. I always did. I wrote in the letter that at no time did either of those guys [including Sukumaran] threaten me.' In December 2005, Rush had testified in the Denpasar District Court that Chan said, 'You do as I say, don't mess around with me. I've got a gun with me and I could kill you.' At Chan's 2006 trial he'd denied making these threats; he was sentenced to death the following day. At the time, Michael Czugaj confirmed Rush's account as being true. Mules Martin Stephens and Renae Lawrence also alleged Chan had threatened them.

Two days after publication, the piece provoked a barrage of abusive phone messages from an expat visitor friend of Rush's who felt the story legally endangered Rush. Then from Rush himself, on 12 May, came an avalanche of exceptionally abusive texts and he physically threatened me. Over our years of conversations, many went unpublished but I'd felt Rush had wanted this off his chest and I was surprised he turned on me.

*

I took a routine family break in Sydney for a couple of weeks in late May. In the newsroom, where I was welcomed back, I felt as though I had returned from war – and, in a sense, I had. The executions were profoundly challenging, unlike any story I had covered.

The prolonged months of reporting such a macabre story – involving people I knew personally – had taken on a surreal twist. I frequently imagined myself in their shoes, tied to a stake in a jungle clearing and facing a firing squad.

On home turf I found a circuit-breaker. A wave of relief washed over me. The nightmare didn't completely subside, but I was no longer in the eye of the storm.

I revisited my fascination for Indonesian terrorism and its radical players, pitching ideas to my editors. I would be filing from Java on the jihadi trail for much of the second half of the year.

On my return to Indonesia in June, I travelled with a guide to Serang in the province of Banten, west of Jakarta, where we visited a small cemetery. A nondescript grave, the only one without a headstone, provided little hint it held the remains of the terrorist who authored the 2002 Bali carnage.

The cemetery was deserted except for a foraging brood of chickens. Buried beneath bamboo groves at the back was Imam Samudra, executed in 2008 beside accomplices Amrozi and his older brother Mukhlas for their roles in the 2002 Bali bombings. I studied the crude grave from every angle, finding it difficult to believe the bomber lay beneath the small inconsequential mound. The topsoil was blanketed with pebbles, a scattering of twigs and dead leaves, with an asymmetrical rock at the top daubed with rudimentary blue letters reading 'Imam'. Samudra had requested an ascetic resting place, his younger brother, Lulu Jamaludin, explained after we met later that afternoon.

The dirt graveyard was only a few metres from Samudra's family home. Seven years had passed since November 2008, when his funeral had attracted a seething hysterical mass of people to his resting place. Jamaludin had escorted his brother's body – freshly executed by firing squads on Nusa Kambangan – in a chaotic procession of thousands of hardcore supporters through his village to the mosque before the burial. Similar scenes ensued in Lamongan, East Java, when the bodies of brothers Amrozi and Mukhlas arrived home to throngs of hardliners – and to the police who stood outside, fearing a backlash. Wrapped in black cloth laid with Koranic inscriptions, Samudra's body was carried through groups of armed police by fist-waving supporters jostling to touch the corpse. Jamaludin, in a white Islamic tunic, chanted wildly amid the uproar.

In his home town, Samudra was revered by a tight-knit extremist network of family and supporters. At the graveyard entrance, a couple of loitering young men told us that vigils were carried out by hardliners gathering in the deep of night 'to feel closer to their hero', who was committed to martyrdom and violent jihad.

Samudra, the engineer and computer expert turned field commander of the Bali bombings, in death, was a magnet.

The radical supporters pocketed handfuls of the stones and soil covering the grave, believing them to be sacrosanct – and Samudra's family regularly replenished them.

The narrow streets in Serang where Samudra had grown up were dusty and hot, the houses wedged between tiny *warungs*, with the mosque in the centre.

My guide had a contact who knew Jamaludin and we drove across town to interview the forty-year-old, a social worker on his lunchbreak, these days dressed in Western clothes. We met him in the lobby of a large hotel.

'Some visitors see [my brother] as a hero,' said Jamaludin. 'Many followers come from Java and Sumatra', hotbeds of jihadist activity.

I'd anticipated a tell-all interview. But why Samudra attracted hordes of hardcore followers to his graveside seemed to elude Jamaludin. Bizarrely, he denied his brother was a terrorist, least of all a Bali bomber. 'I don't believe that my brother can make a big bomb like the one in Bali. There are no facts to support it. I don't believe my brother had anything to do with this. Even when his family asked him, he didn't admit to it.' He added plaintively, 'I wish the police would find the real Bali bombers. I am still questioning who the bombers are.'

Thirteen years had passed since the bombings. Stunned, I turned to my guide for clarification. Clearly Jamaludin was delusional; indeed, he'd meant what he'd said.

'The state killed Samudra, and it was the wrong thing. He was innocent,' Jamaludin continued. He added that the jailed Bali bomber Ali Imron had betrayed Samudra, and that he had been incriminated by Imron's statement alone.

It was true that the remorseful Imron had provided evidence against his brothers and Samudra, and it had helped put them before the firing squad while delivering him a life sentence in 2003.

Jamaludin went on. 'Islamic people who carry out *shaheed* violence are labelled terrorists. This is discriminatory against Muslims. I have jihadist thoughts; there are many kinds of jihad. I would like to die *shaheed* [as a martyr].'

Then he made a minor confession: he knew the Bali bombers' spiritual mentor Abu Bakar Bashir 'a little'. But there, Jamaludin stopped short. Possibly I could interview Samudra's mother and sister, he said when I expressed exasperation. Then he backflipped, deciding his mother was too old and frail.

Rankled, I returned to the village to find his mother, accompanied by my guide. Alighting from the car wearing a headscarf, I felt eyes boring into me from behind drawn curtains, alleyways and buildings. The streets emptied suddenly, and menace saturated the air. I had entered their subaltern world, as Noor Huda Ismail, my counter-terror contact, described it.

'They're living among us, but they have different values.'

As an infidel Western journalist, I was seen to be living under the yoke of imperialism. Anti-government, anti-democracy, the Islamic extremists considered me the embodiment of everything abhorrent. In Serang, I was a vulnerable outsider. Each step we took towards the mosque felt leaden and observed; my guide entered to pray, and mingled. I waited nervously outside like a red flag. When she emerged, she had a description of Samudra's families' homes, just a few steps away. One contained the small shop of Jamaludin's sister, Mila Jamilah, who hid in the back. Samudra's cousin, preparing food, similarly disappeared. His mother, Embay Badriah, was nowhere to be seen.

*

In a chilling echo from the grave, Samudra's legacy endured through his eldest son Umar Jundral Haq. The nineteen-year-old was – as Nasir Abas told me – fulfilling his parents' request when he fought in Syria with Islamic State for almost two years, before he died there in October 2015.

One day, as Abas and I had talked in a plush Jakarta hotel lobby, he recalled Samudra exhorting Umar to engage in jihad. 'Since he was a child, Samudra said, "When you grow up you should be mujahid, carry guns and fight against the government." All of them who went to Syria will get training to carry guns, to mix a bomb, so if they come back to Indonesia … it will be dangerous.'

Jamaludin had denied Umar's involvement with IS. He'd told me his nephew moved frequently and lived in a *pesantren*, whose name evaded him. 'Umar is not interested in radical Islam. He's still a student, he lives with his mum.'

After the young militant's death, a message was passed around radical circles trumpeting his martyrdom: 'My son Umar … is a martyr. Hope is unshakable … May the angels bathe my son, bring fragrant shrouds. May the inhabitants of the heavens welcome with kindness my son's spirit.'

At our meeting in June 2015, Jamaludin had been equally vague about the whereabouts of Samudra's wife. 'Not in a *pesantren* in Solo,' he'd muttered, contradicting my contact, Taufik Andrie.

Andrie had earlier told me Samudra's wife taught at the Ulil Albab Islamic boarding school in Solo, raising her four children on a fundamentalist diet.

Jamaludin's furtiveness perhaps reflected Banten's history of far-reaching tenatacles and binding radical networks. The Banten Ring – part of Samudra's network – was responsible for the 2004 Australian Embassy bombing in Jakarta that killed ten people. It provided recruits for bombings by Jemaah Islamiah and was involved in military training in Aceh, at Sumatra's northern tip. Through Samudra, the ring – a faction of Darul Islam (House of Islam) movement, whose goal was an Indonesian Islamic state – had worked on the 2002 Bali bombings. The radical anti-colonialist movement, now dismantled, was established in Indonesia in 1942 by Muslim militias.

More than a decade on from the Australian Embassy bombing, the son of the Banten Ring's late leader, Kang Djaja, reportedly had a son fighting in Syria, while another member involved in the 2002 bombings, Abdul Rauf, had died fighting for Islamic State. Since the defeat of IS, it was unclear where many of the offspring of terrorists who had survived Syria's battlefields had ended up – but some had returned to Indonesia, and many were lying low. I knew that first hand because those I tracked down were too scared to talk to me.

It was assumed others remained in Syria. The parents did not mourn the loss when their sons were killed, Taufik Andrie told me one evening at the café of my Jakarta hotel. 'They're happy and proud,' as Umar's family had been. 'They often have *shaheed* ceremonies as a celebration.' The lure of Islamic State had equated to 'the new Afghanistan', when Indonesian JI alumni had fought alongside Afghan mujahideen against the Soviet invasion in the '80s.

Over my years in Indonesia, I reported bombings, threats, the rise of splinter groups, frontline roles of women, and the use of social media as a radicalising tool. With the Middle East caliphate a shattered dream by March 2019, there was a void. My contacts pondered, what next? As Western countries grappled with the dilemma of nationals begging to go home, so Indonesia wondered how to handle hundreds stranded in Syrian prisons and refugee camps after fleeing the last ISIS stronghold of Baghouz. While fears prevailed that jihadist returnees would use their combat skills back home, analysts were concerned about militants reorganising at home, and a revitalised Jemaah Islamiah.

Sidney Jones, a terrorist analyst who I had known since 2011, was one of my best sources. The director of the Jakarta-based Institute for Policy Analysis of Conflict, told me in 2019, 'The threat right now is not from foreign fighters, it's from people who never left.'

23

THE LAST TERRORIST

The bonds of terror networks had few degrees of separation, and in October 2015 I met the nemesis of the executed Bali bombers. While on a sunset beach walk, I received a call confirming an interview with the jailed Bali bomber Ali Imron, the sole survivor of the inner circle behind the 2002 atrocities. My interview coincided with the eve of the thirteenth anniversary of the carnage. It was in the palm of my hands – as long as I could reach Jakarta by nine the next morning. I bolted, from beach to home to Bali's airport, brushing sand from my toes in the taxi.

Imron would also participate in a documentary tracking his deradicalisation from violent extremism, shot by South-East Asia terror specialist Rohan Gunaratna and his team. But I would have special access to Imron. As it happened, I spent an entire day with him, immersed in his deranged jihadi lexicon. This aptly bookended my terrorism series, which had taken me on a wild ride through the archipelago.

In counter-terror circles, some said Imron turned extremist lives around. In the process, he became something of a cause célèbre among counterterrorist specialists who picked his brains about how to defuse the terrorist threat. Sidney Jones is one who thought Imron had formed a 'new understanding', her belief fortified by a released terrorist inmate who credited Imron for his deradicalisation.

I wasn't so sure. Despite his remorse for his role in the bombings, I found his empathy for his victims and their families unconvincing and disingenuous. His vociferous rantings and contrariness jarred. And his disturbing outbursts harking back to Indonesia's worst act of terror have lingered with me.

*

Rohan Gunaratna, who headed the Singapore-based International Centre for Political Violence and Terrorism Research, had known I was waiting for this opportunity – but when he called me as I walked along the beach, it was already 7 p.m. in Bali. 'Meet me at 9 a.m. tomorrow at police HQ,' he said over the phone. 'Tito will be there.' He was referring to General Tito Karnavian, the then Jakarta police chief whose astute helmsmanship had fast-tracked him to national police head within a year, and later to Minister for Home Affairs in October 2019.

An authority on Indonesian and regional terrorism, Karnavian had begun his trajectory as a commander of Detachment 88 – or Densus 88 – a crack counterterrorist squad created in the wake of the 2002 Bali bombings. He had masterminded the 2009 killing in Solo of Indonesia's most wanted Islamic extremist, Malaysian-born Noordin Mohammad Top, a financier, bomb maker, recruiter and trainer for JI.

When it came to jihadist ideology and networks, Karnavian was intimately attuned. He claimed his knowledge of interconnected networks of the Afghan alumni, friendship, kinship and marriage groups had been crucial in uncovering the inner circle of Noordin Top. He was also my conduit to Imron, who'd been convicted for helping to assemble and transport bombs in order to kill hundreds of foreigners.

I just made a 9 p.m. Jakarta-bound flight. Only once the plane was airborne did I relax. It was after midnight when I settled at a hotel and grabbed a few hours' sleep. In a change of plan, I met Gunaratna not at police HQ but at his hotel, the JW Marriott. He was a sight to behold in his pressed pin-striped suit and tie, a sartorial achievement in the steamy heat in anyone's books.

The Marriott was a bombing target in both 2003 and 2009. Twin suicide attacks at the Marriott and adjoining Ritz-Carlton hotel in 2009 had claimed nine at the Marriott. To that end, Gunaratna's documentary included the Marriott's upgraded security procedures – so prolonged and punctilious that death by boredom in transit seemed more likely than dying in a terror attack.

We headed to Polda in the city's south, where Imron was detained. Karnavian was keen to draw on Gunaratna's strategies aimed at tamping down radical ideology that spawned politically charged violence. In that vein, the police chief's expansive quarters were sequestered for the unusual event, and a makeshift film studio was painstakingly erected in the conference room. Swarms of undercover cops crowded in, anticipating Imron's arrival from the cells. We mingled in Karnavian's improvised dining room, hovering over the backdrop of an extensive buffet lunch in silver tureens, the contents of which appeared glutinous and unappetising. A weird buzz permeated the room. More police arrived, squeezing into hallways and adjoining outer rooms. Karnavian welcomed me and chatted sanguinely about Imron's ability to propagate deradicalisation strategies to hardline inmates. He worked the room and checked Gunaratana was on track for what evolved into a long day.

A sudden frisson and there he was, like an apparition. Ali Imron, almost an iconic figure, stood beaming, a rictus grin nearly splitting his face. Police absorbed him, wrapping arms around his shoulders, like he was a stalwart mate. He moved easily round the room, basking in the limelight, free from handcuffs. He wore neatly pressed Western attire rather than the ankle-length pants defining the style of radical Islamists. His smile revealed perfect white teeth.

All care had been taken to preserve the remnants of the shocking night of the bombings in the hope Imron's inside knowledge – forensically sifted over the years – would be channelled into deradicalisation prison programs. The general record for prison deradicalisation was woeful, with recruitment, study groups and the creation of new cells, ongoing problems, though in 2018 Taufiq Andrie said there had been a slight improvement, 'nothing drastic'.

That day, Imron seemed eager to ensure his imprint on radical history didn't fade – not that there was any chance it would. Despite his unsettling tirades, he appeared razor-sharp. Twelve years behind bars hadn't dulled memories of a childhood steeped in extremism and a jihadist trajectory that ended in his ultimate act of terror: the 2002 Bali bombings. They were crystal clear. But his eyes – dark, unfathomable pools – led to a seemingly disturbing void.

I searched in vain for something that pointed to a conscience.

Imron didn't eat the lunch. I sat at a table flanked by him, Karnavian and my interpreter. All eyes were on him as I began my interview. Suddenly, in a booming voice, Imron exhorted, 'We are the pioneers of jihad in Indonesia – not ISIS. I and my veteran colleagues … are the Jemaah Islamiah group that initiated terrorist attacks on behalf of Islam. ISIS is the new kid on the block. Let's calculate who has been more involved in jihad,' he challenged, playing to his captive audience. 'ISIS is a kindergarten in my eyes.'

We were all riveted; the room was was deathly silent. Karnavian appeared slightly uncomfortable – this was his poster boy for deradicalisation.

Imron, at thirty-two, had driven a van loaded with a 1.1-tonne bomb close to Kuta's Sari Club in an attack aimed against innocent tourists. He had trained the two suicide bombers who blew up the Sari and Paddy's nightclubs, then escaped on a motorbike. 'I myself drove the car to the Sari Club for the Bali bombing. When I drove back to Denpasar I heard the car bomb explode loudly. I was shocked for a few minutes when I heard the explosion. It was so big. I could not smile. I could not cry. I was just silent. I was glad the operation was successful, but I felt sad that Muslims were killed.'

How had he *felt*, I asked, when he saw the aftermath: shocking pictures of his victims, many burnt beyond recognition, with limbs blown off?

His reply sounded recited, wooden and somewhat weary, 'Many times I have apologised. Whether it was with me or without me, the Bali bombing would have still happened.' However, despite his numerous public apologies for the Bali atrocities, nothing suggested Imron had empathy for his victims. 'The Bali bomb was a big mistake,' he said, staring into my eyes. 'I tried hard to stop the violent operations. I stated I was wrong and I regret it and I've apologised. I admit guilt. I've said that since when I was arrested … I'm sorry about the victims and their families.'

Now paraded as a model of deradicalisation, Imron – who isn't isolated and mixes with inmates convicted of terrorism and narcotics charges – preached 'peaceful jihad' outside jail, proselytising against extremism to youth and radicals. 'I have pioneered deradicalisation programs with authorities. I was the driving force,' he told me proudly.

Had the forty-five-year-old, with his impeccable ties to al-Qaeda-linked JI, genuinely changed, I asked Karnavian later in his office.

A quietly spoken man, he replied, 'No, he is not really reformed. He is still thinking of an Islamic caliphate, he is still aiming at implementing Islamic sharia in Indonesia, but the way to achieving that goal has already changed from violent to non-violent. It's good progress but not fully moderate.'

Yes, Imron affirmed, his goal for an Islamic state hadn't diminished, but he also laid the blame at his brother's feet. 'I was involved in some bomb operations and the biggest was in Bali. I had to be involved for the victory of Islam and I will continue with this goal. I was instructed by my brother Mukhlas, also a senior JI member.'

The photos I shot of Imron that day portray a strange mix of features. He was a slouched and stunted figure with a childlike demeanour, whose middle age had eluded him. His round, pudgy face was defined by a meaty mouth. Slightly cross-eyed, he stared out: dead holes in a doughy mass.

His stints outside jail to promote deradicalisation allowed him more freedom than his victims' families and survivors of the Bali bomb attacks would have liked or could have imagined. For the past ten years he'd published a blog on deradicalisation at aliimron.com under the auspices of the national counterterrorism agency (BNPT), a website that it ostensibly monitors. His life was more fulfilling than perhaps it could ever have been if he hadn't committed his crime. He wrote his first book behind bars – *Ali Imron Sang Pengebom* (*Ali Imron, the Bomber*), published in 2007 – which dealt with the Bali bombing and his professed remorse. Karnavian was encouraging Imron to write another on Islamic State, but Imron professed to abhor IS for its inferior dogma. Running on high emotion, he repeated that JI had everything over IS. He railed and jeered at his IS 'competitors'.

In the 1990s Imron had completed combat and explosives training in Pakistan and Afghanistan, then joined Mukhlas in the Darul Islam (House of Islam) movement. 'Although I disagreed with the Bali bombing, I joined anyway,' Imron continued. 'I wanted a revolution in Indonesia, especially for Muslims, and we tried to establish an Islamic state.' Emboldened by the attention of the crowd in the room, his voice suddenly rose, laden with fiery rhetoric as well as excuses. 'I was the first of the Afghan alumni to prepare a big bomb operation … no Indonesian terrorist had prepared as well as me,' he boasted. 'Our collection [of weapons and ammunition] was much bigger than what other Indonesian terrorists had. No terrorist in Indonesia has carried a one-tonne bomb like me. I have been a militant since I was ten years old.'

Ordered by Samudra, a 'field commander' in the plot, to find the most crowded Bali nightclubs in order to target unbelievers – decadent Americans and their allies – Imron claimed he'd tried to dissuade Mukhlas. 'The motivation was jihad against *bule* [foreigners] in Bali. Mukhlas ordered me. It was against war, oppression. The big boss was Bashir, but I don't know if he ordered the attack.'

Abu Bakar Bashir had always denied being involved in the crime, and a guilty verdict against him for conspiracy relating to the bombings was overturned in 2006. He had then been imprisoned in 2011 for fifteen years for inciting terrorism and financing an Aceh-based terrorist cell. An uproar ended Bashir's chances of a presidential release in 2019, with Widodo accused of courting the Muslim vote ahead of the April election. 'I remonstrated with Imam Samudra on whether bombing tourists was true and legitimate jihad,' Imron said. 'I was against the Bali bombing. I asked if it was justified based on the principles of Islam. The idea was to get back at the Americans for the invasion of Afghanistan [in 2001]. There was no intention to attack Australians, but it didn't matter if other nationalities were involved.'

Mukhlas had approved Samudra's proposal at a meeting in Solo, Central Java. In 1998 a fatwa issued by al-Qaeda leader Osama bin Laden had legitimised the bombings. 'Bin Laden said fighting foreigners was part of true jihad,' Imron went on.

Recalling the rallying call to jihad at age ten from his eldest brother Mukhlas, with whom he had the closest of bonds, Imron described his journey into a heart of darkness, his initiation, and the years of militant training and fighting since the 1980s. According to him, Mukhlas – whom Imron had idolised and obeyed – bore most of the blame. 'Mukhlas was my biggest influence. I looked up to him. It started when I was at elementary school. I was ten. Mukhlas was teaching me how to found an Islamic state when he was at al-Mukmin at Ngruki. Mukhlas was seventeen.' Indirectly, Bashir's radical indoctrination had been the catalyst for Imron's jihadist path. 'Mukhlas joined jihad in [Soviet-occupied] Afghanistan in 1985. I was still at home in high school. I did whatever Mukhlas said. Now I realise the bombing was counter-productive for Islam. It was wrong jihad. I will not do it again and I hope no one else does.'

Imron came across as simultaneously proud of and repentant about his jihadist roots. I couldn't tell if he was angling for sympathy when he disclosed he was considered an apostate by violent jihadists. His cooperation with police and denunciation of jihad had triggered death threats from visitors. 'I am labelled *kafir* [infidel] by my own people. I am not afraid. My blood is halal. It is legitimate to kill me,' he said, referring to sharia law, which was implemented in Aceh in 2005.

Imron then aired an extraordinary new grievance involving Australian and Dutch non-governmental organisations in Ambon. During the 1999 sectarian conflict in Ambon between Christians and Muslims, in which Imron and other JI veterans – including the alleged financier and organiser of the 2002 Bali bombings, Hambali – had waged jihad, he claimed Australians had offered Christians IDR5 million (about A$500) for each Muslim they killed. Hambali, whose real name is Encep Nurjaman, is the alleged operational mastermind of Jemaah Islamiah and has been described as the Osama bin Laden of Southeast Asia. Charged with murder and attempted murder, he has been controversially imprisoned at

Guantanamo Bay without trial since 2006 but is soon expected to face a military court.

'Why Australians became an important consideration by the brothers was because ... when we arrested some [Christians] they said they were paid by Australia and the Dutch. Each head of a Muslim was to be rewarded with five million rupiah. We have to believe it's true because Christians volunteered the information ... it came from Christians we arrested. This is our legal basis for why Australia became a target, because their coalition is American, and Australia was involved in the killing operation in Ambon.' However, 'the Bali bombing was not because of that', he continued; the plotters were unaware that Australians were at the Sari Club.

Many who had seen 'ground zero', the cavernous crater left after the bomb detonated, stood by the theory that the Bali bombers' ammonium nitrate bombs were ill-equipped to cause such destruction and it was a CIA job. Abu Bakar Bashir's claim that the bombs were replaced with a 'micro-nuclear' weapon by the CIA met with derision by Imron, who scoffed, 'Other Muslims said the bomb wasn't made by me, Mukhlas and Amrozi. America was not involved in the Bali bomb. It was purely made by us. I am making this statement so other Muslims can learn the lessons of the Bali bomb. It was wrong.'

A few months before I met Imron, he'd been confronted by two Bali bomb widows, Ni Luh Erniati and Nyoman Rencini, and a Melbourne man, Jan Laczynski, five of whose friends were killed in the Sari Club blast. The confrontation took place during an SBS interview at the jail. I had interviewed the widows previously; they were resilient, but I doubted they came away from the jail that day with a sense of relief or closure. And when Imron had offered his outstretched hand, Laczynski couldn't bring himself to shake it. Speaking about this confrontation, Imron told me with obvious surprise, 'I had no problem meeting them but when I asked to shake the Australian man's hand he refused and he showed a feeling of anger and hatred on his face. When I talked about myself, I felt strongly burdened.' Later, as I turned to leave, Imron smiled at me disconcertingly and said Laczynski had shaken his hand in the end.

Laczynski later strongly disputed this in an outraged letter to the editor and in a Twitter post: 'I did NOT shake his hand! He needs to get his eyes tested or wear glasses! I have no regrets about refusing to shake his hand or forgive.'

At tables piled with empty lunch dishes, police leant in, transfixed, their gimlet-eyed gaze on Imron as he answered my questions in Indonesian and they were interpreted. In the extraordinary interview, Imron pontificated on the differences between JI and Islamic State. He opposed the latter because of its ideological differences with JI. 'I do not respect what it is doing. The ideology of ISIS is not representative of what a caliphate should be. The Islamic caliphate has already been declared by the Prophet Muhammad. It is not written anywhere in the Koran that you can carry out atrocities such as beheadings. Their bloody brutality makes me sick. Also, not all infidels are eligible to be killed. Jihad has its own procedure and ethics. ISIS is very dangerous for Indonesia.'

'Did you regard the bombings as less brutal than Islamic State tactics?' I asked.

'There are similarities and differences in the level of violence. It's different because ISIS is perpetrating violence against Muslim brothers.'

I couldn't establish if he still thought it was acceptable to kill non-Muslims.

Gunaratna had met Imron a decade before and acknowledged that Imron's remorse might not be genuine, but he maintained confidence in him. 'When he was first arrested he showed the classic ideology, that it is permissible to kill non-Muslims, especially Westerners. He has realised it is wrong to kill.' Gunaratna had patiently waited for his interview, and now everyone piled into the conference room with Imron. A blanket of silence fell with the recording of the documentary. 'Is Ali Imron truly committed to peace?' Gunartana began, staring at him. Cue Imron, who spoke tirelessly of his rehabilitation and his influence on other extremists.

The show over, several police officers filed into Karnavian's office, where he sat at the head of an oval table. I sat down too, just as an animated Imron bounded through the door, wrapped his arms around Karnavian and the others, and joined the conversation in an incongruous display of camaraderie.

After a photo shoot outside the HQ, about fifteen of us squashed into the mini-van, minus Gunaratna who travelled separately. As we drove back, one of the researchers behind me repeatedly vomited into a small paper bag. Perhaps Imron had got to him, or the lunch had. In any case, none of his colleagues suggested stopping the van; they just looked out the window. The odour was unbearable, and I was relieved to escape to my hotel.

The following day I met privately with Karnavian. He revealed Imron had appealed to former president Susilo Bambang Yudhoyono to reduce his life sentence to twenty years, but the matter had been unresolved when President Widodo took office in 2014. Shocked, I asked Karnavian what he thought the reaction in Australia might be. 'We encouraged him to try to get a lighter sentence but we think our government will consider the response from the Australian community.' A reduced sentence would likely provoke a backlash, he pondered. 'We suggested he communicate with other radicals to influence them away from extremism.' It was difficult to change the mindset of radicals, he admitted.

Imron's family still lived among extremist networks at the radical Islamic school where the 2002 Bali bombs had been planned in Tenggulun, Lamongan, East Java. His wife had regularly visited him until about 2014. His daughter was in 2015 reportedly enrolled at al-Mukmin Ngruki Islamic boarding school in Solo, the notorious hub for JI recruits the Bali bombers had attended. It was there that Bashir had preached jihad to Mukhlas, Amrozi and Ali Imron, driving the violent cycle that led to the Bali carnage. If Imron were ever released, it would be to his home town in Lamongan that he would return – an unconscionable prospect, no doubt, for the survivors and families of the victims of the Bali bombings

*

Over the next several days I met up with Gunaratna and his team at the Marriott, where they filmed the hotel's Fort Knox security.

One afternoon, before Gunaratna rushed out to see Karnavian, he said, 'Quick, there's someone here you should talk to.' An Indonesian Islamic State supporter, sporting a *kufi* (prayer cap) and long Muslim tunic, sat undisturbed in the plush lobby. He had coolly sauntered through. My experience of the lobby was quite different: while waiting for Gunaratna, I was on each occasion harassed by security staff asking why I was there and for what purpose. Meanwhile the man, named Budi Waluyo, raised no alarm bells. I discovered he had pledged allegiance to IS and planned to join the fighting in Syria. As though preparing for a fun family expedition, he said he would take his two wives and seven children. 'I have heard people are rich, they have a good life in Syria. But money is not the main purpose, an Islamic caliphate is,' he asserted gravely from a stately armchair.

He was among a thousand supporters regularly meeting at a Central Jakarta mosque until they were moved on shortly before I met him. Situated in the well-heeled diplomatic area of Menteng, the mosque had been used to recruit people. Budi and his group decamped to the Islamic Centre in Bekasi on the outskirts of East Jakarta where they freely proselytised.

Capping a strange week was the departure of Gunaratna. One afternoon he suddenly hightailed it from the Marriott to the airport, unshaven and unkempt. Gone was the debonair suit and tie. Gone was his fixed serene disposition. I raced after him through the security corridors – easy to exit. He muttered something indecipherable from his rolled-down window then, with a harried wave, took flight, so to speak.

24

UBUD IN THE FIRING LINE

Ali Imron's tirades were behind me, but a different storm was brewing in Bali. In late October 2015 I attended the annual Ubud Writers & Readers Festival. After an intensive year, I was primed for a freewheeling week of work, mingling with prominent writers, celebrating Ubud's cultural cachet, and eating languorous meals in verdant settings.

First stop, the media centre. The usual bonhomie was subdued. Journalists huddled round a large whiteboard showing cancelled events that would have focused on the fiftieth anniversary of Indonesia's 1965–66 anti-communist massacres. Under police pressure, the festival's founding director Janet DeNeefe had been forced to slash those sessions. I had known DeNeefe for years, and publicly she was her typical unflappable self – but privately she was highly disturbed and disappointed, she told me.

It was my seventh Ubud festival and the first that felt so politically charged. Victims and families who had travelled from Papua, East Timor and Java to discuss their traumatic stories were again fearful. Under the shadow of the massacres, in which about a million people (the real figure is unknown) were killed, some went home.

My Balinese friend Ngurah Termana, a political activist whose sessions on the legacies of 1965 were cancelled, told me his personal story. We had met during the tenth anniversary of the Bali bombings when he'd translated the gruelling stories of Indonesian widows for me. But what he was about to say was new to me. Termana was to speak about a dark family secret: his grandfather's murder. His mother's fear had kept him ignorant of it, along with one of the worst genocides of the last century, for twenty years. He'd grown up in the 1980s knowing nothing of the estimated eighty thousand or so fellow islanders slaughtered in state-sponsored purges. At school, the history of the massacres was covered up, omitted from the curriculum, and replaced with lies and propaganda to brainwash youth and depict Suharto as a saviour of Indonesia.

'Communism and 1965 were used by the state to silence critical thinking, the people and corruption,' said Termana. His schoolteacher grandfather, marked as a communist, had vanished one day when Termana was no more than six years old. 'My grandpa ran away to protect his family, so they wouldn't come after them. My mum said that he suffered ill-health and died. She was afraid to tell the truth because I would have asked many questions and she wanted to silence me. It was very risky. It indicates how effective the killing system was, that even my mother should tell her son lies about the death of her father.'

Not until the fall of Suharto's corrupt dictatorship in 1998, when student-led riots helped to topple him and Termana was at Yogyakarta University, did he learn he had been fed propaganda. The whitewashing of the massacres perpetuated Suharto's ruling Golkar Party in farcical, unchallenged elections for thirty-two years.

The reform era began when Termana graduated from university after Suharto's regime collapsed. Then twenty, Termana discussed 1965 with his mother for the first time. 'So then I asked Mum. But it's hard; it's still very delicate, sometimes she doesn't want to talk about it because it's traumatising. Remembering is still very painful. She worries about us [his siblings] as political activists, talking about human rights issues. She says, "I lost my father, I don't want to lose you."' Termana's relatives and neighbours knew his grandfather was buried in a mass grave in Denpasar 'but no one was willing to dig up the body'.

Now in his late thirties, the Balinese father of a young daughter said another code of silence, drawn like iron curtains over the past, had been imposed to protect the island's lifeblood: tourism. 'Tourists only want the beauty story. The Balinese were very effectively silenced. Tourism needs peaceful, smiling people. But look at their legacy of cruelty and barbarity in 1965. They can be sadistic, as well.'

At the peak of the Cold War, anti-communist purges swept the country under Suharto's militarised, US-backed New Order regime after he ousted left-leaning incumbent, Sukarno. The worst mass killings were in the Communist Party (PKI) strongholds of Central and East Java, northern Sumatra and Bali. Alleged communists and ethnic Chinese Indonesians were targeted. Military death squads, army-affiliated youth groups, *preman* (thugs) and anyone bearing a grudge pitched in to the bloodletting. Thousands more were detained without trial for years. Suharto assured the world the failed coup was a PKI attempt to undermine the Indonesian government under Sukarno, though the now-defunct PKI denied involvement. No one has ever been charged.

In Ubud, Suharto's ghost hung in the soupy air. The festival's aim had been to push for truth and reconciliation. President Widodo, expected to apologise to victims, instead warned the country to be vigilant against the prospect of socio-political unrest, alluding to the turmoil and violence unleashed after the failed coup on 30 September 1965.

The aborted coup had been triggered by the assassination of six army generals by leftist army officers of the 30 September

Movement, with the chilling acronym Gestapu. If Suharto had foreknowledge, it remains a closely guarded secret.

Bali's purges were particularly barbaric. US journalist John Hughes, in his Pulitzer Prize-winning book, *The End of Sukarno: A Coup That Misfired: A Purge That Ran Wild* (1967), wrote, 'By general agreement, the most savage massacre took place on Bali. There the troops had to call the people off, whereas elsewhere they egged them on to kill Communists.'

People were surviving in a dystopian landscape of killing fields, famine, rat plagues, destitution and fear. Crops had been destroyed in the cataclysmic, year-long 1963 eruption of the sacred Mount Agung in Bali's north-east, and the economy was decimated by political instability and Sukarno's penchant for squandering money on monuments, himself and his four wives. The country starved amid hyperinflation and Sukarno's apathy.

Over the course of a few months, people hacked, chopped, stabbed and clubbed each other to death. Brothers fought brothers, and neighbours and families turned on each other – children on parents. I wondered how generations of bad blood reconciled the past on such a small island. Corpses had been scattered round Bali in unmarked mass graves, or thrown over cliffs or into rivers, forgoing the ritual funerals that Balinese Hindus believe purify the soul for reincarnation into higher beings or into a better world.

Only after cremation, can the soul detach itself from the body.

'Offerings will implore God to purify the spirit and return it to earth in an appropriately higher and purer form,' writes Fred B. Eiseman Jr in *Bali: Sekala and Niskala*.

I'd once attended the flamboyant Hindu cremation of an elderly king who was placed in the animal-shaped sarcophagus of a bull (the bull represents the highest caste; other forms such as a lion or deer, lower castes) and on to a funeral pyre; as the bull crackled, flames licked the sides and burst into a blaze; relatives celebrated his ritual passage into the next life, albeit in royal tradition.

Under this belief system, the souls of the victims of the 1965–66 bloodletting remain eternally adrift, unreleased to God and without peace.

*

A subversive frisson suffused the Ubud festival that year as programmed events inevitably veered into massacre territory, and attendees tittered like naughty children. Hastily prepared censorship panels discussed a skittish government unwilling to face the violent past. DeNeefe told me that the cancelled sessions only spotlighted the atrocities. Indeed, as our news stories lobbed around the world, they may have caused some embarrassment for Widodo, who was visiting the White House.

The Ubud festival had opened in 2004 to help Bali recover and heal after the 2002 bombings. It became South-East Asia's pre-eminent literary event; the debut 300 attendees swelled to a record near 30,000 in 2015.

'Out of tragedy good things can happen,' DeNeefe had said to me years earlier – but, it seemed, this wasn't the case in 2015. When DeNeefe reluctantly complied with festival censorship that year, critics admonished her for lacking the courage to proceed with the banned events. In turn, she labelled the government cowardly in its refusal to address the wounds of the past. But her greatest fear was that the festival would ultimately end up bland and meaningless under gag orders. 'I'd rather close it than have it reduced to that,' she told me.

The government backlash prompted counsel from her Balinese husband, Ketut Suardana, whom DeNeefe described in her 2003 book, *Fragrant Rice: My Continuing Love Affair with Bali*, as 'my strength and spiritual teacher'. She told me, 'Even my husband said, "You stop mucking around, this is serious business." If you don't comply, it doesn't mean you'll be having a festival next year.'

Cancelled that year was the screening of Joshua Oppenheimer's disturbing film *The Look of Silence*. It is the companion piece to his acclaimed 2012 exposé, *The Act of Killing*, which depicts real-life killers re-enacting the murders of alleged communists. *The Act of Killing* only circulated on YouTube and in underground screenings due to political risks in Indonesia.

Fear was a useful tool. I had been outside a Jakarta movie theatre in 2009 when journalists gathered to view another politically sensitive film, *Balibo Five*. It depicts the killings by Indonesian soldiers of five Australia-based journalists during the 1975 invasion of East Timor. Moments before screening, government censors banned it. Frustrated journalists pondered proceeding with the screening but then thought better of it. That military thugs might burst into the theatre was a creepy and real prospect and the journalists eventually dispersed.

Oppenheimer sought to expose the regime of fear, corruption and thuggery over which the killers continued to preside. 'I felt I'd wandered into Germany forty years after the holocaust, only to find the Nazis still in power,' he reflected in a news report.

During the 2014 presidential campaign, Widodo – a former furniture salesman without ties to the military or political elite – had committed to reconciling past human rights abuses and ending corruption. Now Indonesians complained of a weak president bowing to pressure from military oligarchs and security forces.

The prospect of a clampdown on freedom of expression spooked festival-goers. For the *Jakarta Post*'s then senior editor Endy Bayuni, the bans were reminiscent of Suharto's iron-fisted regime and the erosion of Indonesian democracy seventeen years after his collapse. I attended Bayuni's panel on censorship, then had a coffee with him. A soft-spoken, middle-aged man, he leant in, asking, 'Did you see the policeman emerging from the audience to photograph me during my session?'

In fact, I'd seen attendees and all four panellists' identities overtly recorded.

'It's like the old days, during the Suharto days,' he said. 'We are seeing indications of regression in the 1965 events.'

Ubud was not an isolated case. A student publication, *Lentera*, from the Satya Wacana Christian University, in central Java, had been burnt for producing an anniversary edition on the purges, and the editor of investigative magazine *Tempo* was summoned over its robust coverage of the massacres. Then there was the sad tale of a seventy-seven-year-old Swedish political exile who was deported as he tried to pay homage to his father at a mass grave in west Sumatra.

At a panel session including Bayuni, participants reflected on the significance of amended legislation to uphold the rule of law implemented after Suharto's fall.

'The ban against public expression is unconstitutional; we can fight through the legal system,' Bayuni told me over coffee. Nevertheless, he was edgy. Press freedom and free speech weren't taken for granted in Indonesia, despite the creation of the 1999 press law, he said. 'It's not secure, we have a wonderful press law but putting it into practice is difficult. They [those in power] see an opportunity to roll back some of the policies. We have a very weak president, people around him are taking advantage. The police ignore Jokowi. For many [the political and business elite], there's now too much democracy that prevents them from doing what they want, stealing money, corruption. This is the trend that we are seeing in all the reforms we have pushed through in the past seventeen years. They are not ready to confront the reality that something horrible happened in 1965.'

Bayuni had been at the epicentre of media censorship, reporting for fifteen years under Suharto's regime. The *Jakarta Post* survived but the government closed several media outlets deemed to have crossed the line. Now, the freedom unimagined twenty years ago was in question. 'But we can't criticise certain groups and powerful business people,' said Bayuni.

'What we are seeing in Indonesia today is only electoral democracy,' warned Andreas Harsono, an Indonesian journalist friend and a Human Rights Watch researcher.

'What we are seeing in power are the oligarchs with links to big business and the military. Jokowi does not own his own political party [the PDI-P, or Democratic Party of Struggle].'

In 2018, I asked Harsono if the 1965 issue would be resurrected. 'It's basically untouchable now,' he lamented.

Bayuni echoed the view but was determined to revisit it on the sixtieth anniversary. 'If you try to bring it up [the purges], they label you PKI. The smear is back in vogue after 2015.'

The following year, Widodo was pressured by hardline conservative Muslims. Curtailed freedom of expression, driven by racial and religious intolerance and Islamic identity politics, was pushed by such hardliners as the Islamic Defenders Front (FPI) – branded *preman* in Islamic cloaks – whose aim was state implementation of sharia law. The FPI had risen after Suharto's fall in 1998. Known for political alliances and smashing up bars, the group manipulated public sentiment towards the religious right. It mobilised mass protests against Jakarta's former governor Basuki 'Ahok' Tjahaja Purnama for blasphemy, which led to his 2017 jailing after he ran for re-election in 2016.

But for all their bluster, when I raced from a café to snap a passing FPI rally in Central Jakarta's Jalan Thamrin in 2017, I found my unease misplaced. Clad in their trademark white, hardliners stopped to pose for me in group selfies. They grinned broadly and delivered thumbs-up gestures. Only in Indonesia, I thought.

The jailing of Ahok, a Christian and ethnic-Chinese, stoked fears the largely moderate Muslim-majority nation was strategising sectarian populism amid escalating Islamic extremism. Indonesia prides itself on pluralism. Its motto, Unity in Diversity (*Bhinneka Tunggal Ika*), enshrined in its coat of arms, signifies the unity of the Indonesian people despite their myriad cultures and ethnicities.

The divisive anti-Ahok campaign arguably changed the tolerant face of the republic and dismantled Ahok's reform-based partnership with Widodo who didn't defend his former ally. Known as a moderate Muslim, Widodo was accused by some Islamic groups of being anti-Islam.

In shows of piety and to the shock of liberals, he chose hardline Islamic cleric Ma'ruf Amin as his running mate in a bid to bolster his Islamic credentials for a second term. Amin, as chairman of the Indonesian Ulema Council (MUI), the nation's top Muslim clerical body, had supported fatwas against religious minorities and called for the criminalisation of LGBTI activities. He was also behind the blasphemy ruling on Ahok.

*

When I returned to the Ubud festival in 2018, I found myself sitting beside the former foreign minister Marty Natalegawa and his wife Sranya Bamrungphong as Indonesia braced for a divisive 2019 presidential election campaign. The couple were relaxed, but I imagined Marty – as he was universally called – was in character as an affable, cautious diplomat.

Marty spoke of the need to consolidate the world's third-largest democracy. Electoral democratisation was secure, he said. 'But what I worry about is the distinction between politics and politicking.

The things that happen in between the elections when we have cajoling for power; that is debilitating and it can devalue and debase the quality of democracy. People are driven by the pursuit of power, and young people, whose formative years are only the *reformasi* [democratic reformation after Suharto's fall], especially can quickly become disillusioned by how the system is working.'

Many young Indonesians had taken to social media indicating they would *golput–golongan putih* – abstain from voting in protest. Intolerance and corruption – notorious in the judiciary – and in the military (TNI), whose political-socio and security role had been stripped in democratic reforms after Suharto's fall, needed constant monitoring, Marty stressed.

'With the *reformasi*, we are meant to do away with the practices of the Suharto era. Where we have been in the past in 1998 was a challenge and it will continue to be a challenge.'

'Are you pessimistic about the nation's future?' I asked him.

'Hardliners is one issue we need to be mindful of. We always prove ourselves to be resilient. Immediately before the *reformasi* the obituary was already being written about Indonesia: [people said] "it will go the way of Yugoslavia".

'Indonesia's body politic is able to sustain and withstand even the most divisive election campaign and in the aftermath ... the country reconsolidates itself and then continues. Many don't really fully appreciate the complexity of Indonesia as a country in terms of its diversity, the various challenges it's facing.'

I had witnessed environmental and social upheaval in Indonesia: volcanic eruptions, earthquakes, bombings, lethal disease and abject poverty. I'd also witnessed people's despair, their desperate attempts to rebuild their lives and the ineffectual bureaucracy for the job. Though Westerners in the region often marvelled at Indonesians' resilience, what choice did they have? I mused.

We were sitting at a table that faced Ubud's lush Campuhan Ridge. Talk turned to Australia, the couple recalling a Sydney visit. On a city street, a man had approached one of the most recognisable faces in Indonesian politics. Much to the couple's amusement, as Marty paused to gaze at his surroundings, the concerned man repeatedly asked, 'Are you lost, Marty?' He got that a lot. Strangers randomly addressed him as 'Marty', as though he were a long-lost friend. 'It's the glasses,' I blurted, of his Harry Potter-style specs. They nodded. The man must have seen him on the box. Without his consent or knowledge, he'd starred in an ad for spectacles; he was not amused.

That Joko Widodo would win the election against his two-time rival, Probowo Subianto – a Suharto-era general with a dubious human rights record, once married to Suharto's daughter – wasn't in doubt. But the great reformist hope was now perceived in local newspaper editorials, civil society groups and by my contacts as weak and disappointing. Political and social coexistence would be tested with a swing to hardline conservative Islam and restrictive piety.

Michael Vatikiotis, an author and journalist in South-East Asia whom I met at the 2018 Ubud festival, voiced his concern on Indonesia's increasing embrace of religious values and 'a more exclusive manifestation of identity'. 'I think politicians are largely to blame for the way in which these boundaries are being reinforced and undermining traditional forms of coexistence and social harmony. Heading to elections there is the drift to a more Islamic, more religious ... embrace of piety. It's a serious concern. Many people are just resigned to the idea that Indonesia will become a different country. The fact that Jokowi has as his running mate Amin ... is a failure of leadership.'

But we would have to let Widodo run his course.

25

UBUD INTERLUDE

The 2015 Ubud Writers & Readers Festival had kicked off in genteel fashion. Authors and journalists gathered for a meet and greet at Janet DeNeefe's sumptuous open-air soiree, sampling Ubud at its magical best. The backdrop was palm-fringed gardens, tinkling glasses and Balinese cuisine. We mingled in the crush of pre-dinner drinks at DeNeefe's Honeymoon Guesthouse before moving on to long elegant tables.

At the end of the evening, guests peeled off until my table thinned to a small group when, as is typical, broader, animated conversation opened up amid new faces. Quietly pushy, a man leant across my fellow diner to chat. I hadn't noticed him until then. A few pleasantries were exchanged, an interest noted. He had a mop of silver-grey hair and an impressive business card. High cheekbones framed a fine mouth, chiselled jawline and an incongruous flat-bridged nose – I wanted to ask if it had been broken in a fight. He was sixty-three, a New Yorker, charming, seemingly unpretentious; his card told me he was an esteemed writer.

I must have joined a vast array of groupies, I later mulled irritably.

He insisted on walking me back to my nearby hotel. We ambled along, two strangers reaching into our familiar worlds of books and news, seeking common ground. Leaning forward from a tall physique, he described inadequately his just-launched memoir that he was promoting on Bali's lit circuit.

The following year, the deftly written book and paean to people's unfulfilled yearnings would earn him one of the world's most prestigious literary prizes, reinforcing his reputation as a brilliant writer. In my realm, the memoir's sporting significance was slightly lost, and it was only after absorbing the book that I appreciated the full depth of its compelling, subjective journey.

That first night, when we reached a corner crossing to my hotel, I thanked him politely. He asked to escort me to the door, but I backed off.

The next morning I was surprised by his email. We had casually discussed meeting at a panel of mutual interest, but his own event coincided. 'Lovely to meet you,' he signed off, adding only his phone number. Did he expect me to call? Were writers' festivals and lit events his pick-up joints? Probably. I was slightly rattled, but the uncertainty seemed ripe with possibility.

The week rushed by in an upsurge of work. I interviewed many whose panel sessions had been cancelled, filing stories on the 1965 banned events. Our encounter slipped into the back of my mind. Then the festival's official schedule wrapped up, and I'd moved on to reporting the arrest of a notorious Indian mafia figure when I received an invite to a peripheral literary panel and dinner at a beachfront hotel.

There he was at the podium. Friends who sat strategically in the centre of the room, just back from the makeshift stage, waved me over to their table. Directly ahead under the platform's spotlight, his gaze bored through me. His co-panellist took over the mic, cracking a few jokes, but the words faded in a background drone. The memoirist seemed a reluctant speaker that night. Down the track, I asked if he liked speaking publicly; he shook his head vehemently, but I felt he was probably at ease in the role. As the event closed, he made a beeline to my table for a drink. We joined several others.

It was obvious where things were headed. He was staying at the hotel's adjoining traditional-styled villas, strangely decorated with wall and ceiling mirrors – not quite my thing.

We hardly slept. Not all due to the passion of the night. Lying in the dark, he spilled details of his personal life, filling in far more than strangers do. He told me he had separated from his wife over four years ago. During his curious, expansive revelations, I wondered if they were prompted by a sense of grief, guilt or perhaps relief. I felt like I'd been given permission to trespass in a very private room. How to respond? He had divulged not only his marriage woes but also a secret life that dogged him across continents – none of which would appear in any article or book. 'I wouldn't,' he told me gravely.

At breakfast, we ordered in. 'Four cappuccinos,' he briefed room service. How thoughtful. When I reached for a cup, he said with a slight smile, 'No, they're all for me,' and proceeded to over-sweeten each cup. Did I want a sip? Too sweet for my taste? What a pity. Everyone has their peccadilloes, I reasoned. We arranged to meet again. His next villa was stranger than the last.

Over the next sixteen months or so, when we went our separate ways, we exchanged many emails, discussing writing, books and people, and swapping articles and some of our personal circumstances. He sent me his memoir, inscribed beautifully, and the first of Elena Ferrante's Neapolitan novels. After a trip to Rome, where he had plugged his book, he disabused me of the notion Italians hail Ferrante as a favourite daughter, despite her prodigious accolades. He told me, 'She writes potboilers for housewives, they think, and they are proud to have never read a word ... So, take that as a Roman warning, I guess.' On finishing the sensational tetralogy, I told him I was entranced – like the vast masses.

We met up in Sydney on one of my trips back; savoured hours together amid his boundless sea of travel. He was again touring festivals, promoting his book.

I smiled to myself when he revealed via email, from Byron Bay, his thoughts on sharing a platform with political satirist P.J. O'Rourke: 'He did his schtick – libertarian curmudgeon conservative – and I pointed out the huge holes in his account of American politics and society. He was funnier, but the crowd was with me.'

We live on different sides of the world. Our lives had intertwined in a sweet, romantic interlude.

26

MAN OF STEEL

On New Year's Eve 2015, I flew south to Lombok to escape Bali's festive madness and celebrate with friends. Just north of Senggigi's tourist strip, on the north-west coast, I strolled round a cerulean infinity pool facing a luminous horizon. My thoughts turned to a different patch of water – one in bitter contention by Bali's Ngurah Rai International Airport.

The Balinese, often depicted in the West as relaxed and peace-loving, could also be quick to anger. In 2016, threatened with cultural and environmental ruination, they steeled themselves for battle at the prospect of a giant tourist resort that promised to engulf Benoa Bay. En route, it would ravage sacred Balinese Hindu sites, a mangrove-rich ecosystem, a fishing industry, communities and one of the last uninterrupted horizons in the south. If approved, the transformation would showcase a Dubai-esque development of twelve artificial islands – a mini city including Venetian-style canals, hotels and Disney-themed parks. This massive 700-hectare reclamation plan was smack in the middle of Bali's golden triangle of tourism spanning Kuta, Sanur and Nusa Dua, which generated 70 per cent of the island's A$80 billion annual tourism revenue.

But the bay had fallen into decrepitude; for years, due to corruption and funding shortages, governments neglected a rancid rubbish dump blighted by toxic industrial waste and accumulated trash. The developer of the glitzy Nusa Benoa project promised 'revitalisation'.

Balinese objectors argued, however, an incursion would annihilate environmental and social harmony. At stake overall was the environmental, human and religious philosophy that underpins all Balinese life, *Tri Hita Karana* – three causes of well-being – harmony among people; harmony with nature; harmony with God. A litany of grievances on the social and cultural impacts of the proposed development spurred ForBALI (Balinese Forum against Reclamation) protests. The campaign multiplied from thirty protesters in 2013 to near 30,000 in 2016.

Despite their outrage, I could not help thinking the Balinese argument weakened under the mountains of rubbish. The developer prepared to dredge and clean as unremitting media coverage and huge protests triggered the most polarising modern battle Bali had known.

Behind the IDR30 trillion (US$2 billion) mega-development was Tomy Winata, one of Indonesia's most powerful, contentious and enigmatic tycoons. Simply referred to by Indonesians as TW (pronounced Tay Way), he'd made his multimillion-dollar fortune in property, banking and construction, and was known to have close political and military ties.

In 2011, US embassy cables obtained by WikiLeaks revealed claims that Winata had used political alliances to further his business interests. The claims provoked a diplomatic storm that went to Indonesia's top echelons. The cables, from 2006, alleged Winata had used a middleman to relay funds to the then president, and retired army general, Susilo Bambang Yudhoyono (SBY), and had sought a channel to fund the president's 2004 election campaign. Both men vehemently rejected the claims.

Poised to begin the Benoa Bay project through his privately owned PT Tirta Wahana Bali Internasional (TWBI), Winata waited for the central government's go-ahead. He labelled the venture 'green'; critics branded it 'disaster capitalism' masquerading as sustainable development. Yet despite his demonisation, the fifty-eight-year-old was almost a myth, so rarely was he spotted or interviewed.

Australian coverage ramped up in the Fairfax media. But reporters skirted around Winata, interviewing his lieutenants at his Kuta Kartika Plaza Hotel in Bali, where an architectural model of the project commandeered the lobby. Why was the only voice that truly mattered absent? Standing beside that cerulean pool of water in Lombok, I phoned a Jakarta journalist friend with an impeccable contact list who provided Winata's number.

My heart skipped a beat when Winata answered my call. Perhaps so few people had his number he assumed it was important. 'Yes,' he intimated cautiously, 'I am interested in an interview.' I felt mildly euphoric, as if I'd won the lottery.

Depending on the content, Winata would see the timing of a foreign news report as propitious. A critical government environmental impact assessment, or *amdal*, of the proposed project was due, and tensions were running high. Jakarta didn't want trouble in Bali, the glittering crown jewel of Indonesia that raked in forty per cent of the country's A$200 billion annual tourism revenue.

Months passed. Winata was frequently away on business, he was ill, VIP meetings arose. 'Bapak [Mr] Tomy is keen, but [it's] just timing,' said Jet, my intermediary – a loyal, long-time staffer. 'He is always impromptu, sorry.' I would learn more about that spontaneity.

In the meantime, I immersed myself in the fightback politics of ForBALI, organised by the nation's environmental watchdog, Walhi. Their slogan *Tolak Reklamasi* – Reject the Reclamation – drove the widespread movement, including an Indonesian diaspora abroad. Regular mass rallies converged across the island; some of the most energised were held near Benoa Bay, where I was swept along snapping photos by throngs in full battle cry and ceremonial dress. At these protests, ForBALI's coordinator and lawyer Wayan 'Gendo' Suardana, feted like a rock star and with his long hair flowing, stood on a platform and shouted into a loudspeaker.

The most powerful demonstration I witnessed was a massive male pilgrimage to Benoa Bay in early April 2016, during which participants were propelled into trances. We proceeded from a temple ceremony in a convoy of motorbikes – with me on the back of one – to the seafront. The only noise was the rumble of hundreds of bikes on a rocky track. At the ocean's edge, a frenzy whipped through the crowd like a mini tornado. Men buckled knee-deep in water, entranced, shaking and crying, their faces distraught. Joining the hordes in their long white ceremonial costumes, I clambered aboard one of the traditional fishing boats motoring out to the bay. Offerings of flower petals, rice and fruit were made to the Hindu deities, while *mangkus* (high priests) sprinkled the masses with holy water.

Then out of the growing dusk, guttural animal sounds perforated Benoa Bay's calm. A Balinese man, the centre of the massive crowd's attention, deeply entranced, convulsed, cackling like a chicken. Next he was a sobbing wounded beast, writhing, his face contorted in pain.

The unnerving spectacle set off a further ripple effect as the boatloads of Balinese on their spiritual odyssey prayed to their Hindu gods to save the contested bay from environmental ruin.

*

A world away, my interview was finally scheduled: I would spend three days with Winata in May on his remote conservation property, a promontory of untouched emerald jungle on Sumatra's south-western tip of Lampung province, specifically to discuss his Bali reclamation project, Winata assumed.

His Sumatran venture – fifty-nine thousand hectares of pristine national forest, a marine reserve and renowned tiger sanctuary – was his passion and a spectacular coastal wonder. Was I expected to endorse Winata's Benoa Bay aspirations based on his Tambling Wildlife Nature Conservation? The rags-to-riches businessman and philanthropist obviously elected his private paradise as a potent environmental message.

'You are lucky,' said his personal assistant, Hanna Lilies Puspawati. 'You're the only journalist to have this opportunity with Pak Tomy.' Publicity for Tambling focused on his lauded Sumatran tiger sanctuary. Journalists occasionally visited but didn't stay so I felt I'd scored a coup.

The refuge was just one cog in Winata's vast Tambling reserve, into which he had ploughed $A40 million to regenerate degraded areas since he'd started running it in 1997. In a mutual agreement with the government, which owned the land, the elusive tycoon managed the sprawling property with a tight rein over illegal logging, hunting and fishing, under his Artha Graha Peduli (Care) Foundation. It was part of the 356,800-hectare Bukit Barisan Selatan National Park, where he also assisted to stem the same illegal activities.

At Jakarta's airport, a Winata staffer hustled me into a black SUV. 'We have strict rules at Tambling: no plastic, no perfume. Is that okay?' he asked, watching me intently. The first wasn't such a peculiar ground rule for an Indonesian wildlife nature expedition, but why the perfume ban? 'Pak Tomy dislikes it,' he replied simply.

I was whisked off to Winata's five-star Borobudur Hotel and given a staff briefing over a rooftop dinner. The next morning, we met at the small East Jakarta Halim Perdanakusuma airport.

Airline staff nodded respectfully as they spied me and Hanna. But when Winata loped in sporting a casual khaki shirt and baggy dark-blue trousers, there was an audible intake of breath. He greeted me, smiling hospitably. But he was distracted. His eyes darted around the room; he muttered to Hanna and airline crew, then looked askance at the tarmac. The moustached man with razor-cropped greying hair was a familiar sight to staff, visiting Tambling monthly, and the routine had to be seamless.

One of Winata's private choppers sat on the tarmac. Silver and sleek, it gleamed under a hazy sun. With Winata's partner Amelia, Hanna, project consultants and an elderly 'mystery' man, we packed the heli, as Hanna called it. Winata ensured I had a window seat. My camera poised, we lifted off, spun and sliced through the thick, smoggy air, the clogged metropolis slowly receding. As we hovered above Jakarta, Winata enthusiastically pointed to a colossal chunk of prime property: forty-five hectares of the high-rise central business district that he owned through publicly listed companies PT Danayasa Arthatama and PT Jakarta International Hotel & Development – before we detoured in the Sunda Strait over the once cataclysmic Krakatoa volcano and its *anak* (child) of Krakatoa still spewing ash.

An hour from Jakarta, we descended to a manicured green airstrip, a generous belt cut between thick jungle. Swirling sea caps fringed the peninsula. A lighthouse near the beach built by the Dutch in 1879 was the only remnant of a community annihilated by Krakatoa's 1883 explosion heard as far away as Alice Springs.

The emerald wilderness of Tambling was extraordinary and otherworldly, but its spell broke under the presence of uniformed armed guards on horseback. Standing to attention, they acknowledged Winata with military-style salutes. Po-faced, young employees deferentially greeted their boss; in turn, Winata nodded curtly before escaping the belting sun.

As I too sought shade, Hanna led me first to an outdoor lectern to sign an Indonesian form. A formality, I thought. Later she said I had signed over copies of my taped interviews with Winata. I laughed off the idea but she pressed me incessantly until our departure. 'What if you get something wrong?' she persisted rather too much.

About sixty guards patrolled the grounds, a couple of whom were my chaperones, ostensibly to protect me against three released 'conflict' tigers that had been rehabilitated and freed. Each morning, on my way to the adjoining dining room, an armed guard escorted me. He didn't talk; he just fell into step.

At some point, I entertained brief flashes that I might be stranded in this sweeping, remote rainforest where I was beholden to Winata and his heli. Was I intimidated by this formidable character in this setting, surrounded by his attendants? I brushed the thought aside; it was a masterstroke to be there.

My air-conditioned 1950s-style cottage – one of an identical cluster circling the meeting/dining area – seemed like an anomaly. But outside the gloomy room, deer, monkeys and peacocks frolicked beneath my balcony.

As one of the nation's wealthiest men, Winata could afford the indulgence of his beloved showpiece. Globe Asia ranked him fiftieth in its 150 richest Indonesians 2018 list, with a US$930 million fortune – though he was not on Forbes' 2018 list; the extent of his fortune would not be for prying eyes, said a source. He presided over his extensive conglomerate through his Jakarta-based Artha Graha Group and Artha Graha Network. The Benoa Bay development would slot into his gigantic property portfolio, including the mammoth PT Jakarta International Hotels & Development and its subsidiary PT Danayasa Arthatama.

At Tambling, Winata took siestas during the enervating peak heat of the day after lunch. He emerged late that first afternoon, as the light dimmed, to show me a spectacular lake, once a poachers' paradise. We took off in a jeep with a couple of guards, Winata standing on the roof beside an enormous sheathed hunting rifle. As we rumbled along well-worn tracks, eagle-eyed he searched for the telltale signs of poachers, decayed forest and tigers. I, too, was glued to the scenery, anticipating a coveted sighting of a wild tiger, not uncommon along that stretch. Alas, none made an appearance.

'The most important thing is conservation,' Winata assured me on the boat, pointing to restored mangroves framing the magical, glassy, wildlife-rich lake from which we observed frolicking water buffalo. 'Tambling is more valuable than any of my properties.' Of his Benoa project, though, he had flashy ambitions. 'We want to attract international tourists who spend US$300 a day. I would like Bali to change and I want to help it … to face the world for the next century. Don't let Bali become underdeveloped and only a cheap tourism destination.' But more than four million – predominantly Hindu – Balinese saw it differently.

Bali was a status symbol for Indonesian property seekers, and the first Benoa incarnation had been earmarked for then president Suharto's youngest son, Hutomo 'Tommy' Mandala Putra, in 1994, but abandoned during the 1998 financial crisis. The advantage of reclamation was that it circumvented exorbitant land prices in Bali's south. On 2019 figures, Winata would save US$2.6 billion on the cost of the US$2 billion project, said Agung Wardana, who has a PhD from Murdoch University on environmental conflicts in contemporary Bali, including Benoa Bay.

At Tambling, Winata turned out to be a generous, if erratic, host, with a penchant for French red over dinner and impromptu meetings conducted anywhere – from his cottage, to the dining room, to brisk walks. At night, about thirty earnest young staffers sat round a table, pens and paper poised, while the four of us ate and drank wine. Like that of a schoolmaster, Winata's voice rose and fell in a soliloquy. The staff took notes. He dismissed them around midnight when they tottered on the verge of sleep. No one left the room until he did.

Of some mystery was his constant companion and partner of several years, Amelia, a large Chinese-Indonesian woman. Winata didn't introduce her to me, despite the fact she translated when he stumbled; for the most part his English, though not fluent, was incisive, and he was good at nuances. Amelia, like other personal topics such as his early background, was off limits and, if pushed, he changed tack. When the pair posed together for a photo, Winata cautioned me, smiling, 'It's only for your personal album, I don't want those Australian men to take her away.' Needless to say, the snap wasn't published.

Though he dressed down in crumpled shorts, T-shirt and Crocs, this man who wielded an uncanny amount of power was clearly held in awe by his staff. Those around him didn't talk unless spoken to; when summoned, they ran. His solipsistic tendencies kept an audience captive for hours, sometimes under a blistering sun. On tenterhooks, his staff tried to second-guess his capricious habits. On his impulsive reserve walks, they accompanied him while he designated chores.

Winata invited me on one such walk. Heading off at a brisk pace, he gathered speed around the airstrip, leaving Hanna and me struggling in the punishing heat. We trailed the others, me with laptop in hand (I had organised a sit-down interview). Eventually, we broke into a run to try to catch up with him. Sweating profusely, and feeling nauseated, I gave up. Hanna called for a golf buggy. Relieved, we piled in, veering wildly as we continued chasing Winata – who upped the ante, striding furiously up the airstrip. Intermittently, I alighted, charging after him for comments while exhausted staff hopped in and out of the moving cart, then resumed at Winata's speed. If he knew what was happening, he gave no hint.

Hanna said Winata, though obsessively private, disliked being alone. While she had known him since 1989, she remained a stranger. 'I've been with him twenty-seven years and I still don't know him personally. I just know he always cares, and helps other people. He has helped me to be a much more disciplined and educated person,' she said, invoking a father figure. She described his North Jakarta home in east Ancol – surrounded by six thousand square metres of green space and caged exotic birds – as modest, like his Tambling cottage. Indeed, he depicted himself as a frugal person with simple habits. During my stay, he ate the same basic Indonesian food, such as nasi goreng, as the staff. 'I never start my projects looking at the profit,' he assured me. 'I only buy for personal use. I can spend less than US$10 in one day ... The gods' hands help me to survive with new concepts and new ideas ... to make my projects successful.'

On the veranda of Winata's simple cottage, we talked deep into the second evening amid hanging red Chinese lanterns and a wildlife cacophony. Winata, an ethnic Chinese Indonesian, was a dedicated Buddhist, and a temple took pride of place in his living room. 'You are welcome to my home,' he said, motioning me to sit at his veranda table. 'I also welcome you to pray. Maybe my god will help you, give you good luck,' he continued with a laugh, showing me his shrine.

*

Winata might still be up against his most intractable opponents yet. What's more, the Balinese promised to take it to the apogee. So much did some opponents see his proposed development as a gross violation of their rights, they threatened mass ritual suicide – or *puputan* (a battle to the end) – if it went ahead. They had last enacted this in 1908 over their subjugation by Dutch colonialists.

Although Winata smiled sceptically about a modern *puputan*, he hadn't expected such intransigence.

In 2013, while visiting Madrid, Winata had appointed the Real Madrid soccer star Cristiano Ronaldo as mangrove ambassador of the Bali Mangrove Care Forum, an arm of Winata's NGO Artha Graha Peduli (Care) Foundation that cleaned up Benoa's rubbish-laden mangroves. Winata had brought him to Bali, and during a charged press conference at Benoa Bay, Ronaldo had planted mangroves alongside former president Yudhoyono and committed to preserve the forests. Both men insisted no financial gain was involved in the role. That was when Bali had rallied.

Though the artificial islands were to be state-owned, TWBI was expected to receive exclusive managing rights for an unspecified period, conferring wider entitlement than land ownership. Winata insisted the process had been scrupulous. The Corruption Eradication Commission (KPK) had spent six months investigating the Bali project, he told me. 'KPK cannot find gratification … because my money is clear and clean. I never do hanky-panky deal. The KPK investigated for evidence. I did not influence anybody. I only ask for fair treatment. I am not hiding anything.'

In November 2018, the Maritime Ministry issued Winata's TWBI a new permit for Benoa Bay following the expiry of his previous one. All that stood in his way was a critical environmental impact assessment, or *amdal*, approval, required ahead of all developments. But a presidential decree remained over the bay: it had been earmarked as a conservation zone by Yudhoyono in 2011, then in 2014 he had surprisingly switched its status to development under a presidential regulation, shortly before leaving office.

Unless this was revoked by President Widodo, Benoa Bay could be developed. In October 2019 the Maritime Ministry declared Benoa Bay a maritime conservation site. Yudhoyono's regulation prevailed due to its higher status, but it would be difficult for

TWBI to pass the environmental impact assessment under the new maritime designation.

'With the combination of Bali style and Palm Beach, do you think it [the Benoa project] will shake the world?' Winata asked me with a laugh. Then he surprised me – so trenchant was the backlash that he suggested he may pull out. Really? 'I'm not always [thinking] I will win,' he replied. He seemed to relish the game as much as the whiff of victory. 'I am not saying I will cancel the project. I am not saying I will continue. I also don't want to throw away my money.' A retreat would be conditional: if at least one million opponents signed guarantees committing to Benoa Bay's continuous environmental care, he might quit. 'If they sign, maybe I will withdraw. For me, the reputation is more important than the money. I am trying to save Benoa for another few hundred years. I love Bali. I have responsibility for the good of the people.'

*

Winata, a self-made businessman, had been born in Jakarta to poor parents, the son of an automobile spare parts trader. He'd left school at fourteen for labouring work in Kalimantan and West Papua, including contracting jobs to build army barracks. 'I went with my parents' blessing. I went from island to island, region to region. When I was young, I passed my days for eight years in the forest. I owe the forest and nature very much. For instance, I have no business in logging.'

After that, his life was a blur. His parents were, he said, the biggest influences on him. 'They made me a good person.' Beyond that Winata refused to discuss his family in any detail, instead inviting me to meet them. 'Whatever I say, people will say it's just window-dressing, like lipstick,' he added with a sigh. In the lantern-lit twilight, I noted his discomfort. Pak Tomy doesn't discuss his personal life, Hanna and Jet had said.

While he proudly disclosed he was a grandfather of eight, he wouldn't confirm he had five children, some involved in his businesses. Indeed, two sons with their respective families featured in beach snaps at Tambling. But none would inherit his fortune; they were expected to work for their money. 'When I pass away all my assets go to the [Artha Graha Peduli] foundation.' Artha Graha means 'house of money'.

Winata asked, frustrated, why I was asking personal questions. He was equally evasive on the subject of the 1998 Suharto riots and pogroms against ethnic Chinese Indonesians. He said curtly that his family had been unharmed. 'We were all in Jakarta, no problem. This is not an issue, this passed a long time ago. Me and all my family never left my country.' Most – who could afford to – fled, mainly to Singapore and China, and vast numbers of their properties were looted and burnt to the ground.

*

Elsewhere, Winata continued to court controversy after those secret cables originating from the US Embassy in Jakarta.

When I probed him about the WikiLeaks allegations, Winata seemed shocked despite his previous public denials. 'I never heard about this,' he protested. 'If you can bring this data, proven and legalised, I will bring [it] to the court tomorrow. What is WikiLeaks? ... I sue them, because why? From 2004 until 2008, I never meet or make any communication with SBY [Yudhoyono]. This is good.' He chuckled. 'I can make money to prove 100 per cent there is no data or chance I can visit SBY.' Suddenly, he asked, 'Do you want to discuss about Benoa or my personal [life]?'

'Everything. It's a profile.' I went on: was it true Winata was an 'underworld figure', as WikiLeaks had claimed? He appeared unable to understand, so I improvised, 'You know, like mafia.'

'What is mafia? Is it a cake?' he responded. 'People always ask me like this, what about mafia? When the bomb Bali happened I am the most supportive person. How come they still say I am mafia?'

Likewise Winata's lifelong friendship with the late Taufik Kiemas and husband of former president and current leader of the Indonesian Democratic Party (PDI-P) Megawati Sukarnoputri shone an unwelcome spotlight on his powerful political connections. Their friendship was viewed as the basis for Winata's political alliance with business. US diplomats in 2006 were allegedly told of Yudhoyono personally intervening in the case of Kiemas reportedly using his continuing control of his wife's party to broker protection from prosecution for what the US diplomats described as 'legendary corruption during his wife's tenure'.

Winata explained his relationship with Kiemas like this: 'We have a long story, we are friends for a long time. We never talk about business, or politics. I never use excellency Mr Taufik, I only was instructed by him when the 2002 Bali bomb happened. He invite me politely, "Please, Tomy, help Bali. Tell the world Bali will grow again." That's why I built up the Discovery Mall in Bali.' Construction of the Kuta mall had started in 2000, and it had opened in November 2002 – a month after the bombings.

'Does politics beckon down the track?' I asked.

'I don't like politics. I just want to be a businessman until the last of my days. People are jealous of my success; they always try to blackmail me with rumours – like WikiLeaks,' he said huffily. 'I only respect the truth. I go to Australia, they have no problem. I go to the US … to England, I have no problem.'

In my later meeting with the former Bali tourism board chief Ida Bagus Ngurah Wijaya, he spoke candidly of Megawati's friendship with Winata. 'She is very good friends with Tomy Winata. He is good friends with everybody. He's a businessman.' The conversation segued. 'It's difficult for Tomy Winata because the army and police have got big money from the government now – their salaries have been increased. During Suharto's and SBY's time they didn't have any money, and that's why they relied on Tomy Winata. He still runs the "military business" starting from when he financed uniforms, then graduated to guns.'

When I contacted Damien Kingsbury at Deakin University – an expert in international politics and security issues in South-East Asia, and in Indonesian army (TNI, or Tentara Nasional Indonesia) business activities – he described Winata as among an elite handful of powerful people in the country, using his influence in subtle ways.

I asked Winata, as we chatted through the balmy Sumatran evening, if he had current military partnerships. He said, 'I have no business with the military. My partner[s] [are] not military. We make a business with the retirement foundation, not army. I am very close with the grassroots people. I am friends with everybody, the army, civilians, police.'

In 1988 Winata had worked with the Indonesian Army Foundation for veterans in order to rescue a troubled local bank, Bank Propelat, and subsequently changed its name to Bank Artha Graha. The army foundation (YKEP), or the Kartika Eka Paksi Foundation, was started in 1972 under Suharto to improve soldiers' welfare. 'We took over the bank to become Artha Graha. If we can do something with the foundation to save the bank and to save the people money, it's a good thing,' he said defensively. 'The bank went public.'

In his 2005 book *Power Politics and the Indonesian Military*, Kingsbury wrote that YKEP became a successful conglomerate, owning some twelve primary businesses. Kingsbury found that the

TNI owned 20 per cent of Winata's bank Artha Graha and 30 per cent of the overall holding company.

Given Indonesia's entrenched corruption, I asked Winata, 'What is the key to running an ethical corporate empire in your country?'

'This is not my area and I have no idea about this. I only say everything must be done legally and with transparency. I have no comment.' When I tried a different tack, asking what it took to be an upstanding businessman in Indonesia, he said, 'I am loyal to my government's policy, I don't make entertainment, I don't lobby government people. I never come to the high-ranking official party and I do not join any political party.'

Though Winata balked sometimes, he was in no hurry – I suspected he was, in a sense, enjoying himself. Team Winata included eighteen legal advisers to ensure 'they protect and guide us' and a bevy of other staff around the country. Yet, chimed in Amelia – who had barely spoken to me until then – he couldn't navigate the internet. 'I cannot look at the internet, I cannot open my email. I have no time,' he said with a laugh. 'Every day, I'm thinking about how to make a green project, serving the poor people, serving the micro-financing, from morning until night.'

Beneath a changeable, shrewd and, often gruff, exterior, I wondered what drove Winata.

Long a devotee of mega developments, he envisaged Jakarta as the new Manhattan and planned the world's fifth tallest skyscraper. Now he dreamt of a dazzling Bali icon. The concept would be 'a bit US Florida, Maldives, Santosa Island, Singapore, with the culture of the Balinese and modern, international facilities'.

Was it profit that motivated him? I asked. No, he repeated, he wanted to help poor people and preserve the environment. After all, 'saving the planet is still business', he muttered.

Perhaps Jet best summed him up. 'He's a great guy, but very tough, disciplined, never gives up and dreams high.' I pondered the *never gives up* part – the quality that was haunting Bali.

Since Winata had started his Tambling ecological venture, the lush regenerated reserve had seen about a hundred endangered species, including elephants, rhinos, wild buffalo, monkeys, sambar deer and turtles, return and flourish. Tambling was also home to thirty-five endangered tigers, with a rescue and rehabilitation centre then housing seven 'conflict' tigers that had previously attacked and killed humans and livestock in Sumatra. In the past decade, five had been released into the conservation area with GPS tracking devices. They were fed live pigs, bred at the reserve.

With some reticence, I asked Winata to show me the refuge during feeding time. We would wait for 'guests' – local officials – who were being collected in the heli. A staffer explained that feeding was every three days but it had been delayed to induce an extra bloodthirsty session for Winata's guests. I watched men pile out of jeeps wearing red T-shirts emblazoned with the words *Satgas Anti-Narkoba* [*Taskforce Anti-Drugs*], *Lampung*. They crowded round a wire-mesh enclosure separating the tigers. A small squealing pig was dragged by its tethered trotters and dumped inside. The tigers ignored it.

This standoff continued for about an hour. The men were getting antsy; Winata's staff cut to the chase, flinging pigs into small tiger cages. In one, I watched the pig freeze in fear, its haunches rigid in a half-sitting position. A ferocious Sumatran tiger paced, surveying its trapped prey. Suddenly it lunged. Bloodcurdling screams resounded around the compound. As though signalled, the other tigers tucked into their lunch. Colossal paws and teeth tightened around the pig's neck, deftly and savagely taking it down. The pig writhed, its legs madly peddling the air until it succumbed. 'That's nature,' Winata said with a shrug, acceding to the law of the jungle.

Winata's floating development was to tap into a market irked by crime upsurges targeting foreigners, trash and gridlocked traffic. Using a sanitised Bali brand, it would try to re-create what had once been defined as a unique, peaceful paradise. Critics continued to bemoan the development, arguing it was yet another example of Balinese property being expropriated for tourism with a complicit government contravening regulations.

In Denpasar, ForBALI's coordinator, Gendo, told me, 'We don't have any problem with Tomy Winata, but we do with anyone who wants to occupy Benoa Bay with unethical methods. This is a war. The only person who can overturn the reclamation is Jokowi [Widodo]. But Winata is very powerful. He can negotiate with everyone.'

On the last morning at Tambling, Winata called a staff meeting at his cottage. At his balcony table, he ate a leisurely breakfast of nasi goreng and dumplings while dispatching instructions to silent, glum faces. A couple of hours later, enveloped by the roar of the heli, we hovered above the jade belt. Looking out the window, I watched the exuberant waves of grinning staff recede into the distance.

'I hope this will be good for Pak Tomy,' Jet later texted about my article.

'It will be balanced,' I responded.

27

THE SMILING GENERAL

By the time the silver heli returned to Jakarta, Tambling's verdant forest had woven its spell on me. I understood why it was Winata's passion. But business was his drug. Probably money too, though he denied that.

Journalists apprised me of strange Winata stories. A couple of unappreciated articles had legal implications and I girded myself for his reaction to my piece. When it was published, I was almost disappointed by the thud of silence. My editor had forensically combed my work, removing anything remotely litigious; she heaved a sigh of relief. I was slightly dissatisfied, curious about Winata's opinion. But I thought it impolitic to inquire. The silence perhaps signalled displeasure, but at least he wasn't complaining.

*

Suharto's shadow was never far away. Hard-won reforms after his collapse were not necessarily set in stone, corruption remained and civil society worried the military was gaining the political power that had been stripped after Suharto's fall.

But the divisive political-Islamic extremism that erupted in Jakarta in 2016 brought some nostalgia for the 'old days'. In 2017, Jakarta lawyer Wirawan Adnan – with whom I had a long connection over Bali Nine cases – told me he longed for a return to the economic and social stability of Suharto's reign and a halt to the hardline mass protests Suharto would have efficiently crushed.

That Suharto's brutal rule had been toppled by student-led riots, political chaos, the 1997 Asian financial crisis and corruption didn't disturb Adnan's daydream, and he wasn't isolated in his fears for the country's future.

Intrigue still surrounded Suharto. Much about him remained as hearsay. He had preferred to be viewed as a benign sovereign but, like many, I speculated on what lurked beneath his deceptive smile.

When the opportunity arose to interview the Balinese man who had been Suharto's aide, bodyguard and near-constant companion for twenty years, I flew to Jakarta. Little did I suspect that the seventy-two-year-old Nyoman Suweden lived in a fantasy devoted to Suharto's memory and his family, in denial of known facts. I arrived at his office ahead of my interpreter and the moustached Suweden, wearing a batik shirt and dark pants, spoke no English so I stumbled along in my Indonesian. I had arrived at the tail end of Jakarta's annual floods, and my interpreter was stuck in traffic; when I explained this to Suweden, he promptly ordered an elaborate Javanese morning tea.

The retired lieutenant colonel had remained the adjutant of Pak Harto, as he was known, after he'd been forced to resign in May 1998. Then asked by Suharto to be his personal bodyguard, Suweden could not have been more honoured.

In his office, which fronted the Australian Embassy, his amateur artworks of lush Balinese landscapes adorned the walls. Behind glass cabinets were countless photos of Suharto with his children and his wife Siti Hartinyah (also known as Ibu Tien; *ibu* means 'mother' or 'Mrs'), and on 'incognito' impromptu visits to villagers. The office was like a small shrine. In one image, Suweden obsequiously bowed from the waist, clasping both hands over Suharto's extended one; there was Suharto with Suweden overseas, the autocrat wearing his perennially enigmatic smile and black *peci* (cap); and Suharto on his hospital deathbed hooked up to tubes, surrounded by Indonesia's power elite paying last respects to their immutable leader. Suweden proudly showed me dozens of images of himself posing with Suharto: at the Great Wall of China in 1988, in Hawaii, in war-torn Bosnia-Herzegovina and Croatia in 1995 under tight security after a UN summit to Copenhagen, to Western Europe, to Japan and to Washington, DC. 'In Bosnia he was given a flak jacket but he gave it to his assistant – he wasn't afraid of death,' Suweden marvelled.

Much has been made of Suharto's inscrutability, and Suweden recalled that quality with vicarious pride. 'He was never emotional. He was stable. He followed the Javanese proverb: *Don't be too proud; don't be too curious*. He followed it for his own emotional stability. He never showed anger, he had self-control. He believed in God, that God protected him. He was self-confident. Suharto was very wise. I loved him as a friend, he was very loyal and good to me. Yaah, yaah,' Suweden blurted repeatedly. 'He was very kind.'

Later, when I asked my Indonesian sources if they knew an unbiased Suharto source, I was met with derisory smiles. I had naively entered Suweden's office.

After the death in 1996 of Ibu Tien, rumours abounded that she had been shot by one of her children. As did speculation that Suharto's *wayhu*, or divine power and inspiration, had dissolved with her demise. Descended from minor Javanese royalty in Solo, Ibu Tien was believed to have conferred the *wayhu* on her husband. Suweden, scoffing at the theory, pointed to the 1997 Asian financial crisis and subsequent unrest that triggered Suharto's downfall.

Suweden, the devoted servant, would rise at 3 a.m. to go to Suharto's home in Jalan Cendana (meaning Sandalwood) and wake him for morning prayers at 4.30 a.m. 'I helped him with breakfast, laundry, exercise until 11 p.m., sometimes later, until he died in 2008.' When Suharto had a stroke in 1997, Suweden's duties intensified and he tended to his boss's every need, including showering and letter-writing. Until then, he said, Suharto had played golf, gone deep-sea fishing in the Thousand Islands off North Jakarta's coast and to his cattle ranch in Tapos, Bogor, in West Java, with Suweden joining him. 'After the stroke he was shaky, he couldn't speak properly, but he could still think well.' Reports emerged his frailty was initially overplayed, and that he had been spotted playing golf and jogging.

Suweden would have lived at Suharto's house, but he had his own family. Sometimes he stayed overnight instead of returning home to East Jakarta. However, he said vehemently, 'Pak Suharto was *keluarga* [family] Number 1. As a Balinese man I fulfilled my duty and *yes*, I felt honoured.'

'What sort of man was Suharto?' I asked.

'Pak Suharto was not a dictator, like people said he was. Many spoke badly of him, few people talked about his goodness. At the office he was the commander-in-chief; he implemented government rules and regulations. But at home he was a different person. He never looked down at people, he never embarrassed anyone and he was caring.'

Why is he defending a long-dead, ruthless kleptocrat? I thought.

When I mentioned the cronyism and nepotism that had marked Suharto's rule, Suweden denied it. 'It's blatantly untrue. Suharto never gave his children preference. Businessmen actually approached his children to take advantage. There is no proof Suharto was corrupt.' Apparently the Smiling General had definitely not looted billions of dollars of state money – further, Suharto hadn't even had any money. 'The money went into foundations. Suharto didn't have a bank account. There are accusations he had accounts overseas but there is no proof of that.'

When Suharto died, aged eight-six, he had escaped prosecution for corruption by declaring himself too ill to stand trial. He was accused in 2000 of embezzling US$600 million of state funds through charitable foundations to bankroll businesses controlled by his cronies and his children. In 2004 Transparency International ranked Suharto top of the leaders' corruption ladder for misappropriating up to US$35 billion during his three-decade reign, with his family and cronies beneficiaries.

Yet Suharto had simple tastes. Along with a partiality for basic Javanese food, 'tofu and tempe', his house was modest and old-fashioned. 'He didn't want to live in the palace,' said Suweden. 'He didn't want to be perceived like a king. His father worked in the rice fields, he came from ordinary people.'

Suharto had been born into a poor family in the village of Kemusuk outside Yogyakarta, in Central Java. His parents divorced soon after his birth. For much of his childhood he was passed between foster parents and carers. It was through a relative that he met Kiai Daryatmo, a noted Javanese *dukun* and healer, whose mystic arts left a lasting impact on Suharto's life. Yet Suweden strangely insisted that Suharto hadn't practised mysticism and had adhered only to the Muslim faith – fanatically, in fact. 'He prayed five times a day. He did not practise mysticism.'

In later life, Suharto visited sacred sites, among them mountains, caves and rivers. In his autobiography, he revealed parts of his early childhood spent in Wuryantoro, Central Java, with his aunt: 'I was ... given spiritual training by my stepfather such as fasting every Monday and Thursday. I did it diligently and with strong belief.'

Endy Bayuni, the *Jakarta Post*'s senior editor whose journalism was sorely tested during the Suharto era, said the dictator was very open about his mysticism in the '70s.

'Three members of his Cabinet were *dukuns*. One was with the Jakarta-based Centre for Strategic and International Studies; he was a special presidential adviser. He said Suharto consulted him to gain extra power. The *dukuns* (in his Cabinet) shared the stories,' said Bayuni.

The prevailing view among Indonesians was that Suharto was surrounded by mystical forces that later portended his demise. Spiritualists pointed to omens – not only his wife's death in 1996 but landslides near her burial site and the death of his spiritual mentor four months before he was overthrown in May 1998. At his deathbed, *dukuns* expressed awe that despite multiple organ failure, Suharto's spiritual power had sustained him several times.

I found it extraordinary that Suweden refuted Suharto's mystic pursuits. Even former president Susilo Bambang Yudhoyono had claimed sorcery was deployed against him during the 2009 presidential campaign. 'Many are practising black magic. Indeed, I and my family can feel it,' SBY was quoted as saying by Antara, Indonesia's official news agency.

Javanese cultural genetics, the convergence of the real and transcendental worlds, was widely acknowledged and practised. Syncretic Islam, or Abangan – a blend of Hinduism, Buddhism and animism – integrated with Javanese Islamic belief.

A nominal Muslim until the 1990s, Suharto undertook a Hajj pilgrimage to Mecca in 1991 to shore up his religious and political legitimacy and exert greater control. But throughout his life he was a devotee of the Javanese tales of *wayang kulit* – shadow puppetry – taking values from the *wayang* as a basis for his political power. In the *wayang kulit*, derived from Indian narratives that trace from the first century, the *dalang*, or puppet master, manipulates and controls leather puppets whose shadow images are viewed by audiences. Based on the legendary Hindu epics *Ramayana* and *Mahabharata*, life is a battle between anarchy and order, the goal to achieve the latter through mystical endeavour. Popular in Java and Bali, the shadow plays allegorically mirror the politics of the day.

In 1974, the year before Indonesia invaded East Timor, Suharto invited Australian Prime Minister Gough Whitlam to a mystical Javanese cave named Gua Semar (Semar Cave) on Central Java's Dieng Plateau, where Suharto had meditated. Indonesians observed Suharto took Whitlam into his confidence. Australian documents released in 2000 reveal that around this time Australia gave tacit approval for Suharto to invade East Timor.

'It was during this visit that Whitlam agreed to turn a blind eye to Indonesia's imminent invasion of East Timor; as a sign of gratitude Suharto took him into the Cave of Semar, sacred to Java's greatest native deity,' wrote Richard Lloyd Parry in *In the Time of Madness*.

In Javanese mythology, Semar is a pot-bellied, comical but all-empowering mystic clown-god of the shadow plays. This entity's name also invokes the document on which Sukarno signed over his presidential power to Suharto on 11 March 1966: it was called Supersemar, the abbreviation of Surat Perintah Sebelas Maret (Letter of Instruction, 11 March), a wordplay on Semar. In the document, Sukarno handed Suharto authority to restore order by whatever measures deemed necessary during the chaos of the anti-communist massacres.

*

In his adolescence, Iskandar Wawo-Runtu had been a regular visitor to the Suharto household. He was one of five children of

Bali's legendary Wawo-Runtu family, whose iconic 1960s Sanur hotel drew celebrities and royalty from afar. It was in Jakarta that the family found themselves amid the most influential of all.

Now in his early sixties, Iskandar guided me through Suharto's home and personal life as he spoke to me in a phone interview from Yogyakarta.

The Suhartos had been neighbours during a tumultuous period between 1963 and 1967 in Jalan Haji Agus Salim, in the well-heeled Central Jakarta district of Menteng. During Suharto's dethroning of Sukarno and the subsequent 1965–66 massacres, Iskandar was in junior high school. 'We lived in No 94 and Suharto's house was No 98,' Iskandar said. 'I grew up with his six children. My sister, Fiona, was close to Tutut' [Siti Hardiyanti Rukmana, the eldest Suharto daughter].

Significant benefits flowed to Suharto's neighbours. 'Definitely it was an advantage to us kids being neighbours as Suharto became the most powerful person in Indonesia. The whole street was closed to the public; we could bike around freely; we watched movies every weekend at Suharto's house. They showed a lot of Western films, he would have had access to the censors. In those days it was a great luxury.'

Iskandar, then aged about thirteen, recalled the austerity, hunger and economic paralysis that marked the period under Sukarno, the charismatic but authoritarian founding president. In their blocked-off street, the Wawo-Runtu family were sheltered from Jakarta's bloody rampages and riots.

It was in Suharto's personal life that Iskandar gleaned the banal and mystical Javanese side of the man roundly feared. 'Suharto came from the village; he followed simple habits and ate very simple Javanese food, rice and noodles,' Iskandar recalled. 'He dressed casually in the Javanese tradition of a sarong while indoors. If he had visitors, he changed into pants and a batik shirt.'

Inside a simple, semi-modern 1940s Dutch house were displays of gaudy souvenirs and trinkets. Neither his brother Yaya nor Iskandar remembered seeing books. 'They didn't have a sense of beauty, they put everything together, there was a stuffed tiger. It was tacky.'

As then head of Kostrad (the first-line warfare combat unit of the Indonesian army), Suharto had a modest salary. But in 1967 when the family moved to Jalan Cendana, a fifteen-minute walk from the former home, it was furnished in the same gauche fashion. Suharto had a penchant for caged animals, keeping orangutans and forest cats on the property in the tradition of army generals of the day. 'It was a hobby of the powerful. When they moved to Cendana they had to become international and they spoke no English. They called my great-aunt [Jane Wawo-Runtu], also a neighbour, and she taught Suharto and his wife English.'

Of greatest interest in Suharto's house was one room. 'As a kid, I could go to an area of his house nobody visited. He had a room containing all his mystical objects, collections of spiritual artefacts from sacred sites, called *pusaka*, such as his kris,' said Iskandar. The kris, a Javanese dagger, is said to possess mystical powers and provide protection, though the blades could render good or bad luck. 'Suharto had a strong, traditional Javanese background. He had to respect the *pusaka* – give offerings and observe the calendar. It was an intense [thing] to them.' The *pusaka* purportedly maintained Suharto's hold on power. 'I was curious about the objects. Certainly it's a room you don't want to enter unless you're taken.'

Suharto's two older sons, Bambang Trihatmodjo and Sigit Harjojudanto, with whom Iskandar had grown close, invited him into Suharto's sacred room.

Iskandar recalled Suharto as a 'calm' man who smoked cigars but didn't drink. The 'calmness', or absence of expression, was

312

known to deflect analysis of a thirty-two-year unchallenged rule synonymous with repression and cronyism.

Just as Suweden described Suharto's inscrutable face, Iskandar witnessed it. 'He never showed his emotions. He was a very controlled person; that's very much the behaviour of Javanese elders. That's how you earn respect, by having self-control, people don't know your position, if you're angry or not.'

It also commanded fear. But to the young Iskandar, Suharto was a nice man – a president at that – who waved and called out his name from his car window while passing. 'What president would do that?' he marvelled on the phone.

When the first family moved to Jalan Cendana, Iskandar rarely saw them. 'We had completely different lives.'

But the connections ran deep. Iskandar's English mother Judith had sold her paintings and jewellery from her shop, Rama Sita, at the family's Menteng home, and Suharto's wife Ibu Tien – derisively nicknamed Madame Ten Percent, for her unscrupulous money-skimming exercises – had sold her batik fabrics there. A running joke quoted in a 1996 obituary reported she was known to be in the 'mining business': 'That's mine, that's mine.'

'She was a very aggressive merchant,' conceded Iskandar.

*

As I was leaving Suweden's office, he handed me two tomes depicting Suharto as a beneficent ruler, published by his daughter, Tutut. One, titled *Pak Harto: The Untold Stories*, is an anthology of hundreds of anecdotes by politicians, aides, army personnel and acquaintances. The foreword is written by former vice-president Jusuf Kalla.

Most tales referred to Suharto's Islamic fervour, none to his mystical endeavours. The overwhelming sentiment was of a sage and unpretentious leader blessed with unalloyed control. In one account, a former interpreter Quraish Shihab recalled asking Suharto, 'Sir, what made you decide to take over the command when the G30/PKI [30 September Movement] coup attempt took place in 1965?' Suharto replied, 'I don't know, Quraish, I just had this very strong push in my heart to do it. I also did not know precisely how I eventually managed to appear so convincing.'

I later messaged Suweden, asking if his mentor had gifted him property or concessions. He didn't reply.

28

FULL CIRCLE

Seeking respite, I nipped across to tranquil Lombok in April 2016. The former Indonesian lawyer for Bali Nine mule Renae Lawrence was an island resident, and when I called she excitedly disclosed she had a new villa venture in Kuta. Would I like to stay a night?

I'd known Anggia Lubis Browne for years, a middle-aged woman from Medan in North Sumatra who'd married an Australian man. I regularly quoted her in my stories but this was a peep into her private life. Collecting me the next morning, she smoothly navigated her SUV over the ninety minutes from Senggigi's tourist strip. In her laid-back but coolly shrewd voice, she chatted about Kuta's neo-building boom. I thought, *She's a lawyer, she understands the scams, the problems.* And if anyone got hurt, it wouldn't be this woman.

The villas were bungalows, small and a bit gloomy, more of a guesthouse. We ate lunch at the attached *bale*-style Indonesian restaurant, an oasis amid swaths of sandy fallow land waiting to be cultivated with lush plants and vegetables. But Lubis Browne was riding the crest of a lucrative investment wave at Kuta's new frontier; she had several properties and boundless enthusiasm. Not only was she excited about this particular venture where I was a guest, but she also had a novel plan for it.

It was nearly sunset when she surprisingly advocated that Lawrence serve parole under her custodial care at the property, if the prisoner were permitted; she was nearly eligible for parole, but she would require a guardian in Indonesia. Her father, Bob Lawrence, seeing no prospect of that, had discounted the idea. 'I trust her,' Lubis Browne continued. 'She can teach the local children English, gardening and cooking.' The media-savvy lawyer had methodically thought it through.

She went on, discussing the void stretching before the remaining six on life sentences. To her, it was indefensible they still languished behind bars a year after the 2015 executions of Chan and Sukumaran. 'It's time the six Australians on life terms are released on humanitarian grounds,' she said. True, they had virtually disappeared from the face of the earth. Only the two still at Kerobokan jail – the youngest, Matthew Norman, thirty-two, at my time of writing, and Si Yi Chen, thirty-four – continued voicing hope for release. 'Send them back to Australia. While they are still alive, they should never give up,' said Lubis Browne. 'They were just mules. They have done their punishment. They're just boys, give them a chance. Don't play God,' she implored her government from afar.

We moved to a restaurant on the beachfront. As the blazing sun slid into a tangerine-streaked sky, she proposed a lifeline: she would write to Widodo requesting clemency for the six whose legal appeals were exhausted. (There are now five after the death of Tan Duc Thanh Nguyen in May 2018.) Beyond a merciful president or a revision to the penal code – which sat on the backburner – prospects crumbled.

'They were naive and young and worked in poorly paid jobs. When the offer came to go on this trip they didn't think about what they were doing,' Lubis Browne said. Failing clemency, she would happily take them into her custodial care, also – they could start a school and teach locals to surf. 'It could be the Bali Nine Surf Camp,' she joked, yet also seeing the attraction. 'Jetstar would resume flights.' (The Australia to Lombok leg had been ditched due to flat demand in 2014.) We laughed at the whimsical idea. Prisoners serving life weren't entitled to parole: life means life in Indonesia.

Invoking comparisons with Schapelle Corby – whose first lawyer had been Anggia's sister, a rookie, Lily Lubis – she went on, 'Why [did] the Australian government only [fight] for Corby? What is the real story behind Corby's release? What was the reason? I don't believe she should have been.'

The following day it was sundown when we left Kuta for Senggigi. Along the way, Lubis Browne suddenly remembered committing to a girlfriend's birthday party. 'Do you mind if we stop?' she asked, already swerving off the freeway to Mataram.

The apartment was abuzz with excitable Indonesian women, music, food and alcohol, though most weren't drinking. Here was Lubis Browne, shedding her cool, closed lawyer exterior, in the groove among friends. It wasn't a face I had seen on her before. Generous and inquisitive, the giggling women plied me with homemade spicy food.

The party girl's Australian husband, an older man, sat on a stool with a beer, extolling the virtues of local women before proudly showing me a renovation he had built above the swimming pool. It was a tiny retreat for visiting family, he said. We had to climb a ladder to reach it; probably his man shed, I thought.

For the next few months I quizzed Lubis Browne on the progress of her clemency letter but she kept stalling and the idea eventually fizzled. Realistically, she was with Bali Nine lawyer Wirawan Adnan, who nailed his colours to political conservatism. Pardons for drug crimes were patently futile – although Frenchman Michael Blanc had bucked the trend as the first foreign drug criminal to walk free on parole from a Jakarta jail a month before Corby did in 2014. Also granted a presidential reduction of his original life sentence, like Corby he never admitted his crime, and he too became a cause célèbre at home. But Corby's parole had been bitter and polarising, provoking a local backlash with anti-drug campaigners trying to overturn her clemency. She'd caused then president Susilo Bambang Yudhoyono huge political damage, said Adnan.

Lawrence was released in November 2018 to a media scrum after serving thirteen years, including six of remissions for good behaviour. She was deported smartly, but not before the Lubis sisters farewelled her inside Bangli prison.

*

I came full circle on a trip to Sydney in March 2017.

I had reviewed Sukumaran's first art exhibition in Jimbaran, southern Bali, in September 2010, and it had given me a palpable flutter of excitement. In iconic Andy Warhol-inspired style, a pastiche of portraits depicting the Nine titled *The Brady Bunch* had nearly missed the opening. Still wet when it was hung, the centrepiece sold for $300 to a Western man who wished to remain anonymous but 'wanted to help them'. Sukumaran told me he was intrigued to know who it was.

Seven years later, I took the train to the Campbelltown Arts Centre in south-west Sydney to Sukumaran's posthumous, first major exhibition, *Another Day in Paradise*, a couple of months after it was launched. Many of his disturbing self-portraits, painted in Ben Quilty's style using thick oils, had been created in his last days from Kerobokan and Nusa Kambangan jails. He had turned the mirror on himself, as Quilty suggested. In so doing, the world witnessed the personal savagery of execution. Many paintings had also been wet when they were unveiled to journalists on Cilacap's dock, across the strait. The darkness engulfing Sukumaran as he awaited his fate was on display, the politics of the death penalty in defiance of his oppressors never more confronting. What depths did he plumb as he painted an execution chair and cross on which he would be tied in preparation for the firing squad? It was beyond comprehension.

Embedded in my subconscious is an anguished double self-portrait. A haloed, otherworldly Sukumaran on the left joins his human self, holding a voluminous pure-white cloth over his heart: the point of entry for the bullet. The bi-facial images – alarmed and sorrowful – were like gaping wounds. I had seen the painting and others in Indonesia; in this setting, the urgency had passed but not the impact. If anything, they seemed starker and more subversive.

I wandered slowly around the exhibition space in a trancelike state, viewing each painting lining the white walls. This was a far cry from the pandemonium of screeching sirens and macabre preparations surrounding them in Cilacap, Central Java, two years previously. But still the raw self-portraits screamed out.

Co-curated by Ben Quilty, the exhibition had attracted crowds but it was nearing the close, and I was relieved to be alone to reflect on Sukumaran's violent end-journey, the catalyst that had brought the pictures home. I felt I was reliving this horror story. But the portraits of his grief-stricken mother, brother and sister, depicted as old beyond their years, cut to the bone.

A female assistant accompanied me after a while, curious to glean something tangible of Sukumaran and the Bali Nine members, whose representations hung like alarm bells in a row, each personality laid bare on canvas. Sukumaran had, I thought, got them right.

It was the closest they had been to the outside world since their arrests. Who knew if the six surviving lifers would ever see beyond the slammer?

I lingered, reluctant to leave. A personal attachment to the Bali Nine story gripped me. Sukumaran's nightmare and crusade for mercy, giving credence to the futility of the death penalty, filled the sanitised space.

I wondered what it meant to viewers who knew him from a distance as an infamous painter who had destroyed his precious life, transformed himself and begged for mercy.

*

It was the end of an era. After a decade of living in Indonesia I was ready to return to the West – and my family, whom I missed every day.

This journey had left me suspended between two worlds, pulled as I was to the customs, people, foibles and magic of Indonesia. In the end, though, I'd been a foreigner in a foreign land. As an outsider, I was also regarded with suspicion by some Bali expatriates decrying negative exposure of their home. But along the way, I made firm friends with Indonesians and expats, some of them with me from the start.

Exposed to the good, bad and vicissitudes of the tropics, I had one day in April 2018 woken to the ravages of dengue fever. I couldn't move. For a month, in the midst of writing this book, the mosquito-borne virus rendered me useless. I lay on my back hammered by a vicious hangover, cared for by a good friend between hospital visits.

On the flip side, one morning I opened my PC to find I was a Walkley Award finalist for my terrorism work. I had to read the email several times before it registered; it was a wonderful way to wake up.

But with Joko Widodo – the continued reformist hope – at the helm in his final presidential term, fears abounded that the country was lurching into hardline Islamic conservativism.

When I asked leading Indonesian author and astute chronicler, Eka Kurniawan, his view of the shifting political tone, he spoke pragmatically of a dynamic culture. 'The rise of conservative religion is part of the tension in Indonesian politics. It's not beautiful, of course, but not something new, too. Socially and politically, Indonesia is like a laboratory, where various experiments are inserted into a soup bowl. Sometimes we find it tastes good, but also it's erratic. Communism, liberalism, democracy, pan-Islamism. These ideas are mixed, sometimes mingling, more often smashing each other. This is what creates all the beauty of this country, as well as its tragedy.'

Over a decade, I had become entwined in that tapestried tragedy and beauty. The erraticism is a worrying trend, the concern that Indonesians, known for pluralism and religious tolerance, may be forsaking their liberal democracy. Yet for all of Indonesia's paradoxes and difficulties, I couldn't have imagined the extraordinary experiences and insights I would gain along the way, nor my addiction to the resilient, cheerful people who live in diverse circumstances, many with nothing. Coming back from this journey, I saw life in broader brushstrokes, in a larger context with a heightened sense of light and shadow.

One night, early on, I had ordered a motorbike taxi and waited some time in a central tourist spot. Growing impatient, I was about to cancel it when an esoteric message flashed across my phone screen: 'I am in the Heaven.'

My heart sank; I imagined the driver lying in a pool of blood, reaching out for their phone, this text a last gasp. What to do? I wandered off feeling helpless. Five minutes later, when I looked across the road, a young woman was sitting on her motorbike beneath a hotel sign: The Haven.

Many things were not as they seemed in Indonesia, but as though it was a vision I had stared at for too long, I had missed the obvious. So too, while immersed in this mysterious, mystical country, I had missed the lifting of a burden from my shoulders. No longer was I haunted by the corpse of my relationship or my dispirited self. Without thought, I had moved on.

GLOSSARY

adat – custom, customary law

amdal – environmental impact assessment

anak – child

arak – cheap rice spirit, local firewater

ayam goreng – fried chicken

babi gulung – suckling pig

bale – open-air hut

balian – traditional healer

Banjar – Balinese village council

bapak / pak – sir, Mr, father

becak – rickshaw tricycle

beli emas – buy gold

besok – tomorrow

bule – foreigner, especially Caucasian (not necessarily offensive)

bungkus – takeaway food

bupati – mayor

campur – mixed

canang – small woven basket made from coconut leaves

cap cay – stir-fried mixed vegetables

dukun – shaman

fado – a type of singing originally from Portugal

gang – alleyway

golput – derived from *golongan putih*, or white group; refers to a voting boycott *ibu* – mother or Mrs

jam karet – rubber time

janda – widow or divorcée

jero – the title of a Balinese commoner who marries into a high caste

joglo – traditional Javanese bungalow

kafir – infidel

kampung – village

kawin kontrak – short-term marriage contract

kebaya – traditional long-sleeved blouse

keluarga – family

keronkong – traditional music originally from Portugal

kost – cheap rented room

kufi – prayer cap

losmen – hostel

mangku – high priest

musholla – Islamic prayer room

nasi – rice

nikah siri – unregistered marriage

niskala – Balinese belief in the unseen world (as opposed to *sekala*, the tangible or seen)

niqab – a garment worn by some Muslim women; it covers the hair and face but not the eyes

pacar – romantic term for boyfriend or girlfriend

pak / bapak – sir, Mr, father

pasung – the practice of restraining the mentally ill using stocks, shackles, ropes, cages and locked rooms

peci – Muslim cap

pembantu – housemaid

penjor – curved bamboo poles decorated with flowers and laden with fruit offerings

pesantren – Islamic boarding school

pinisi – Suluwesi schooner

polda – provincial police

preman – thug

puputan – Balinese mass ritual suicide

pusaka – sacred tokens, magic charms or talisman

puseh – navel

puskesmas – community health centre

reformasi – democratic reformation after Suharto's fall

sekala – the tangible or seen world (as opposed to *niskala*, the intangible and unseen)

shabu – crystal methamphetamine

shaheed / syahid – martyr

siri – secret, refers to unregistered marriage

sonket – ornate gold-threaded sarong

sop – buah sticky milk drink

susuk – magic charm implanted beneath the skin

taksu – Bali's divine Hindu spiritual energy

tamping – leader

tirtha – holy water

udeng – traditional Balinese head cloth with religious significance

warung – restaurant or stall

wayhu – power, inspiration

ACKNOWLEDGEMENTS

This book developed over nearly a decade of my assignments and life in Indonesia. More a series of adventures than work, I thank those I met on the road who freely gave me their time, knowledge and wisdom.

There are numerous people to whom I owe my gratitude for their assistance, generosity and support – both personally and professionally – many of whom are within these pages.

To the survivors and families of the 2002 Bali bombing victims I am deeply indebted for sharing painful memories and emotions to ensure the lives lost in the atrocity are never forgotten. I am particularly grateful to Barry Wallace and Danny Hanley.

In my investigations into Indonesia's web of terrorism, some of the world's most expert counterterrorists helped me dig beneath the surface. Among them I am grateful to Noor Huda Ismail, Taufik Andrie, Sidney Jones, Badrus Sholeh and Rohan Gunaratna.

I owe thanks to countless refugees who shared their shattered lives with me, not least Mohammad Bagherian and his wife, Shirin, who tirelessly drove me round Jakarta at all hours.

I thank my wonderful children, Jake and Ruby, for their encouragement; Pamela Robson for reading my early drafts and providing inspiration and insight; Philippa Ellis for her unflagging patience in retrieving my stories from *The Australian* newspaper's archives; Asana Viebeke Lengkong for her indefatigable insights and friendship; Agung Wardana; Andreas Harsono; Endy Bayuni, for his historic perspective; Janet DeNeefe; Michael Vatikiotis; Justin Hale; Jane Walters; Russell Darnley; Richard and Gilana Poore; my assistant Firdia Lisnawati, who periodically worked impossible hours; the Dyson family; Yuyun Ismawati Drwiega and the Balifokus team; Luh Ketut Suryani and her colleague son, Cokorda Bagus Jaya Lesmana; Ida Ayu Puspa Eny; Dr Putu Anda Tusta; Jason Childs; William J. Furney; Paul Lupton; Marian Carroll; Daniel Rudi Haryanto; Jeff Hammond; Vicki Czugaj; my editors at *The Australian*, ever generous with their time: Patrick Lawnham and Steve Waterson; *The Australian* newspaper and *The Weekend Australian Magazine*, without which this book would not have life; my friend and agent, Margaret Gee; Brigitta Doyle and HarperCollins and ABC Books Australia.